CHAPTERS IN A LIFE

Written by God, lived by all

MARTIN BOOKER

WestBow
PRESS
A DIVISION OF THOMAS NELSON

WestBow Press books may be ordered through booksellers or by contacting:

WestBow Press
A Division of Thomas Nelson
1663 Liberty Drive
Bloomington, IN 47403
www.westbowpress.com
1-(866) 928-1240

Because of the dynamic nature of the Internet, any web addresses or links contained in this book may have changed since publication and may no longer be valid. The views expressed in this work are solely those of the author and do not necessarily reflect the views of the publisher, and the publisher hereby disclaims any responsibility for them.

Any people depicted in stock imagery provided by Thinkstock are models, and such images are being used for illustrative purposes only.

Certain stock imagery © Thinkstock.

ISBN: 978-1-4497-1095-8 (sc)
ISBN: 978-1-4497-1096-5 (dj)
ISBN: 978-1-4497-1097-2 (e)

Library of Congress Control Number: 2011923845

Scripture taken from the HOLY BIBLE, NEW INTERNATIONAL VERSION®. Copyright © 1973, 1978, 1984 Biblica. Used by permission of Zondervan. All rights reserved.

Printed in the United States of America

WestBow Press rev. date:4/1/2011

DEDICATION

To my very, very, very, beautiful wife. For years I've secretly asked myself why it seemed as if you were a lot stronger than me. I thought that what I was seeing and feeling about your strength verses my strength couldn't be possible, because the bible says that wives are the weaker vessel. Its funny how we miss interpret many things in the bible. Now that I know I was misinterpreting 1 Peter 3:7 that was speaking only of a woman's physical strength, I now know that what I've said in the back of my mind is true. You are so much stronger than me in many ways. You always hold me up when I'm weak. You are my better half. I'm just your other half. You're much greater and stronger than I believe I can ever be and I humble myself to you. Thank you for giving me encouragement, support, and a reason to live throughout the fifteen years of our heavenly marriage bond. I'm proud to tell the world that I am your servant. I love you, and I thank you Patty, for loving me.

To my eternal treasures Ethan and Seth. Thank you Ethan for helping me develop Jacob's character and his hilarious pronunciations of words in this story. You are a mood changer who makes it hard to lock laughter up when you're around. Although your only seven years old, I can already see what type of man you're going to become.

Thank you Seth for helping me develop Heath's character in this story. Just like Heath in this story, no one on earth has ever asked me questions about God that are almost impossible to find the answers to in the bible than you have. Sometimes I wonder if you're really nine years old. I couldn't be more proud to be the father and servant of you both.

THANK YOU

Thank you God for allowing me the opportunity to possibly stand before you and receive a heavenly crown. Although I'm not worthy to speak your name and ask anything of you, I pray that this story you have given me will motivate others to try their best to earn a crown. May this book also remind us all that you are coming back soon.

I'd like to thank my mother Dortha Booker and my father Luther Booker for introducing me to God at an early age.

Thank you Carol Thomas of A-1 Editing Service.

CONTENTS

PROLOGUE
DEATH AND LIFE

Absent from the body, present with the Lord, or could it be that my body and soul have been asleep for centuries and I'm dreaming that I see Jesus as I sleep in my grave? Maybe my soul is in the temporary heaven where the souls of the Old Testament believers in Christ were held before Jesus died on the cross. I remember studying and discussing the subject of what happens after we die during the time that I lived on earth. The promise that everyone would be absent from their bodies and present with the Lord in Philippians 1:23-24 became a major debate in my theology class one day when it was noted that Apostle Paul said he'd rather be absent from his body and present with the Lord. How the verses became a promise for everyone that was ever created became a mystery that day. My entire class searched for weeks for an answer that connected the verses to all believers in Christ, but failed to find a way they applied. It wasn't long before the whole school joined in on the search and failed to find the answer.

It wasn't until many years later after I graduated theology school when I found the answer. But before I was able to finish writing a sermon that I had planned on getting published as a book to reveal the truth behind the controversial verse—I died. I don't know how I died, but I know I did. Whether this experience is a dream I'm having while I sleep in my grave or my soul is in a temporary paradise or it's in the third heaven with Jesus. I know now what happens to the souls of believers when they die. But one mention of anything I see in the new life after death would make the souls of millions of believers in God leap out of their bodies and cause a premature Rapture. I can only say that the things I've seen now that I'm on the other side of life makes death a beautiful and magical reward for all my earthly sufferings.

The last thing I remember on the day my soul left my body is returning to the church to get the lottery ticket that I had left in my desk. Thursday night choir practice had ended as usual at 7:30, but Sister Waters and Tom, the choir director, were still there. *Now, why are they still talking at the front door an hour after choir practice has ended?* I wondered. They were probably getting each other caught up on the latest church gossip. No matter how much I preached on the sin of gossip and the harm it can do to people, it still managed to find its way into the hearts of my flock. As I got out of my car, Tom and Sister Waters had begun making their way down the steps of the church.

"Evening, evening," I said to them.

"Hey, Pastor Shoemaker. What brings you out at this time o' night?" asked Sister Waters, a plus-sized Black woman who was still trying to understand all of the controversial sermons that I had preached. After years of study at the nondenominational theology school I attended, I had discovered that not one of the so-called Bible contradictions was actually in the Bible. All the contradictions and controversies came from misinterpretations. This discovery was wonderful news I thought, but for some reason no one I shared it with saw it the way I did. Maybe it was because it went against everything they had believed about the Bible their whole lives. Or maybe their pride was the reason they resisted the truth that I was trying to teach them.

"I left something in my office that I need," I responded. "But what's got y'all out this late?"

"Oh, we were just discussing the sermon and the Scriptures you preached to us on gossip and how it's impossible to love one another by spreading gossiping rumors that are hardly ever even true."

Tom was clearly stunned by the lie that Sister Waters had told me. Out of the corner of my eye, I saw him quickly put his fingers in a T shape to form a cross and displayed it to Sister Waters when I turned my head away for a second.

"Good Sister Waters, I'm glad to hear that my parishioners are paying attention to my sermons. I'm not going to hold y'all up; I know you have to go to work in the morning."

"Yeah, hopefully," said Sister Waters.

"What do you mean, 'hopefully'?" I asked.

"Well, my company is threatening to have a lay-off tomorrow or next week."

"Mine, too," Tom added in his Cajun accent. "Rumor has it that my company is closing their doors and going out of business for good." Tom was a middle-aged White man from Louisiana who had moved to Arkansas to start a new life after a hurricane destroyed his hometown.

"Well, you both know that those jobs are not our real jobs. They're just places that God is allowing us to work for a time, and only He knows how long. He provides our daily bread. Put your trust in Him and not in your job."

"Amen and everything like that, Pastor. But you've just started teaching us about how the Bible never command us New Testament believers to tithe and-and-and how it's impossible to tithe correctly today because tithing dealt with food, animal sacrifices, and all kinds of other offerings like burnt offerings and sin offerings—but never a money offering or a tithe involving money."

"Isn't that great news?" I said, purposely interrupting Sister Waters because I knew that the smallest big word in the Bible and elsewhere was coming next.

"Yeah, that's great news, Pastor. But . . . ."

There it was. I knew it was coming. That small but big word *but* that plays a very important part in translating important key verses in the Bible. Never has the word *but* carried good news both before and after it. It has always connected good news with bad news or bad news with good news. I knew that there would be some uncertainty or some negative thinking after she finished her sentence.

She continued, following up on the word *but*. "Every since you preached on that, it seems like things have gotten worse. A large number of people in our church have been laid off from their jobs, including you. After eighteen years of teaching Christian studies at that two year college they decide they no longer need you. I mean, what's really going on? I read the Scriptures and understand all that you said about tithing to be true, but . . . you kind of took our hope away by telling us that. Now we have no hope at all that God is going to bless us and protect us during these hard economic times. The churches that I see tithing are being blessed it seems like to me."

"Well, Sister Waters, would you rather know the truth or would you prefer to hold on to false hope? Jesus holds me to a higher standard than my congregation, so I'm going to teach His Word as correctly as I can. If I'm ever proved wrong about a verse or something I've preached on, I'll come back and admit it. I believe I proved that when I gave my testimony on how God broke off a limb and straightened me out on the seriousness of purposely miss teaching his word. Never again will I teach tithing to fit in with other pastors and to receive a little extra in the offering plate and get another whipping with a limb from the Lord God's hands. When it comes to money, even the best of us pastors can be tempted by Satan. I knew I was wrong when I was teaching my flock that tithing was required if they wanted to be blessed. For the rest of my life, the lesson I learned from my mistake will remain as a thorn in my side that God will not remove. Even as a pastor who had just graduated with a doctoral degree in theology, I failed to trust God when times got tough. I believe the reason God has still given me the honor and privilege to continue teaching at this church today is that I didn't let my pride step in the way when the spirit of God led me to shame myself and admit to the church that I purposely misinformed them to fit in with the in crowd. I could've easily lied and said that I misinterpreted the issue of tithing, but God was listening, so I humbled myself and told the truth."

I could barely hold my head up as I remembered the day that God convict my heart of my intentional false teachings. "That's why on issues such as tithing, Bible contradictions, controversies, and anything else that makes the Bible look to be untrue," I assured Sister Waters, "I can tell you that I'm three hundred percent sure on a scale to one hundred that I'm telling you the truth. I'm not going to sugarcoat God's Word for anybody just so a lot of people will like me for this short time we're here on earth. Life is just a journey to the beginning of no end. Through Jesus Christ, our new life begins. Death is the beginning of eternity with our awesome God. No other hope or promise is better than the promise of being with God forever. Think about what Jesus said about worrying in Matthew 6:26. Just as God feeds the birds of the air, He'll take care of you whether you tithe or not if you trust Him. Just ask any rich person you know who doesn't tithe."

"So are we just supposed to suffer?" Sister Waters said in a teary voice. "Is God going to let us lose our jobs and our homes and everything we've worked so hard for years for? Tom and I want to know what we can do to get blessings and prosperity today, right now, while we're here on earth since you say we can't get them by tithing."

I could tell that she was trying hard not to break down in tears, but the fear of losing a job during a bad economy almost guaranteed that we wouldn't find a new job anytime soon.

I reached out my hand and touched Sister Waters on her shoulder to comfort her and show my compassion for her burdened heart. "God didn't promise us that we'd be blessed if we tithe any certain percent. I wish He had; that way we'd all be rich. The only people He promised He would bless if they tithed were His people, the Jews—not Christians or Buddhists or Hindus. God never asked us to tithe. The purpose and principle behind tithing was for us to learn the nature of God and how He blesses those who helps others who are in need. Now, I've shown you that just because the Bible says that God said He's going to do this or that for His servants, his saints, his people, and sometimes even Christian believers, doesn't always mean that everyone that breathes the breath of life is the group of people He was talking about. God will bless those of us who give money to the church, but God never promised us Gentiles a blessing through tithing ten percent of our income. The Bible says that we will suffer as long as we roam this earth, but—" I broke off abruptly.

"What you looking at Pastor?" Tom asked.

"I thought I saw a flash of light or something inside the church."

"I set the alarm already, so if someone was in there, the motion detectors would have picked them up by now," Tom explained.

"All right, like I was saying. People today want to become beautiful, harvestable crops without going through the storm and rainy seasons that it takes to become that sweet watermelon or that tall healthy cornstalk. You can't just have all sunshine and expect to grow. You have to be nourished with storms in life as well. Don't sow your seeds in the field marked blessings and prosperity only. 'Let the good times roll, hold the storms, and give me lots of blessings and prosperity on the side, please' isn't a restaurant order that's going to get you the proper nourishments you need when God sends his angels down to harvest us from this earth. That field is going to be gathered up and set on fire as unharvestable crops. I hate to do you like this, but make sure you come on Sunday; I'm going to give you all the answers to what we can do to get blessings and prosperity in my sermon."

"I ain't gonna be here Sunday, so tell me now," said Sister Waters.

"Me, neither. The Rapture might come before then, so tell me now, too," said Tom.

"Let me get on in here and get what I came here for," I said, laughing. "Y'all will be here; you're just trying to pull it out of me before Sunday."

"That ain't right to make us wait; what's the answer?" Sister Waters complained.

"Don't play, Pastor. Go on and tell us now." Tom added.

"It wouldn't be right to tell you the ending of a good book or movie before you finished reading it; it would spoil the whole story, don't you think?"

"Naw, not me. I don't think so. Do you, Tom? I like finding out the endings of books and movies first."

"I'm OK with spoiled endings," said Tom. "I learn the lesson and moral to the story a whole lot faster working in reverse, so let's hear it."

"Come on in Sunday and find out how. You're not going to believe it when I tell you, anyway. If people believed it, they wouldn't be trying to tithe, fast, light candles, and all the other stuff they do to try to earn a blessing."

Ok, we'll wait 'til Sunday," Sister Waters said. "Be expecting a three-way wake-up call from us right at 12:01A.M. Sunday morning so you can tell us the answer; in the meanwhile, you make sure you lock the door behind you because this economy has got people doing unnecessary stuff to pay their bills. It almost feels like we're living in the Tribulation times. I know the Rapture hasn't came yet, because we're still here. Matthew 24:40–41. I memorized that verse, Pastor. A husband and wife will be working in the field and the woman will be taken and the ex-husband and all other evil people will be left. Thank you, Jesus, for takin' me and leavin' my ex-husband to stay here and suffer through the Tribulation after he left me and the kids for some—"

"Hold it!" said Tom. "We're on the church grounds. I know what you called her the other day so keep it holy."

Sister Waters and I laughed, and she did a little dance.

"I know that's not exactly what it says. I had to change it like everybody else changes bible verses to make myself feel better about my husband leaving us after twenty-three years of marriage. I loved him. Sometimes when I'm struggling to pay my bills and feed our kids I find myself wishing he'd go to hell for cheating on me," said Sister Waters.

"Forgiveness, Sister Waters, forgiveness. Speaking of end-time events; Revelations 19, verses 17 through 20, talks about the angel that stands in the sun and calls all the birds of the air to gather for the great supper of God and eat the flesh of kings, generals, mighty men, and all people, free and slave . . . . If you didn't know any better, you'd think that all people free and slaved included us, because we're people, wouldn't you agree?"

"Yeah, you're right, Pastor," they both agreed.

"But since we know all believers both dead and alive will be caught up in the Rapture before that time comes, we know that we can't be a part of that group of people. You see what I mean. And on top of that, God promised not to destroy those who believe in Him. All the people who are on earth at that particular time will be nonbelievers who missed the Rapture. Some people don't believe in the Rapture because they have their eras mixed up. God's going to set up his kingdom right here on earth for a thousand years. That kingdom will be similar to the kingdom of heaven but different. When people misunderstand these two kingdoms as being the same kingdom, they can misinterpret the events described in the parable of the weeds in Matthew 13 as saying that the burned weeds are the people who will be taken away in the Rapture. Verse forty-one shows that separation of kingdoms that I'm talking about. Jesus is going to send his angels to weed out of His earthly kingdom the people who don't make it through His thousand year reign of total peace here on this earth. This isn't the rapture of us believers. After we're raptured up we're going to reign with Him during those thousand years. The very next verse tells us what's going to happen with the people who don't overcome after our rapture and the tribulation period. They will be burned and there will be weeping and gnashing of the teeth. They will be taken away or raptured if you will and placed in Hell. Not the kind of rapture that places them in the presence of God forever. Simple misinterpretation . . . and a new Bible contradiction is born. Of course, it's a parable and Revelations goes deeper into detail as to how the removal of all non believers is going to happen."

"Yeah . . . . OK, now, that example helps me see that plain and clear. I don't want to be a part of that group of people," Sister Waters said, laughing. "Uh-uh. God ain't giving them nothin' I want. Shoot. I don't want no birds eating my flesh. No, Lordy. Uh-uh, baby."

"Oh, my God," Tom said.

"I want you to know that there are more of us here that support your way of teaching than there are of us who don't," Sister Waters said. "I don't understand how some of our members can hear the truth for years and then decide to believe something else because it's the new thang and everybody else is doing it. I guess Satan knows that a holy mess of confusion will cause many people to not believe."

"That's right. Every so-called Bible contradiction that exists today came from misunderstandings of God's true words. Take the word *storehouse* where the tithes were commanded to be taken for instance. Is it singular or plural?"

"Singular," Tom and Sister Waters answered together.

"Well, explain to me how it can be changed to mean over one million churches to take your tithes and offerings to today. It's a good thing the word *sins* is in plural form. You'll see what I mean when I start preaching a three-month-long series on Bible contradictions and controversies that I've been working on. Y'all have a good night."

I wasn't sure if they understood what I was trying to tell them because they stared at each other with confused expressions before they wished me good night.

As they started to walk to their cars, Tom held up a makeshift cross sign with his fingers to Sister Waters again.

I couldn't help stopping to watch them and listen as I fumbled with the keys to find the one to the front door.

"This is going to burn, but it's for your own good," Tom said. "Come out of her in the name of Jesus."

"The Holy Spirit lives in me; I ain't scared of that mess no mo'. I know better. You better quit before you burn yourself trying to cast spirits out somebody. I'm fire protected, baby." Sister Waters did a little step with one hand on her hip and her other hand waving above her head.

"I ain't never lied to a preacher the way you just did," Tom said. "You know good 'n well we were gossiping 'bout him and you had the nerve to lie 'bout it on the steps of the church house," Tom said.

"That's why I started walking down off the steps." Sister Waters laughed. "You'll never be able to prove to Jesus I lied. All my sins have been forgiven and forgotten about. That makes you a liar when you accuse me of sinning. Tell my Jesus to show you in his records one of my sins." Sister Waters placed her hand on Tom's shoulder. "If he pulls out any kind of a record, grab it and accidentally tear it up for me, hear."

"You're a raw crawfish in cooked gumbo," Tom said as they both laughed.

"You know I'm just kidding, but ain't it good to know that He's not going to bring up our long sin records when we stand before him?"

"Woo! Thank you, Lord," said Tom.

As I found the right key and walked up the steps to the front door, I felt a little weary and burdened. Maybe it was because we had been talking about the depressed economy and its effects on the lives of everyone except the rich and powerful. I opened the door, turned on the lights, and rushed toward the alarm keypad, but slowed down because I noticed that it was silent. I knew that it could mean only one thing: Tom hadn't set the alarm.

"They were so busy gossiping that he thought he turned the alarm on," I mumbled. I still felt weary for some reason so I not only locked the door, but I put the alarm on stay mode and headed toward my office.

Sister Waters's comments about my lay-off situation had stuck in my mind and I thought about them as I walked down the hallway. I hadn't been called for one interview during the nine months since I had been laid off. I knew that time was winding down and my unemployment benefits were going to end in the next three months. The pressure was great on me. The money I made from preaching wasn't enough to pay the bills. I had no idea how God was going to provide for my family and me, but I had faith and trusted Him to make a way out of no way. I had never played the lottery before but out of desperation, I'd decided to play. Since the tithing sermon that I had given approximately three months before I got laid off, the church offering had gotten on the low side. There were times that I asked the deacons not to pay me in full so we could keep the doors of the church open. We'd lost a lot of members who preferred to hear sermons that promised good favor for the tough situations they found themselves in. Sermons that gave them earthly hope instead of biblical truth were more satisfying than the messages I had to give.

I lifted my key to unlock the office door, but it was already open. The secretary, janitor, and the head deacon were the only ones with a key to my office. Tom only had a key to the front door of the church, so I knew it couldn't have been him. This could mean only one thing, along with the coincidence of the disarmed alarm. People were so worried about the economy and so unwilling to trust in God that they couldn't remember simple daily task. Right then and there, I knew that my upcoming sermons would be on "worrying about tomorrow."

I turned on the lights, sat at my desk, and reached to turn on my desktop computer, but it was already on. The strange things that were happening caused me to believe that my destiny to win the lottery was presenting itself to me. I opened the drawer where I had left the tickets and felt a jolt like an electrical shock that numbed my tongue. The tickets were not there. Every hair root on my body itched as if millions of fire ants were gnawing on them from beneath my skin. The lottery numbers for four hundred and seventy-five million dollars had been drawn the previous day, Wednesday. On Thursday afternoon, the local news reported that the winning ticket had been purchased at the same gas station where I bought my tickets.

Angry and confused, wondering who would steal from a pastor, I snatched open every drawer, rearranging my neatly organized desk as I searched hard for the tickets. All of a sudden, the electric current that flowed through my body faded away. I found the tickets in the top middle drawer even though I was certain that I'd left them in the top right-hand drawer. Someone had been prowling through my desk, but I told myself I'd worry about that problem another time. The winning tickets to Arkansas's largest lottery were possibly in my possession. Only a couple of clicks with the mouse separated me from the knowledge of my fate. Dial-up was all the church could afford, so I patiently waited to see if I possessed the winning ticket. I remember talking to myself out loud. "Come on, come on. High-speed Internet is the first thing on the list to get if I win," I said to myself as I got one click away from either a huge disappointment or a life-changing experience of winning the big one. All the strange feelings I had been having came crashing down as I clicked that last click of the mouse. I read and checked each set of numbers twice, only to find out that . . . "I won the lottery!" Four hundred and seventy-five million dollars, thank you, God!" I yelled as I got out of my chair and jumped up and down.

While I was in midair, I thought I heard a noise. I immediately grabbed my keys and unlocked a small safe I had built into the wall behind the books in my bookcase. I'd been staying late at the church a lot after I had gotten laid off, so I kept a handgun there just in case I ever needed it. I left the lottery tickets and my keys on the desk and went to investigate. As I reached the doorway of my office, I swung the gun around quickly to the right and then to the left side of the hallway. Seeing no one, I tiptoed down the right side of the hallway with both my hands sweating on the gun. I was so nervous that I didn't even notice I had the barrel of the gun pointed right under my chin.

I was a good preacher, but a good gun handler was something I needed practice on. I passed the first door on the left side of the hallway, which was closed and I presumed to be locked. I didn't think to double check it because it was only a closet that the janitor used to store whatnots in. As I neared the first open doorway to my right, I raised the gun closer to my chin and leaned forward to peek inside.

Despite fearing that someone inside would take my gun away and send me to glory, I offered my head as a quick flashing target, darting it back and forth inside the perimeter of the doorway twice before deeming it safe to pass through. Just as I was about to walk through the doorway, something in the corner of my left eye caught my attention and startled me. I turned and jumped quickly to my left and lost my balance.

When I stumbled toward the left side of the hallway, it was as if I had fallen through the wall into the arms of two angels. In what felt like a two-second ride on a bullet, the angels had me standing in front of Jesus. I didn't see God the Father, which led me to wonder if I was in the third heaven that Paul mentioned in 1 Corinthians 12:2 where God lives, but I was overjoyed to see the Lord Jesus that I had praised, worshiped, and talked about all my life standing before me in his Angelic form. I recognized Him instantly out of all the angels. He was much more glorious than I had imagined He'd be. Billions, maybe even trillions, of angels were all around us as far as my eyes could see, cheering for me and for Jesus.

A seraph with six wings said in a loud powerful voice as he placed me in front of Jesus who was standing at the huge entrance of the Books of Life Library. It looked more like a temple than it did a library from its outward appearance. The walls gleamed white like snow and its dome roof was made out of pure gold, "Another one you have saved from our enemies."

Jesus smiled at me and said, "Well done."

All the angels cheered again. Louder than millions of fans in thousands of fully packed sports arenas, their voices roared all over the beautiful place the angels had brought me. The seraph bowed before the Angel of the Lord and spoke for seven other seraphim who wanted to honor Him with a song. As the sounds of musical instruments poured out of their mouths, thousands of angels began to sing Robin Marks version of the song "Be unto Your Name." What sounded like an orchestra of instruments combined with thunder and stars and comets burning through space poured out of the angels' mouths. They were so loud that I thought all the people on earth could hear them although they were zillions of light-years away. Still having my earthly mind, I couldn't help thinking earthly thoughts about my family and the other people I loved.

Jesus came over to me and said, "Behold, the angels are cheering for you and you have tears of sorrow?" Will you wonder forever what happened to you on earth during the last chapter of your life story, or will you rejoice in the new life with me— the creator of all things that you read about in John 1:1-18. In the beginning, I was the word that was with God and the one in verse three in which all things were made. I'm the Lord God who created the heavens and the earth that you read about in Genesis 2:4. Through me, you will see God the father."

There was no way I could even think about lying to Jesus. I no longer had the sinful human nature inside me, so I told the truth after I got over my initial shock that I was talking to Jesus— the creator of all things face to face. "Lord God, I'll always wonder what happened to me unless you wipe it out of my memory. I must have fallen and accidentally shot myself or hit my head too hard or fallen and broken my neck. What happened to me? I hope and pray that you don't think I'm being ungrateful for asking about my past life on earth. I'm grateful to be in this place with you Lord."

I paused and thought about what I had just said and asked, "I don't have to pray anymore now that I'm talking to you face to face, do I? Will I stay here with you permanently or am I being granted a short time to talk to you before my soul is placed back into my body to sleep until the rapture?"

"The prayers you prayed were no different from talking to me face to face," Jesus answered. "We communicated with each other the same then as now. I spoke to you through everyone you knew."

"My family and loved ones that I preached to—are they coming?"

"Since the time has not yet come for my bride to be with me for eternity, I'll allow you to watch for as long as you like . . . the fulfillment of the chapters of your life through a portion of your only son's life story. The good deeds you left behind will live forever in the hearts of many people. Watch part of your son's life story to see how your life's story affected his. Then the ending of your life's story will be revealed to you."

"Will my son and . . . ?" I began, but Jesus answered my question before I could finish thinking about it.

"The fate of your only son's soul after his life story has been fulfilled, and of your wife and friends, and all of your other questions will be answered in part of your son's life story."

"Thank you, Lord. But how can my good deeds live on? I never got to tell Sister Waters, Tom, and everyone else in my congregation what they could do to be blessed,"

"All have sinned and come short of the glory, but you have led others to the truth? Well done, my good and faithful servant. I'm sending another angel like you to give to them the message that you would have given if you had lived."

"Angel?" I began, puzzled by this reply, but then I remembered that the Bible refers to human messengers as angels as well as the heavenly angels, and I knew that He was sending a pastor or a witness of some sort to deliver the message that I had intended to deliver. "Never mind. You answered my question again before I could ask it."

Then I remembered my last moments and confusion crowded my mind again as I wondered again what had happened to me. Had I accidentally taken my own life? If so, did that count as suicide? If so, how could I have entered the gates of heaven? I knew the answers to all of my questions, but out of nervousness I began questioning things I had found the answers to in the bible. The fact that Jesus didn't answer my question as to rather or not I was seeing him temporarily or permanently before the rapture came was more than likely because he knew I already knew the answer. Jesus had said that part of my son's life story would reveal what had happened at the end of mine. I guess we really are all connected as one body like the Bible said. An angel of the Lord came out of the Books of Life Library and bowed down before Jesus and held up two books for Him to take.

As if in answer to these thoughts and questions, Jesus handed me one of the books which had my son's name on it. When I opened it, I saw that the pages were not covered with written words like I had expected them to be. Instead, the pages recorded every second of his life in real time as he lived it in the flesh. This realization confused me because the Bible says that our names were written in the book of life. I had always imagined that our life stories were handwritten so I asked Jesus why the pages contained no words.

He smiled and said, "Do you know how many people I've saved since I died on the Cross?" Jesus winked at me after I answered "no" and said, "I had to upgrade."

I laughed and thought, *Wow! Jesus has a sense of humor.*

As a drop of blood appeared on the tip of his finger, Jesus opened the other book of someone's life story and signed His name inside with his finger. Then He closed the book and sealed it with a drop of His blood. He showed me the front cover just before he gave it to an angel,

"All of his works and deeds have been recorded, and his purpose has been fulfilled," He said to the angel. To my surprise, the title was *The Life Story of Pastor Johnny Shoemaker*, and below the title was a picture of me. Jesus sealed the book on my life story and had the angel place it in the library with the life stories of all who accepted Him as their personal savior. He didn't mention anything about my sins being recorded when he closed the book of my life story. After seeing the title and purpose written on the front cover of my life story, I quickly turned to the front cover of my son's life story to see what the Lord God had titled his life's story. I was extremely proud of what the title his life story said he grew up to become. When I turned to ask about my son's title that described his life's purpose, I found myself all alone.

I walked inside of the Books of Life Library to see if Jesus had gone inside. There were two huge chairs made out of precious stones of some kind with rubies, emeralds, and diamond decorations all over them sitting side by side on the side of a beautiful table made of pure gold in the middle of the library. The thick massive table had earths, planets, moons and stars etched all over it in a raised 3-D design. It was fifty foot long, twenty foot wide and twelve feet tall. The chair on the left side facing me had the name Jesus Christ, Son of God, creator of the heavens and the earth perfectly engraved at the top of the backrest of it. The chair on my right had the name God the Father, Lord God and creator of the heavens and the earth perfectly engraved on it. Twenty four thrones were seated against the wall behind them in two rows of twelve with crowns placed on them. On the far side of the library, there was another chair sitting by itself. Engrave on it were the words *Great White throne*. It appeared to me that all of heaven was preparing for the coming judgments from God.

I sat down Indian style under the table and began to watch apart of my son's life story and find out the ending of my own. Already knowing what happened in his life from birth to twelve years of age, I skipped those chapters, because I was very curios to see how he had gotten the title that the Lord God had given him on the cover of his life story. I was also anxious to find out what happened to me. All I learned from chapters twelve through twenty nine of his life story was how bad the memory of my death hurt him and kept him away from God.

CHAPTER 1

Seeking Understanding

Seventeen years had passed since Pastor Shoemaker's funeral, and his young son, Chris, was now a man of twenty-nine with a wife and two small sons. Seasonal weather patterns in Arkansas were unpredictable that year. Hot temperatures and a drought replaced April showers for the first time ever. By the time May came around, temperatures were averaging 102 degrees. Meteorologists had predicted a small chance of rain, with a cool front behind it expected to pass through the state later that night. The ground had not been saturated since mid-February, when three inches of snow had melted. Even the vegetation was confused as to what season it was. The unseasonable weather patterns that fluctuated from winter to late summer had caused the grass and the trees to stay in their dormant winter stage, even though it was May.

Down by the river at Riverside Park in Little Rock was the hot spot for antique car shows and other events. Chris and his friends arrived at the park around four o'clock that Friday afternoon to attend a car show they had entered their hot rods in three weeks earlier. Harold drove his '69 Firebird, Bryan drove his '69 Boss Mustang, Tony drove his '69 Dodge Charger, and Chris turned heads in his '73 Chevy Nova. After parking side by side and setting up their cars for display, they walked around and looked at other antique cars, enjoying the food sold at various booths and the music played by a live band on the stage under a large blue-and-white pavilion.

Around six o'clock, temperatures were still at one hundred degrees, but the beauty of all the old cars had somehow taken their minds off the scorching heat. A rare find near a three-foot-tall retaining wall had caught Tony's eyes. Since there were not many people around it, they decided to hang out there for a few minutes to conduct their weekly male bonding meeting.

"A 1969 Dodge Super Bee," said Tony, who lusted over the car's beauty as if it were a woman. "Man, it looks brand-new. This had to be a frame-off restoration. It's *too* clean!"

"I agree with you, man," said Chris. "This is a beautiful work of creation."

"I disagree with both of you," Bryan chimed in. "It's not as beautiful as the works of creation getting ready to cruise past us in ten, nine, eight, seven …" Bryan positioned himself to get a good look, as the greatest of all the creations at the car show walked by them. "Y'all know the routine: wait 'til they pass us, and don't forget the three-second rule. Act like our wives are with us, and see all you can for three seconds. Don't make it a practice to look any longer than that. Trust me. You'll defiantly get caught."

After the beautiful women had cruised past them, the men continued with the scoring game they liked to play when their wives weren't around. While the judges made their selections and picked the top-ten most beautiful cars, Chris and the boys picked their own top-five beauties they thought were suitable for awards. They also made a list of what cars were the most beautiful at the show.

"Oh, my goodness! Oh, my God! Surely, God will grant any man pardon who surrenders to the beauty of the one on the right," Bryan said as he pretended to bow to a queen. "I'd follow her straight to hell. Her beauty will put out the fire! And if she loved me forever, I wouldn't feel the pain. What you think about them, Chris?"

"Almost as beautiful as the back end of a '69 Camaro."

"A '69 Camaro doesn't have anything on those beauties, my friend," Bryan replied.

"Aren't we married men?" put in Harold. "I can't believe what I'm hearing here. Neither of them are as beautiful as heaven. And if you fall for her beauty, pain is all you goin' t' feel both now and forever from your wife and from what you thinks gonna be a beautiful fire in hell. Y'all better wake up, and get your minds right." Before Harold could finish his unwanted comments, all the guys took turns yelling at him.

"Be quiet, Harold. Don't spoil our fun," said Tony.

"Go jump in the river, and wash your sins away after we're done judging; we'll forgive you later," Chris joked as he put his arm around Harold's shoulders and laughed.

"Married or not, you gotta admit the one on the left is prettier than candy paint on a Cadillac. Man, just her shadow alone will cause a preacher to get amnesia on the thou shalts and thou shalt nots. He'll be asking questions like the devil. Did God really say, 'Don't pick but one woman'? She so fine, she'll make you understand the Scriptures differently than what they really mean," Tony said.

"Don't let Harold fool y'all. He be looking too," said Chris.

"Actually, I go blind when beautiful women are in my presence. I don't want to risk fallen down like y'all and hurting my wife and family," replied Harold.

"Harold must be getting along with his wife right now," Bryan said. "Wait another a week or two, and see what he says. She'll be done turned on him by then. He'll be wantin' one of us to bring him a cross and a fire truck full of holy water to cleanse her of that evil spirit that hides behind a woman's beauty once she becomes your wife."

He looked Harold in the eyes and continued. "Your wife is always gonna be a woman. You're crazy if you think she's gonna change. That's one thang I've learned after being married to four different races of women. White, Black, Hispanic, and Brazilian women I've dated and been married to are all the same, so don't let them fool you. All of them give you the same problems, but in different ways."

"When they goin' t' stop fooling you? If women are all the same, why you keep getting married and cheat on your wives?" Harold responded.

"I can't resist their beauty. There is nothing more beautiful than women to me. I need some kind of help to stop me from falling into the addictive beauty of their mind, body, and soul. A drug addict can stay away from the drug houses to get away from his addiction, but what can I do? There's nowhere I can go without seeing what I'm addicted to not dressed in tight jeans, sexy clothes, and half-dressed for my eyes to see."

"I was just messing with you man. We know it's hard. Yeah, it's true that Audrey and I have been getting along real good lately. It took some years of praying, but it was worth the wait. I wouldn't trade my wife for nobody. We've been blessed with our mortuary business for three years now. I thought I'd get used to seeing death every day, which I have, but … when I get someone in that's young, just like me or my wife, I can't help but think about me and my family. I even think about you guys and your families. When it's me or my wife's time to take a nap in that casket, I don't want to think about how I should've loved her. I don't want her and the kids to wonder if I'm going to heaven. I want to know for sure what's going to happen with the souls that lived in these bodies of ours when they fail us. I want to know for certain my family is going to heaven."

"OK, man," Tony said. You're not dying of anything, are you? If you are, don't tell us, here? This isn't the right time and place to share this kind of thing. I don't want to be seen crying in front of all these people. I gotta image to maintain."

"Naw, Tony," Harold explained. "I'm just saying that I realize that we all believe in God, so we need to start living right or whatever it takes to get to heaven. We're going to be laid on a table one day. It's just getting hard for me to do my job without asking myself if I will see this person's face again in heaven, or if they did something in their life that no one knows about that's going to cause them not to make it to heaven. Is this little girl or this little boy going to heaven? My job is starting to be more than just preparing dead bodies to be buried in the ground. We can't change anything when we're dead. Whatever we believe or don't believe is nonnegotiable when we leave this place. I know the economy is bad right now, but I'm gonna have to find something else to do for a living if I don't get some kind of understanding about life and death. Heaven or hell is what I wonder now when I'm working on someone."

"Take you a vacation and have yourself a drink, buddy. You'll forget all about it," said Tony. He looked over at Chris and said, "Hey, Chris. Your dad was a preacher. Did he ever tell you what all it took to keep your salvation and not lose it?"

Chris was hesitant to answer the question. He knew the answer, but he felt confused. What he learned from his father—that you got to heaven by simply believing Jesus died for everyone's sins—contradicted what he had heard from other preachers and friends who quoted other Bible verses that contradicted the ones his father used. The sinful way his father had died only complicated the issue of salvation.

"I don't remember," Chris lied.

There was a moment of silence among the crew of hot-rodders. They had been friends since any of them could remember. They had many awkward moments during their friendship, but when it came to the death of a loved one, no one knew what to say to comfort the other.

"Sorry, man; I didn't mean to bring your father up in this. We all seemed to stop going to church after he . . . ." Tony paused. He couldn't think of a good word to describe what had happened to Chris's father, so he used the big D word as carefully as he knew how. "Died," he said in a very sympathetic voice.

"We should find a good church to start going to," Bryan suggested.

"That's a good idea, especially after Harold's words of encouragement on . . . dying," said Tony, trying to shift the conversation away from the terrible, sinful, tragic death of Chris's father. "Sounds like another place to drive our cars on the weekend to me."

"Let's start 'round September when it cools off, though," Harold suggested. "It's too hot to go to church right now."

"You the one brought up going to church, and now you want to stop blowing hot air in the balloon and let it crash," Bryan replied.

"But it's so hot on the weekends, 'specially on Sunday mornings for some reason when some football, basketball, or some type of sport comes on before church is over," Harold explained.

"All the talk about hell does make Sundays feel like the hottest day of the week. I feel you there," said Tony.

"I think the whole idea of tryin' to find a church to go to is a waste of time," Chris said.

All the guys stood with their mouths wide open as they tried to grasp what they were hearing come out of the mouth of a preacher's son.

"How can you say something like that, man?" Harold asked.

"Sometimes, I believe in God and, sometimes, I don't. This one time when I was looking for a church to start attending, I was forced to give up after visiting five different churches. I went looking for God and couldn't find him. I asked the pastor at one of the churches to give me some Scriptures to read to make me feel better about a problem I was having at work with a coworker." Chris took a seat on the retaining wall as he replayed in his mind what had taken place that day and tried to explain to his friend's one of the many excuses that had caused him to stop going to church.

—

It was ten years after his father's death when Chris began visiting different churches in search of a new church home. After the pastor of The Better Covenant Church finish his sermon, Chris hurried to catch him as he walked down the hallway on his way to his office.

"Reverend Clyde, you got a minute? I need to ask you something," said Chris, he unintentionally blocked Reverend Clyde's path, which didn't sit well with the good Reverend.

"Boy, if you don't move out from front of me!" said Reverend Clyde. He was a tall, skinny Black man with glasses and a four-inch-tall Afro who looked to be in his early forties. "You new ain't you? I ain't never seen you befow. You on my church roll?"

Chris apologized and stood next to Reverend Clyde.

"Sorry sir about standing in front of you. Yes, I'm a visitor. I've been having a lot of problems in my life, and I decided to try to get back in church and get close to God in hopes that he'll make everything all right," Chris said in a voice of desperation.

"Wuss yo' name?"

"Chris Shoemaker," Chris answered. Reverend Clyde put his right arm around Chris, never taking his eyes off the beautiful, plus-sized, brown-skinned woman he had been staring at when Chris blocked his view.

"You pay yo' tithes today?" Reverend Clyde asked.

"Yes sir, I did," Chris answered.

Reverend Clyde's smile shone brighter than hundreds of blinding flashes from cameras photographing swimsuit models on a dimly lit runway.

"You don't need to look nowhere else; you done fount yo' new church home. Since you new, let me inform you one thang, one very important rule we have here at this church. Listen carefully. Pay . . . yo' . . . tithes . . . first—before fixiating yo' mouth to ask for anythang from Gawd. Don't 'speck! Gawd to grant you favor to approach me for permission to pick out of the flock any woman you choose to offer him as a sexual sacrifice for yo' sins." Reverend Clyde took his arm off Chris's shoulder and used his hands to describe the coveted favor he believed God had granted him for his new church and newly formed religion. "Gawd has granted this church a covenant for our sexual gratification. We offer sexual sacrifices instead of animal sacrifices like they did in the Bible. A rib from a bull would go good after our sacrificial ceremonies, but that can get expensive. Sex is free to recycle as long as a woman don't charge; barbecued animals ain't. So we choose to exchange the animal sacrifice part of the Bible with the sacrificing of our bodies for Christ. The animals don't fit in our church budget like they did in the Old Testament days."

Chris made a weird face and tried to cut their conversation short. "It was nice talking to you, but I got a long list of things to take care of," he said. He knew from what he was hearing that Reverend Clyde was changing the meanings of certain Bible verses to benefit himself and to justify doing what he wanted to do instead of what the Bible said to do. Chris didn't know the Bible that well, but he knew that Reverend Clyde wasn't right.

Reverend Clyde pushed a little harder to try to gain Chris as a new member completely ignoring his signals to end the conversation.

"The spirit of Gawd spoke to me one morning after I was passed out drunk in the middle of the Street of Plenty. I took my last drink, threw away my last fix, and checked myself into rehab that day."

Chris tried once again to break away by looking at his phone. He positioned his mouth to speak and cut Reverend Clyde off from talking, but Reverend Clyde ignored the signal and continued trying to impress him to join his church. "Our statement of faith at this church is that we believe that all sins are derived from sex. Everyone lies for sex; everyone steals for sex; every reason for every sin committed can be traced all the way back down to sex." Reverend Clyde had finally taken his eyes off the beautiful woman standing in the hallway. "That's why we've made a covenant with Gawd to offer sexual sacrifices. We are the only church you will find in the world that has been granted permission to do this." Reverend Clyde placed his arm back around Chris's neck and gave him three tugs. On the third tug, he pulled him in close. In a low voice, he told Chris. "You's a young mayun. Look at what you wouldn't o' got to see if I wouldn'a stood you next to me, boy," he said, referring to the beautiful woman in the hallway. Ain't no beautiful, sexy women like that in heabin. This is it! Earth is the last stop for sex. Ain't no mo' after this life."

Reverend Clyde removed his arm from Chris's neck and bounced up and down three times as if he were jumping rope without his toes leaving the ground. Then he swung his left arm upward twice with his fist balled as if he were getting ready to shout for joy. With his teeth gritted together, he made a grunt that sounded as if he had waited too late to use the restroom and said, "You better sin all you can before we leave here. All you have to do is offer God some type of sacrifice for yo' sins like the people did in the Old Testament. See, a lot of people be missing things like that that we can still apply to our lives today."

Chris grew confused. "I thought heaven was supposed to be better than any sin we can think of committing and that we don't honor God by doing that kind of . . . ."

Reverend Clyde interrupted Chris in the middle of his sentence. "You show me in the Bible where it say that at!" Reverend Clyde yelled. "What church you been going ta?"

Before Chris could answer him, Reverend Clyde interrupted him again, stomping one foot at a time as he spoke. "I just hate it when other pastors and churches confuse people by teaching Gawd's Word like that." Reverend Clyde retrieved a handkerchief from his pocket and wiped his forehead. "You done got me to preachin' off the clock, and now I'm a' have to explain to the church why I'm taking a extra hundred dollars from the offering for overtime to try to get us a new member and correct the misteachings of Gawd's Word."

Reverend Clyde paused to catch his breath. "I came up with and prayed about my idea I had for this church, and Gawd answers prayers. Several years ago when I was in the sex, drug, and alcohol rehab center. I read in the Bible where it said 'ask, and ye shall receive.' Gawd is a good gawd. I have received by faith this church." He smiled proudly. "I'm trying to teach people how to use common sense and read between the lines when they read the Bible. That's the only way you'll ever understand the Bible. I'm a' just have to take a little mo' from the offering for overtime so I can explain this to you. Listen, 'cause I'm fixin' ta go deep. The Bible says that it is better to put your seed in the belly of a whore than to cast it on the ground."

"Where does it say that at? Isn't that adultery?" Chris asked, confused.

"Did Gawd call you to preach?"

"No, sir."

"Then why you questioning His Word? You don't question Gawd!" There was a pause as he got himself together after yelling at Chris. All of a sudden, Reverend Clyde put his left hand on Chris's shoulder and his right hand on top of his head and began to preach to Chris in an old Southern-Baptist–style preaching voice. He dragged and stretched out his words as if he were singing a hymn.

"To answer your question, the Lord told me to tell you if there is a mutual—mm-hm—agreement betweence you and your wife or girlfriend, then it's OK. Abraham gave Sarah permission to play house with Pharaoh. Sarah then let Abraham play house with Hagar. God used Abraham and Sarah to be leaders and bless those who bless them. We follow along in the footsteps of Father Abraham and Mother Sarah so we can be blessed."

Reverend Clyde threw both hands into the air and did a quick praise dance before placing both hands back on Chris's shoulders. "Just the thought of adultery is the same thang as committing adultery in the flesh. Might as well do it. You might as well do in the flesh what you do in yo' mind, mm-hm, 'cause it's the same thang." Reverend Clyde began to settle down. "Thank you for your Word, Master," he said to God and then spoke to Chris again. "Gawd will forgive you yo' sins. It's written in His Word." After delivering a quick message from God, Reverend Clyde took his hands off Chris and acted as if he didn't know what had just happened to him, giving Chris an almost believable impression that he had just received a new revelation from the Holy Spirit.

"I hate to rush you, young man, but what was it that you pulled me to the side for? They's waiting on me to officiate the sacrifices down in the basement. You mo' than welcome to come if you wanna, but you got to bring yo' own bottle of ceremonial wine. This economy has got the church on a budget. We goin' t' have to use the lights from our cell phones for candles down there next month until I'm able to put back a little of what Gawd gave to me in the tithes and offerings to support my flock."

"I was just wondering if you could provide me with some Scriptures to read that relate to how to deal with people who do you dirty on your job," Chris said.

"Oh, that's easy. Read the hundred and tenth number of Psalms, verse one, I think where it says, "The Lord says to my lord: 'Sit at my right hand until I make your enemies a footstool for your feet.'" Yes, sir, I like that promise. God promised us right there that he'd knock our enemies down so we can step up above them who try to knock us down. Glory to God!"

—

Chris faded back into the present day with his friends at the car show as he neared the end of his story of the weird religious encounter. "He told me that God would make my enemies a footstool for my feet. All I had to do was just do what the verse said and get closer to *Gawd*. He motivated me with the enemies being a footstool for my feet verse at first, but I left with nothing. I still don't know how to get close to God so He'll bless me instead of making me suffer like I've been doing."

"What kind of church is that?" asked Tony. "Man, that church sounds like some kinda cult, but believe it or not, it's a lot of churches like that all around the world. But I heard that's in the Bible about God making our enemies a footstool for our feet. I haven't read it for myself, but I believe it's in there 'cause a lot of people say it is, so what's so wrong with that?"

"How many of your enemies are you above?" asked Chris. "I have to agree with what Bryan said earlier. Sometimes our wives can be our worst enemy. Which one of us is truly the ruler over our wives? My problem with that verse is this. Many of my enemies have defeated me while I held on to that promise. When I turn on the TV, I see millions of people suffering at the hands of their enemies. Here I am with a college degree and I can't get a job 'cause my hair and other features are different than someone who's fully White. No offense to y'all," Chris added to Harold and Tony who were both thirty year old Black men. Bryan, the only White guy in the group was twenty-eight. At twenty-nine, Chris had still not figured out which color he wanted to claim to be because his father was Black and his mother was White. With his skin tone, Chris could pass as a light-skinned Black man or a White man with a Black man's physical features and facial features.

"I've never thought about it like that. I see what you're saying 'cause if that verse on making your enemies your footstool were true then all the good people would have all the good jobs, wouldn't be suffering and struggling to pay the bills and stuff like that." said Tony. "It seems like people who don't even try to do right get blessed the most."

A thought had dawned on Harold about Reverend Clyde, and out of nowhere, he blurted it out as he tried to recall where he had heard Reverend Clyde's name. "Wait a minute, the Street of Plenty!"

"Dude, what you talkin' bout?" Tony asked.

"The street of plenty where you can get plenty of drugs, plenty of alcohol, and plenty of everything sinful you can think of on one street over in the east end!"

"Oh yeah, I know what street your talking about." Bryan answered.

"I know who he is. I went with the coroner over there one time and he was over there . . . ." Harold paused. "Well, I'm not trying to make a preacher look bad for what he does in secret, so I'll just say he's a well-known celebrity over there so I'd be careful on believing anything he says."

"I didn't believe none of it," said Chris.

"I heard a preacher interpret that verse as a promise from God the father to His Son Jesus that He was going to make this earth and His enemies on this earth a footstool for His feet so He could be king over the earth or something like that," said Bryan.

"I'm surprised you know anything about the Bible judging from the way you live," Tony said, laughing.

"Shut up," Bryan replied. "I ain't never seen any angels flying around your shoulders. You ain't no better."

"I believe that's why my father did what he did—because of them church folk he preached to and his job." Chris paused. "They were my father's enemies, but they won't be mine. I'm a' own my own business someday. I'll never preach, so I don't have to worry about church folks doing me like they did my father. Criticizing all of his sermons, overlooking him for promotions on his job. He worked hard for his enemies. Getting up there telling folks lies about a book that's supposed to be the truth, shaking the Bible at folks every Sunday, and then they talk about him and each other as soon as they leave church. Ain't happening with me." He tapped himself on the chest for emphasis. "With all the knowledge Dad had about God, I just can't understand why he did what he did. He must have found out that the Bible he preached from wasn't true before he. . . ." Chris paused. "That book has way too many contradictions for me."

All the guys were uneasy. They all believed that what his father had done was unforgivable and shameful to the family members he left behind to deal with the embarrassing end to what could've been an honorable memory of his father. A preacher, of all people, doing what he did only caused greater doubt in the minds of both believers and nonbelievers who discussed the incident in secret.

"It is now time to announce the top three winners of today's car show," said the announcer over the loudspeaker. "In third place, we have the owner of the customized 1954 Chevy pickup, Michael Brown of North Little Rock. In second place, we have the owner of the 1967 Camaro, Benny Johnson of Maumelle. In first place, we have the owner of the 1969 Dodge Charger, Tony Brooks of Little Rock."

"We won again!" said Tony, referring to their club as he gave high fives to the rest of the crew.

"Go get our trophy. Another one for the collection," said Bryan.

Tony proudly walked up the stairs and shook hands with the other winners on stage as he passed them. A young woman who was assisting the judges presented Tony with his trophy. As the assistant and all of the winners all posed together for a picture, Tony, who was facing the crowd, noticed that Chris was no longer with the rest of the guys who were cheering him on. Chris had somehow eased out of sight from his friends and had gotten in his car.

When the ceremony was over, Tony made his way down from the stage, clutching his trophy and scanning the crowd for Chris. He glimpsed him fifty yards away closing the hood on his car and preparing to leave the park.

"What happened with Chris?" he asked the guys as he joined them. "Is everything all right?"

All the guys began looking around to see if they could spot Chris.

"Where did he go?" asked Harold.

"I saw him getting in his car when I was getting our trophy. He's leaving the park now," Tony said pointing out Chris's car through the crowd.

"Let me call him and see if he's all right," said Harold.

—

Being careful not to run over any spectators or their kids, Chris drove slowly through the crowd, shaking the ground beneath their feet with the rumble of the 454 cubic inch engine he had rebuilt with the help of his hot rod friends. Each light touch he applied to the gas pedal aroused the shiny, chrome-out, seven-hundred-horsepower engine. It responded with a deep, low-frequency growl that sounded like a lion warning his enemies. Dangerous power hid within the beauty of the custom orange-and-cream leather interior and matching candy apple orange body with cream racing stripes.

As he left the car show without saying good-bye to his friends, he thought about his wife and kids and remembered a promise he'd made to himself never to abandon them like his father had left him and his mother when he was a child. That was how he thought of his father's death—as abandonment—because he couldn't bring himself to say or even think the word *suicide* in relation to his father. All the comments that his friends had made about life, death, families, and his father raced through his mind as he entered the freeway. Chris normally soothed his frustrations on the weekends by making a few passes on the racetrack. The sound of an angry engine going over one hundred miles per hour was like therapeutic music to his ears. Preoccupied by his thoughts but dimly aware that it was Friday evening, the official start of the weekend, Chris pretend the long stretch of freeway in front of him was the weekend racetrack where he loved to put the beast of an engine he and his friends built to the test. He gripped the steering wheel as he entered the interstate and yelled out, "Ah!"

As he prepared to make a run, flashbacks replayed in his mind of when he was twelve years old and sitting in the front row at his dad's funeral. "It hurts, it hurts!" he said with great emotion as he pounded on his steering wheel. Pain overflowed and consumed his emotions. Years of pain recycled itself inside his soul because of what his father had done. "I just can't take it! Where are you, God! I wish I could just run over you for being so cruel!"

Chris stomped on the gas pedal and sent the Nova fishtailing. He eased up on the gas pedal enough to regain control as he used the freeway as his own therapeutic racetrack. Most of the Friday nighters had already made it to their hangouts, which left the interstate uncongested. The touch-screen television/radio installed between the dashboard and console area and tied into his cell phone flashed in the corner of his eye. He quickly looked down and saw that it was Harold calling. Instead of answering the call, he stomped the gas pedal to the floor as if going faster would make it stop flashing.

"He didn't answer," Harold told the crew. "I'm a' call him again."

The screen flashed again as Harold tried a second time to contact Chris.

Chris slowed down and took deep breaths as if he were the one doing all the work it took to move the Nova over one hundred miles per hour down the interstate. Finally, he answered the phone.

"Hello."

"What's up, man? We're about to go get something to eat. Where you at?"

"I'm heading to the house to do the family thang; I'll holla at y'all tomorrow."

"All right, then. Holla at us if you need anything."

"I will."

"All right. Love you."

The phone got quiet. None of the guys had ever said the big L word to one another before. It took Harold a few seconds to realize what he had accidentally said.

"Hoo-wee! Aw, naw, wait. Hold on. I'm sorry, man. That was out of habit. I'm so used to saying it just to be saying it when I get off the phone with my wife that . . . . Man, you understand. My bad."

Chris held the phone away from his ear with a disgusted expression. He was getting ready to respond but decided to pretend that he hadn't heard him. He hung up, hoping to save Harold and himself from an embarrassing moment.

By now, Chris had realized that he was on the interstate and slowed down to the speed limit before he caused an accident or got a ticket.

"Whoo, good. He already hung up," Harold said as he put his phone back into his pocket.

But it was too late. The rest of the gang had overheard Harold's romantic interlude and teased him without mercy.

"Oh, Chris, how I love thee," said Tony.

"I can't wait to see you again, my sweet Chris," said Bryan.

"Say one mo' thang and I'm a' kick the car of whoever wants to be cute," Harold said. "I tell ya that now, so try me."

"I'm jealous; I've never had a man to tell me anything so sweet," Bryan said as he placed one of his wrists on top of the other and held them in front of his waist, blinking his eyelids rapidly as if he were a shy young lady.

"Knock it off, or I'm going to put a dent in it, I mean it man," Harold said as he walked toward Bryan's' car.

"Take it easy. I'm just joking," Bryan said with a frown.

"Well, Harold what did he say? Is he going to get his wife's permission and meet us there later or what?" asked Tony.

"Naw, he said he'll catch up with us tomorrow. Let's ride and get us something to eat."

CHAPTER 2

Wrestling with an Angel

For eight long years, Chris and Angel had sent prayers up to God asking for everything except the rights and title to the earth and the universe in which he made. Little did they know, God had answered everyone of their prayers, but they never noticed it, because he didn't answer their prayers to the exact specifications that they requested? There was nothing wrong with the home they lived in, but they had known when they bought it that they'd grow out of it once God wrote kids into the chapters of their lives.

Chris and Angel lived with their children, six-year-old Heath and four-year-old Jacob, in an old subdivision behind a new subdivision in Forest Acres in Bryant. Driving past the new subdivision every day to make it home reminded them that God had not yet answered their prayers for a new home.

It was about 7:45 P.M. when Chris arrived home. Angel was talking on the couch with Harold's wife, Audrey, and didn't hear him come in. Chris overheard her complaining about something when he opened the door and decided to tiptoe in and eavesdrop. Just like Chris, it was hard to determine Angel's race by looking at her because of her olive-colored skin that darkened in the summer and lightened to that of a Caucasian woman in the winter. Her shoulder-length black hair had the thick, silky texture of African American woman. Her eyes were black, and her physical features were those of a slightly muscularly toned athlete. At five-foot eleven inches tall, Angel stood slightly taller than Chris who was five-foot eight. Audrey was a big boned black woman who wore hazel green contacts and a natural afro of medium height.

"Yeah, I know what you mean, girl," Angel said. "What good is having a man and submitting to him like we're their kids, but yet we go to work and pay bills just like they do? We're doing everything a man does these days including playing the father role for our kids. Men aren't men anymore. Lord knows if a man can't take care of his wife, he's not gonna do much for the kids. Hanging out drinking and acting a monkey like he ain't even got a family. He makes, me, sick!"

Chris stood quietly in the kitchen and leaned over close to the doorway so he could hear all of her complaints clearly.

"Harold is right 'long with him. All men are alike."

"Yeah, girl, I used to think that if I married a preacher or a preacher's son that my marriage and life would be blessed, but that ain't true. Humph. Seems like the devil stays in them more than he does the sinners in the streets."

"I've had several pastors try to holla at me," Audrey said. "I know exactly what you mean."

"Chris's dad taught him a lot about the Bible, but he doesn't even pick it up anymore. All he wants to do is be by himself and work on old rusty cars. I could be driving a brand-new car for what he spent on that orange juice machine on wheels, but every time he makes some extra money, he spends it on that car and never ask me if I want or need anything. I wouldn't be mad or fuss if he'd be considerate or thoughtful enough to think about me like he thinks about them old, raggedy cars he gawks over. You'd think that somebody who loves cars as much as he does would have a nice one for his wife, but, no, he's got me driving a '85 Ford Escort."

That remark struck Chris as unfair. He had done a fine job restoring the Escort. It looked like brand-new and even smelled brand-new thanks to Tony's upholstery skills. He had created beautiful two-toned designs and traced them with white pin-stripe ropes to separate the navy-blue-and-beige leather designs. Harold had helped Chris rebuild the motor and Bryan had helped with the paint and bodywork. They had clothed the RS turbo tuner car in midnight pearl blue with lots of shiny metallic and made ghost flames and racing stripes out of carbon material. The car looked brand-new, but it had one flaw: It wasn't the 2005 Cadillac that Angel had wanted.

Angel continued venting. "And had the nerve to put some racing stripes on it like I want to be seen passing somebody in it," she said.

Chris covered his mouth to hold in the laughter bubbling up in his gut. He tiptoed over to the door, closed it hard enough for Angel to hear, and began making loud noises while he fumbled through the cabinets.

"Jacob! Heath!" Chris yelled as he went through the house opening and slamming doors for the sole purpose of getting Angel's attention. He grabbed the one-gallon jug of purified water from the refrigerator and a glass from the dishwasher and poured himself a glass of water before walking into the living room.

"Hey, Audrey," he said as he entered the room. Turning to Angel, he asked. "Where's Jacob and Heath at?"

"They're spending the night over at my mom's house so you can stop yelling and slamming doors." Angel beveled her head down and gave Chris a dirty look. "You can get over being mad that I asked you not to hang out late some other time. Don't think I don't know you after eight years of marriage, buddy."

"When did you plan on asking me could they spend the night?"

Angel tightened her lips and raised her hand stiffly to shoulder level, giving it a quick jerk as if she were saluting by touching her lips instead of her forehead.

"If you knew what was best for you you'd hold that water in your big mouth like a camel holds it in the humps in his back and get out my face. You don't legislate nothing over this committee at this residence," said Angel.

"You said you wanted help with the kids earlier on the phone and they ain't even here," said Chris.

Angel got up, walked over to Chris, pulled him by the arm, and led him to the kitchen.

"I'm sorry. I said I was going to work on my attitude and I see my attitude getting messy. Audrey is going to be leaving in a little while, and we can spend some quality time together. In the meanwhile, think about what I can work on that will keep you from putting up roadblocks in the path of your love for me, OK? I know you don't believe me, but I really want to be a good wife. I'm sorry that I lost control and flew Jacob's metal airplane into your arm the other night. I want to make it up to you. That's why I sent the kids to my mothers."

"You mean my head!" Chris said referring to the metal airplane.

"I don't want to argue," said Angel. I said I'm sorry, OK?"

"Control your anger and tie your lips in a knot; that'll move all the roadblocks," Chris mumbled.

"What! That's not fair. If you don't provoke me, then I'll never get angry."

"So I can't tell you the truth. You want me to lie to you and be miserable about things you do that I don't like so you can be pleased with yourself? Is that it?"

"Look, we'll talk about this later when Audrey leaves . . . without fussing." Angel went back in the living room and sat back on the couch.

What a mistake it was to decide to come home from doing something I loved doing to hang out with my wife, Chris thought. So he went through all of the cabinets looking for his whiskey, but it was all gone. Then, he stood behind the couch that Audrey was sitting on and interrogated Angel.

"Where is my stuff at?" he said in a demanding voice, using body language to signify that he was speaking of his whiskey.

Angel fired back with a few of her own custom-made kinesics, which Chris had learned how to read during their eight years of marriage. She looked at Chris with a grin, shrugged her shoulders, and wiped her hands together sarcastically to signify that she had thrown it away.

Chris grabbed his keys and went to use the master bathroom where he found five empty whiskey bottles on the side of the Jacuzzi. He had planned to stop drinking, but it frustrated and angered him that Angel would treat him like a kid by making the decision for him. He went back into the kitchen and headed toward the door that exited to the garage.

"Where are you going?" asked Angel.

"To replace what you poured out. I'm not your child. You need to respect me as a man," Chris replied as he pounded on the counter with his fist.

"Yeah, I sure did pour it out, and I dare you to bring some more back in my house, too. As a matter of fact, hand me the keys, Chris. I don't want you drinking." Angel got off the couch and walked toward him.

"There you go again, Jesus, with all your power and authority you think you have over me. I give the commandments in this house, not you. You need to start giving me my respect," he told Angel.

"We need to talk, so give me the keys, and we'll talk about this later when our company leaves."

"No, Momma," Chris responded sarcastically.

"I ain't yo' momma, and thank God I'm not. I'd feel like I let God down by raising such a sorry weak boy who ain't nowhere close to being a man. If it weren't for my help, you'd be a drunken monkey with nothing.

You seem to have forgotten who makes the most money around here, haven't you?"

"Thank God He didn't give me a little girl to raise to break her of her mother's werewolflike instincts," Chris replied. "And if I didn't have to put up with you, I wouldn't have a reason to be getting drunk." Something started happening to Angel. Her posture and all her emotions changed as she locked in on Chris like a hungry tiger that hadn't had a meal in five days. The look on her face terrified Chris, but he tried to hide it. She walked past Chris with her eyes locked on him and locked the door, never taking her eyes off him, and stood between him and the door. Chris stepped to Angel's left side and so did she. Then he stepped to her right side, and so did she. He wanted to leave without putting on a show in front of Audrey, but Angel blocked the only path that led to the garage.

"Are you calling me a werewolf?" she asked as she grabbed him by his shirt.

"Let go of my shirt and let go of me! I'm not going to stay here and argue with you!" Chris demanded.

"You're not going anywhere until we talk! Why is it that I have to put up with mistreatment at work and at home? I'm not happy, Chris. And just the thought of you calling me a werewolf to my face in front of our friend and then trying to lie about it just makes me mad!" Angel said as she snatched on his shirt and ripped it.

"You done tore my shirt; I just got this shirt!" yelled Chris. "Let me go, Angel! I'm not staying here and putting up with this now! We're getting a divorce." Chris paused, remembering that he made a promise to himself that he'd never leave his family for any reason other than death. Deep down inside of his heart, he knew Angel was the kind of loving wife who helped him raise their two boys and pay the bills without complaining, and said more calmly, "I'm not in the mood today Angel."

"Take the shirt off, and the pants, and I'll let you leave," said Angel. "I helped pay for them, so leave them so I can sell them and get my money back. I'm part owner of everything you own. You don't make no money to buy nothing on your own."

"Let me go and I will," Chris replied. Angel let Chris go and he went into the bedroom to take off his pants with Angel trailing right behind him. "Can you leave the room, please?"

Angel left and went into the kitchen to finish putting up the dishes to ease and clear her mind.

In a moment, Chris came out of the bedroom and back into the kitchen.

"Who were you calling a werewolf, Chris?" Angel asked without moving her jawbone.

Clang! Clink! Angel threw a plate at Chris, but missed it and hit the wall followed by a glass, and then picked up another glass, poised to throw it.

"Don't you throw! Stop! That's my favorite glass; put it down!"

"Here!" Angel said as she flung the glass at Chris, barely missing his head. It shattered against the wall.

He decided that it was time to fix his bad judgment in calling his beautiful wife, Angel, a werewolf.

"Do you have a daughter?" Chris asked.

"Don't ask me a stupid question like that; do you have a brain, smart dummy?"

"Do you have a daughter?" Chris repeated so that he could try to end the argument that he knew was about to escalate out of control.

Audrey continued to sit extremely still on the couch as she watched their disagreement as if it were a soap opera.

Angel gave Chris one of her looks that said, I know what you're up to and you're not getting off the hook this easy.

"No, you don't." Chris answered his own question for Angel. "So how could I have been talking to you?"

"A daughter is a mother's child." Angel straightened her posture, relaxed a little, folded her arms, and leaned against the wall. "Oh, I see. I'll be sure to let my mother know just how you feel about her. She hasn't done nothing to you and you want to call her names behind her back."

Realizing that he was still locked in the cage-style boxing ring with no key to let himself out, Chris tried to surrender.

"I didn't mean it the way it sounded, baby. I had a rough day, and I can tell you did, too, so ah, ha, ha," Chris said, laughing to loosen up the tense situation. "Let's just start over." He put his hands on Angel's shoulders.

Angel looked at his hands with a frown and her shoulders began to feel as if they were hot skillets coming off a hot stove. He quickly snatched his hands away.

"Look, I'm coming through the door. I'm just getting home." Chris opened the door and closed it. "Honey, I'm home," he said.

Just as Chris got ready to give Angel a hug, she stopped him and said, "We had better not hug. I don't want to squeeze you to death nor give you a slobbery kiss. I haven't turned back into a human yet, and I haven't had my shots."

"Oh, come on, Angel. Will you stop?"

"I'll stop when you tell me who you were calling a werewolf. Just tell me the truth and I may look over your ignorance. I know you can say things that you don't mean out of anger, so I'll take that into consideration," Angel said and fold her arms.

It's finally going to be over with, Chris thought. "OK. I admit it. I was talking about you, but I didn't mean it. You called me a little boy, so what's the difference? We're even. You called me a name . . . and I called you a name."

Chris held out his hand in hopes to finalize the deal with a good firm handshake or a hug.

Angel looked at his hand and backed away. Smiling, she said in a polite voice, "I need to finish putting the dishes away. I haven't put the knives up yet."

Chris stood there with his hand stuck out, waiting for Angel to shake his hand and trying to figure out why she didn't. He backed up to the door and put his hand on the doorknob just in case if he needed to make a quick getaway.

Angel went to the dishwasher, grabbed several knives, and placed them on the countertop. She gave Chris an evil smile and with a knife in her hand, she cocked her arm back but had to uncock it immediately because her target had already moved out the door as quickly as a ghost or an angel. By the time Angel ran through the doorway and into the garage to chase him down, Chris was already in his Nova that he had parked in the detached one car bay garage he used as his shop on the back side of their home.

"You better run, rabbit!—bounce!" Angel yelled at Chris as he started to back into the driveway, rolling up the window and locking the doors with a look of fear on his face.

CHAPTER 3

Facing the Storm

"My usual please, single room, queen-size bed; second floor, preferably," Chris said sadly as he checked into his home away from home, a motel twenty-five minutes away in Little Rock. Angel never knew where Chris ran off to whenever they had a misunderstanding.

"You've spent enough money here to own part of this motel," a giggling voice replied from behind the counter.

Melody was a young White woman of about twenty-five. For several years, she had regularly assisted Chris with renting a room when fights with his wife forced him to leave home. "At the rate you're going, a divorce would be cheaper than keeping her," added Melody, who was going through a divorce after two years of marriage.

"I've told myself the same thing, but I don't want my kids to grow up without a father like I did," Chris replied. "Not having my father in my life because he left me has been like waiting twenty years for a death sentence to be carried out for a crime you didn't commit. If I had the choice, I would've taken capital punishment over the sentence of life without a father that I received. I just can't do that to my kids on purpose."

"Here's your key," said Melody. "I don't have kids so I can only imagine what you're saying. Most people I know today get divorces and figure out their kid's sentence later. It's something to think about."

Chris's cell phone rang moments after he settled into his room, but he ignored the call. He turned on the TV, lay on the bed, and contemplated on whether he should call Angel back or turn off his phone to avoid a long night of arguing over the phone. Before he could make his decision, his cell phone rang again.

"Dang it, Angel, leave me alone!" he said to himself after checking his caller ID. Finally, he answered the phone.

"What! What do you want?"

"Who are you yelling at? And where are you?" Angel asked.

Chris didn't answer.

"Look, I'm tired of us arguing. Can you stop and get us some Chinese on your way home?" Angel asked in a sorrowful voice.

"I'm not coming home. You can glue some of them plates you threw at me together and make all the air steaks and potatoes you want for all I care."

"I'm sorry about throwing the dishes at you." Angel paused. "Can you come home? I know you're mad and I was wrong. It makes me mad that you just don't see how much I love you. You're always threatening me with divorce over small stuff. How am I supposed to trust you with my heart when you constantly put me in defensive mode with your threats of divorce? Aren't you going to apologize for your wrongdoing?"

Chris hung up the phone and grabbed his keys. He wasn't going to let a sincere apology convince him to return home—not this time. He had made up his mind: A divorce was the only answer. He could do nothing to restore his marriage. He had tried it all, from counseling to reading books on marriage. The one thing he hadn't tried was prayer. He thought that prayer was a waste of time. A bottle of brown liquor was his temporary solution to seemingly permanent problems that would never go away.

Silent lightning strikes illuminated the night clouds, warning of an approaching storm as he started to leave his hotel room to get Chinese food and whiskey for his private pity party dinner. Before he could close the hotel room door behind him, his phone rang again. Standing in the doorway, he wound his arm up to throw his cell phone into the wall but changed his mind and tossed it onto the bed instead, slamming the door tightly behind him.

Returning to his motel room twenty minutes later, he turned on the local news to find out what caliber of storm was approaching while he ate the Chinese food that Angel asked him to bring home and eat with her. In Arkansas, all storms have the potential to become tornadoes without warning. Interstate I-30 ran through the middle of the state and through Bryant where Chris lived and was one of the most frequently used paths that the storms blew threw. His phone began to ring just as he opened his brand-new bottle of whiskey to officially begin his pity party. There was no doubt in his mind that it was Angel calling, but he checked the caller ID to make sure. It was indeed his wife. To avoid cursing her and saying things he really didn't mean, Chris ignored her call.

"Twenty-two missed calls," Chris said to himself as he laid the phone on the table. "This doesn't make any sense at all." The phone began ringing again immediately. Even though he didn't want to talk to her, he answered the phone.

"What?" Chris yelled.

"Why are you being so mean to me?" Angel said in a tearful voice. "We need to just stop this, Chris."

"We!" Chris yelled. "You're the one messin' with me! When did one start equaling two?"

"I shouldn't have done what I did and run my big mouth. You tried to get us to start over. That's been playing on my conscience, and I'd hate for something to happen tonight and I'd never see you again. Come home and close the door again. Let's start over. Just come home and say, 'Honey, I'm, home.' I promise I'll control my emotions and we can have a good night."

"Let me think about it," Chris replied.

"OK." There was a pause. "You're not still thinking about leaving me, are you?"

Chris ignored the question and began smacking loudly on his orange chicken and rice dinner while Angel waited for a reply.

"Just tell me this. Do you still love me? If you don't, then I'll leave. I don't want to be a burden to anyone. You're a good man, Chris, and I know it. No matter what you hear me say about you sometimes, I really don't—"

"Then why the heck do you say things to put me down, then?" interrupted Chris rudely. He took a deep breath and calmed himself down. "Look, I don't want to talk right now. I'll call you later."

"Are you coming home? I don't want to stay here by myself with these storms moving in. I have a bad, strange feeling, and I'm scared."

"I'll let you know in a minute after I get done eating my Chinese."

Hurt by his selfishness, Angel kept her composure instead of waging war with a new argument; Angel chose the humble approach to deal with the consequences of ignoring Chris's white flag earlier that day. Angel had admitted that she was wrong, but it hadn't been enough to stop Chris from pitching his tent and setting up camp away from the presence of Angel's love. No forest fire, high winds, or sincere apologies would cause him to retreat from his position and take cover in the same city as his wife Angel.

"I'll call you back," he said. Then he hung up the phone.

About thirty minutes later, the local ten o'clock news came on. Chris had already drunk a half a bottle of whiskey, and knew he wouldn't be able to drive home. The local weatherman gave a brief analysis of the approaching storm. Severe thunderstorm warnings had been posted for the central area of the state. Chris loosened up with a few more swigs after hearing that the approaching storms were not likely to produce tornadoes. Small swigs became huge swigs until there were no more swigs left.

Thunder rumbled, telling Chris that the storm was getting closer to the motel in Little Rock where he had taken refuge from Angel's wrath. He decided to stretch out on the bed and rest his eyes for a few minutes.

While he slept, the storm knocked out the power, and the angry winds threw all kinds of debris against the motel walls, shattering windows and tearing off part of the roof. At 2:20 A.M., three hours after he emptied the contents of the whiskey bottle into his stomach, he woke up to a dark room. As he felt around for his cell phone to see what time it was, he noticed that the window had been broken. The floor was covered in glass, and the carpet and his clothes were drenched from the rain. Emergency sirens screeched and flashing lights reflected off the walls in his room, causing him to wonder if something more than a thunderstorm had passed through. He felt sprinkles of rain hitting the top of his head and looked up. The flashing lights revealed that sections of the roof had blown away, leaving a huge hole in the ceiling of his room. With the help of the lights, he found his cell phone and keys and rushed outside to see if the storm had done any damage to his car.

The far end of the motel had been destroyed by the storm, which he later learned had killed three people. Unable to walk downstairs to the first-floor level because debris from broken walls blocked the stairway, he climbed over the railing and tried to ease himself down to ground level. But the whiskey he had been drinking robbed him of his coordination, and he fell approximately six feet to the pavement of the parking lot, landing on his left side.

People were standing all around talking on cell phones, but no one noticed that he had fallen. They were all too busy describing to their friends and loved ones how they had just made it through a tornado that weather forecasters had incorrectly predicted as a thunderstorm. As Chris passed one bystander, he overheard the man say into his cell phone, "The tornado came out of nowhere. It started in Bryant and it's still on the ground in Faulkner County." After overhearing that the tornado had touched down in his hometown, Chris rushed to get his keys from his pocket and stumbled over his feet several times as he raced toward his car. Checking for damage to his car suddenly became the last thing on his mind. Two seconds wasn't fast enough for Chris to get home to check on Angel, who he now feared might have been hurt or even worse, taken away by the storm. Luckily, his car was parked on the side of the hotel that had escaped the tornado's fierce winds and hadn't suffered any damage. Not drunk, but very tipsy, Chris got in the car, put it in reverse, and called Angel. With his foot on the gas, he slammed the car from reverse to drive and came very close to locking up the transmission. The high-powered big block engine sent the Nova fishtailing to the right with smoke running away from the burning tires. Angel didn't answer her phone. He called her several more times with the same results. The interstate had small amounts of debris on it, which made Chris even more anxious about Angel's safety as he got close to Bryant city limits.

"Please let Angel be OK, God. Please, God, answer my prayer," Chris pleaded.

The closer he got to Bryant, the bigger the pieces of debris became. Chris seemed to have forgotten that a few hours earlier, he was sure that he didn't love Angel anymore. He had also been sure until that moment that prayer, just like his marriage, was a waste of time.

Less than one hundred feet in front of him was a refrigerator blocking most of the right lane and part of the left. Fifty feet past the refrigerator, a washing machine completely blocked the left lane of the interstate. Chris slowed down from one hundred to ninety miles per hour and swerved first to his left to avoid the refrigerator then immediately to the right to avoid the washing machine. He missed both obstacles, but then the right side of the car veered off the road. Chris pulled the steering wheel gently to the left to try to regain control. The wet streets from the heavy rains wouldn't allow the left side of the car to gain any traction, causing the whole car to slide off the shoulder onto the wet soaked ground.

Panicking, Chris pulled harder to the left and lost control. The Nova went airborne, flipping three times in the air. The driver's side door swung open, ejecting Chris, who had forgotten to put on his seat belt, across the access road on the side of the interstate into a batch of three-foot-tall grass.

The car landed upside down on the access road, flattening the top of the car before it rolled over the guardrails of a twenty-foot-long bridge without touching them and came to rest in four feet of water under the bridge.

Chris's vision was blurry as he started to regain consciousness. Squinting in the darkness, he tried to focus on a group of men at the crash site who were walking down the embankment preparing to turn his car over with chains hooked up to a pick up truck, presumably to save the lives of people they thought might still be inside.

Chris stood up groggily and saw his car lying upside down in the water. He tried to walk toward the men by the truck but stopped and put his hands on his head. One of them heard Chris yelling for help and came over to check on him. Chris fell back down to the ground and lay on his right side.

"Is there anyone else in the car?" asked the Good Samaritan.

"No . . . my Angel. My Angel," Chris replied in a dazed voice.

"He said no one else was in the car with him but his angel," yelled the Good Samaritan to his friends, who didn't know that Chris was referring to his wife.

While his back was turned, Chris managed to stand up. Blurriness and dizziness overcame him, and he passed out, falling straight forward and hitting the ground with a loud thump.

Sometime later, Chris woke up in a hospital bed. One of the three men who were helping him had called 911 after he passed out. He was taken to the nearest hospital, which was on the southwest side of Little Rock, because the code gray had the Bryant hospital backed up with those who had been injured in the F3 tornado that had blown through the town.

The first thing that came into his field of vision when the blurriness cleared from his eyes was a middle-aged Black nurse who was standing beside his bed checking his IV and reading his vital signs.

"How are you feeling, Mr. Shoemaker?" the nurse asked.

"Angel," Chris said soft and slowly.

"Thanks for the compliment. I hate to admit this after a nice comment like that, but I'm not an angel. My name is Felicia, and I'll be your nurse for a few more hours until my shift ends." She placed a cuff around his arm and checked his blood pressure. "Does anything hurt you, Mr. Shoemaker?"

"My head hurts," Chris replied.

"Do you remember what happened to you?"

"I remember rushing home to check on my wife. A bright flash of light blinded me, and the next thing I knew, I was out of my car on side of the road. I stood up and I remember someone asking me if there was someone else in the car with me. That's it. That's all I remember."

"It must have been an angel," Felicia said.

"Huh?"

"The flash of light. That's what I hear they're made of when they're not in human form," Felicia replied.

Chris laughed lightly. "Oh," he said and then rolled his eyes at the thought that Felicia believed in mythical beings.

"You suffered a concussion. I can only give you a low dosage for your headache until some of the alcohol you drank clears out of your system. The alcohol should temporarily hold back most of your pain."

"My wife!" he said as he remembered that a tornado had touched down in his hometown and he had not yet contacted Angel to confirm that she was unhurt. "Where's my phone?" Fear wrapped itself around Chris's throat, cutting off his air supply as he tried to hold back his tears. With wires and tubes hooked to him, he fought to get out of bed to find his cell phone

"We've already contacted your wife, Mr. Shoemaker. She's on her way up here to see you."

"Oh, thank God," Chris sighed.

"Dr. Tutts will be in later to go over the results of your CT scans and talk to you about your injuries. I'll be back to check on you in a little while."

CHAPTER 4

A conversation in the clouds

Still wondering whether the tornado had come close to his neighborhood, Chris turned on the local news to learn more about the tornado's deadly path of destruction.

"Good morning, Terrell," said Charles Martin, a local news reporter, from the scene of a neighborhood hit by the tornado. "It has been confirmed that the tornado that touched down late last night was an F3 with winds above two hundred miles per hour. Four people have been confirmed dead and an estimated twenty-five to thirty people have been injured and those numbers are steadily rising. Looters have been arrested for stealing salvageable property from the tornado victims. Police are warning the public that looting is a crime and that anyone caught taking anything from these storm-damaged homes will be arrested. Reporting to you live from Bryant, this is Charles Martin. Back to you Terrell."

Terrell, a veteran African American anchorman, began reporting another news story on the economy. "Wall Street closed at another record low yesterday, bringing the recession, very close to the days of the Great Depression," said Terrell. Chris continued searching from channel to channel to find out if the path of the tornado had spun close to his neighborhood.

Suddenly, the tempo of the voices coming from the television slowed and everyone he saw walking past his room began slowing down. The birds flying outside his window, his body movements, his breathing—everything that moved began to move in slow motion. A flash of light, as bright as a nuclear explosion, appeared inside his room.

As the brightness of the light faded away, he found himself on top of the clouds above the airport where he worked. There were hundreds of cherubim and seraphim all over the sky. Chris walked around on the clouds in total amazement. Slowly, the angels turned themselves invisible, hundreds of them at a time until they all disappeared except for one brightly lit angel that was descending from the blue sky above the clouds. He knew, somehow, that it was the Angel of the Lord—Jesus in His angelic form.

The angels reappeared. The mighty cherubim angel's formed a perfect circle about a half a mile in circumference around Chris while the seraphim hovered fifty feet above them. As the Angel of the Lord continued to descend, all the angels bowed down in silence as the Angel of the Lord, entered the circle and stood next to Chris.

"Is this the end of the world?" Chris asked some of the angels in the circle, but none of them responded.

As Jesus began to speak, all the cherubim and seraphim transformed into vapors and disappeared into the clouds, leaving Chris alone with Jesus in his angelic form. "I know you, and in your heart, you know me. I'm the one you learned of in story books when you were a child in Sunday school… The one who told Noah to build the Arc, the one who told Moses to part the Red Sea, and the one who placed him in a cleft in a rock and allowed him to see my back as I passed him by," said Jesus, whose thunderous voice was so powerful that it vibrated the earth and echoed through the heavens. From the moon came a loud crackling that sounded like rocks falling from its mountains. A cloud of dust poured off the moon in a straight line as if the sound of the Lord's voice had cracked it in half.

"Are you God the Father?" asked Chris.

"I am, who I am," replied the Angel of the Lord.

The Angel of the Lord adjusted the power of his voice and formed a bench out of the clouds for Chris and Himself to sit on. Chris could hear a loud noise coming through the clouds. The Angel of the Lord called out to an angel and said, "Protect them." In less than a half a second, the angel moved to the bottom of the clouds where the airport was visible and guided a duck away from the path of an ascending Boeing 747 passenger jet. The huge jet burst through the clouds with its wings coming approximately three feet away from where Chris and the Angel of the Lord were sitting.

The Angel of the Lord said, "On that plane are one hundred and three people with one hundred and three times five hundred different burdens and problems. I know only twenty-four of those souls. Too many do not believe in me though I show myself to them daily with splendid beauty between the sunrise and the sunset of each page of their lives. Through all of my creation I speak to them everyday, but they ignore my messages. I send my angels to protect them. If not for my grace and mercy, that duck would have flown into the engine of that plane, causing it to crash. Seventy-nine would have died. I've given them another chances to get to know me. Twenty-four already live forever because they believe in me. The second death for the seventy-nine and many others who are not saved will be the most painful for me. For I shall say, I know you not, depart from me... If only they would believe in my Fathers plan, and come to me for I am gentle and humble in heart."

Chris sat quietly in a state of shock. All he could do was repeat the name Jesus in an awed whisper.

The Angel of the Lord continued to speak. "I know what's on your mind. I never intended for mankind to carry their burdens alone. The burden of carrying my Father's children's sins is light and easy." The Angel of the Lord held His hand out and a section of the clouds began to part, giving Chris a clear view of the earth fifteen thousand feet beneath them. Then he touched Chris's eyes while they were open with the tips of his fingers and asked him, "See that farmer sixty miles south of us working in the field?"

"Whoa!" Chris replied. "I can see insects in his hair like they're on the back of my hand. Wow!"

The clouds turned into dirt and in the blink of an eye, Chris found himself in the field with the angel of the Lord as they both watched the farmer work. Jesus picked up a handful of dirt, grabbed Chris's hand, and poured the dirt into it. Then He looked Chris in the eyes and told him.

"I have opened your eyes. Test my soils. For soil is the main ingredient of my greatest creation. Test my soils."

"How do I test them, Lord?" asked Chris.

"Some soils grow harvestable crops. Some soils lack the proper nutrients to yield crops through all growing seasons." Jesus took Chris by his other hand and poured dirt into it, too. Chris stood with both hands full of dirt and a confused look on his face.

"Test my soils."

"I don't understand," said Chris.

"Sow my seeds of truth and test the soils." With both hands, Jesus reached down and scooped up more dirt with both hands. He stood up and released the dirt back to the earth, but before it hit the ground, it formed into a white bald eagle and flew away. "Sow my seeds and test my soils. I shall give you strength to fly like an eagle through the storm," said the Angel of the Lord.

The ground transformed back into clouds and Jesus began to ascend high into the heavens where the angels were waiting. "Tell them to come . . . . Tell them to come unto me. Come to me, and I will give them rest. Come to me . . . . The voice of Jesus slowly faded away and He transformed into clouds, along with the angels. Chris stood there in the clouds still starring into the heavens. Still having two handfuls of dirt in his hands, he looked at them and looked back towards the heavens to ask Jesus a question, but He and the angels were gone. He then asked himself the question that he was going to ask Jesus.

"Where can I get seeds of truth to plant?"

CHAPTER 5

In the Hospital

"Mr. Shoemaker. Wake up, Mr. Shoemaker. Your wife is here to see you," said Felicia.

"Hey, Angel," said Chris.

"Well, I'll let you two be alone for a while," said Felicia "I'll be back in to check on you in about fifteen minutes OK, hon?"

"All right," Chris answered as Felicia left the room. "I was worried about you," he said to Angel. "How come you didn't answer your phone?"

"If you were so worried about me, you would've came home when I asked you to," Angel replied with a smirk on her face.

"Did we get hit by the tornado?"

"How should I know? Me and the kids, who were left alone, spent the night at my mother's house," Angel said. "And what did the nurse mean, 'hon'? I don't think that's appropriate to be saying to someone else's husband. Humph. Is that some kind of secret code y'all made up? Doesn't she have her own husband?"

"She's a middle-aged woman. Furthermore, I'm insulted. You act like I can't be trusted or something. That makes me mad after I've worked so hard to be nothing but faithful to you. You come along and accuse me of being unfaithful and take away my pride in being a faithful man. I might as well do what you accuse me of doing."

"You shouldn't have to work hard at it if you love me. I started to stay away and leave yo' butt up here by yo'self like you did me and the kids last night."

33

"Angel, what is your problem, huh? Just what in the heck is your problem?"

"Well, there's my answer," Angel retorted. "Ain't nothing wrong with you. You're just fine. You got the strength and the nerve to argue and get smart with somebody after God done blessed you to be alive."

"I swear! Why are you still married to me, huh? You just use me for your—" Chris cut himself off.

"Use you for what, Chris? You got a college degree, but you work as a janitor. You ain't got nothing. You spend all the money on yourself."

"That's not true and you know it. Spending money is never a problem as long as it's for something that benefits you. Look, this isn't the time or place." Chris bowed his head and put his hands up to his face as if he were getting ready to pray.

"Praying hasn't done anything for us yet," Angel said. "I'm tired of that. I don't know why I'm still with you. Evidently, there's some kind of curse on you."

Just as Chris was getting ready to respond, Felicia walked into the room accompanied by a doctor who was an American Indian.

"Hello, Chris, I'm Dr. Tutts, I know you're probably ready to get out of here and go home to rest in your own bed. It looks like you'll be able to do just that. I'm going to give you some medication for a mild concussion. What type of work do you do?"

Chris thought about the comments Angel had made and became embarrassed about his occupation. "Nothing strenuous that would require me to miss work or anything," he answered evasively.

"I just want to make sure that I don't give you medication that will cause drowsiness if you drive or operate machinery or something like that for a living. You'd end up back in here and I'd feel bad for prescribing you the wrong medicine."

"Oh. Well you need to be a little more specific," Chris said, avoiding Angel's eyes. "I'm a CCSA over at Raven Jet at the new airport in West Little Rock." CCSA meant Customer Contract Sales Associate, but he kept that information to himself. "Does your job require you to fly?" Dr. Tutts asked.

"Yes, it does," Chris lied.

"See what I mean? I'm going to have to ground you for a week. High altitudes could cause your brain to swell and worsen your condition."

"Great. I can take care of a lot of paperwork I'm behind on."

"I'm just kidding, you'll be fine. Felicia is going to unhook your IV and disconnect you from all these machines, and you'll be free to go. Drink plenty of water, get lots of rest, put an icepack on your head, and take the medicine I'm going to prescribe to you only when you need it. It was nice meeting you both. Take care." Dr. Tutts shook hands with Chris and Angel and then left, followed by Felicia, who had unhooked all the machines as the doctor spoke.

Chris got dressed and had picked up the remote to turn off the TV when the newscaster announced a change of ownership at Raven Jet where he was employed. Rumors of a major layoff and the possibility of the company completely closing its doors were circulating. Chris and Angel watched as the newscaster announced that Willie Stewart, a local black millionaire in his fifty's who had won the lottery and more than doubled his winnings over many years of great investments had purchased the struggling aircraft company.

CHAPTER 6

Going Home

"Did y'all know they had the company up for sale?" Angel asked on their way to the front entrance of the hospital.

"No, we sure didn't. Hopefully it won't change anything," said Chris as Felicia wheeled him along side of Angel in a wheelchair. Chris and Felicia waited on the curve while Angel pulled the Ford Escort around to the designated pick-up area.

On their way home, Chris thought about what had happened to him and wondered why he was still alive, why he was still married, and why God didn't love him. He remembered the dream he'd had in the hospital, but he passed it off as just that . . . a dream. He thought about how awesome and great the Lord God appeared to be in the dream he'd had while lying in the hospital, but he still refused to acknowledge God as great, because he believed God had failed him too many times.

"Chris?"

"Yeah."

"Do you love me?" Angel asked in a sincere voice. "Be honest."

Chris was still a little upset from the arguments the night before and from the smart-mouthed comments that Angel had made in the hospital earlier that morning. His temper had cooled down to a temperature that was still hot enough to weld sheet metal together with the palm of his hand. Reflecting back on the previous night when he thought he had lost Angel in the tornado, he decided to try to end the friction between them by forgiving and letting the past go . . . or trying to let the past go. After a moment of silence as he looked into Angel's sad face, Chris finally answered her question. "You're the mother of my kids," he said. "Of course, I love you."

"Why did it take you so long to answer the question? You don't really mean it, do you?" Angel said in a squeaky teary voice as she held back her tears and waited for Chris to agree.

"Yes, I do," Chris replied.

Angel could sense that he was becoming irritated as he added, "What difference does it make? Next week, you'll say you're sorry again and force me to agree that we're both wrong—as if we always mutually agree to start these arguments at the same time or something."

"I guess I deserved that. Maybe I don't know how to love, but I do love you." Angel started to cry. "I'd give anything to learn how to love. Even though God hasn't answered our prayers for some reason, I'm still going to pray that He'll have mercy on our marriage and show us how to love each other the way He wants us to."

Angel's tears brought out Chris's sensitive side. "I made a promise to myself that I would never abandon my family the way my father abandoned me and my mother," Chris said. "You can leave me, but I couldn't live with myself if I left you and the kids. God may not have kept his promises to me, but I'm going to be the man God hasn't been. I'm going to be a man of my word."

Dead silence interrupted their conversation for a moment. Angel wiped away her tears, cleared her throat, and sniffed.

"I guess now that you know I don't plan on ever leaving you for any reason, you can just continue treating me how you want to, huh?" Chris asked.

"No, Chris. Believe it or not, it's hard for me to trust you or anyone because of God. Maybe that's why it seems like I mistreat you sometimes. How can I trust you with my love when I don't trust God with it? What you said years ago about the bible being contradicting stuck in my head and changed my life for the worse. How can anything in the Bible be true if one or many things in it are untrue? I never told you this, but for years now, I've been uncomfortable living because I'm not one hundred percent sure of what's going to happen to me when I die. I'm realizing that I'll never be a good wife to you feeling so confused about this life we're living. I agree with you that the bible isn't all true. I use to believe it was, but since I can't prove that it is. I'm lost and confused."

Sidetracked by their location, Chris didn't respond directly. "Here's where I ran off the road right up here," he said. He pointed to a billboard at

First Baptist church located a few miles before entering Bryant. "Humph. That's weird. That sign says almost the same thing that Jesus said to me in a dream I had while I was in the hospital. 'Come to me, all you who are weary and burdened, and I will give you rest'."

"Why don't we go and hear what the pastor has to say? Maybe God's trying to tell us something. Service starts tomorrow at nine."

Chris shrugged. "It's been a while since we went to church," he said. "Why not? After surviving the tornado and a car wreck, it just might be worth trying to find God again."

"Why did you lie about your job to the doctor this morning?" asked Angel.

Chris didn't answer. She had made him feel less than a man with her comments about his job and because she made more money as a paralegal at a criminal law firm than he did as a janitor.

"You know I didn't mean any of that. I was just mad," Angel said.

Traffic became more congested as they got closer to the street that led to their home. Police officers were directing the traffic because of the power outage caused by the tornado and cruising the neighborhood to stop people from looting. A barricade blocked traffic from turning left. Chris and Angel began to wonder if they had a home to go home to. Angel put on her signal light while Chris signaled to a police officer that they wanted to make a left turn. The officer came over to the car and motioned for Angel to roll down the window.

"Are you residents of Forest Acres?" The officer asked.

"Yes! Did the tornado hit our neighborhood?" Chris asked as he leaned toward the driver's side window.

"Yes, sir, it did. I'll need to see some ID to verify your address before I let you through."

Fear of finding out that the tornado had destroyed their home or that someone they knew had been killed in the storm had begun to rob their brains of oxygen.

"Maybe it missed us. Maybe it missed us. Please, God, let us still have a home. Answer this one prayer, please." Chris pleaded.

Forest Drive was a hilly road. As Angel drove up and over the first hill, they could see several rooflines in the neighborhood that they normally couldn't see. The wall of trees that normally blocked their view had been reduced to twenty-foot-tall stumps, all the same height as if a carpenter had measured them for a perfectly even cut. When they reached the top of the second hill, they could see the extent of the devastation. With the green space of trees that use to block the view of the neighborhood out of the way, it was apparent that another prayer had gone unanswered. It was all gone. Everything they had worked hard for was gone. Angel parked the Escort as close as the debris allowed her to and they walked to the rubble that used to be their home.

"How much worse can life get? Oh, I guess I should thank God for allowing the storm to save the mailbox. We don't have any place to stay, but we can still pay our bills. That's always how it goes." Chris looked up into the sky and finished thanking God. "'Preciate you. Can't say I don't have anything to be thankful for," he said before kicking the bricked mailbox and hurting his big toe.

Something on one of the four Bradford pear trees evenly planted on both sides of their driveway caught Chris's eye.

"Look at this! This business card must have cut into the tree like a razor blade." As he got closer to the tree, he noticed a white tack pinning the card to the tree. "Wait a minute. Someone tacked this card to the tree," he said.

"What's it for?" Angel asked. She sounded calm, but her face was pale as she stared at the ruins of their home.

"A Detective Grant wants me to call him, probably to ask questions for an accident report." With no place else to go until their insurance agent came out to survey their home, Chris and Angel decided to stay with her mother, Amanda, for a few weeks or months. They began loading up as many personal items as they could salvage from the rubble, including his NIV study application bible he spotted lying on the floor of what use to be his bedroom. "I forgot I had this," he said as he kneeled down to pick his bible up from the floor. On top of his bible was corn seeds placed neatly in two piles. "Where did these seeds come from," he said out loud. After they finished gathering up a few of their personal belongings, they drove to Amanda's house.

CHAPTER 7

More Troubles

Hearing them pull up, Jacob and Heath opened the curtains in the living room as wide as they could and waved at them with big smiles.

Angel's mom lived in a town not to far from Bryant called Hope. The three-bedroom, 2,148-square-foot home provided shelter for now to replace their home that was blown away. The brown brick home with tan-colored siding was the last house on the right on a dead-end suburban street. Deer, coyotes, and other wildlife drank from and bathed in the stream that flowed between the end of the subdivision and the woods located fifty-five feet away from the dead-end road.

Amanda lived alone even though her husband, Angel's dad, was still alive. He sent money to help with the bills, but a separation that was supposed to have been temporary was still in progress after twenty-two years. They feared getting a divorce for religious reasons. Living separately was their way of getting past the judgments and laws of the non-Christian faith they practiced and believed in.

Chris received a call from Harold as Angel put the car in park. "I'll be in after I'm done talking to Harold," he told her.

"I'm going in and tell my mother and the boys what happened and that we're going to have to stay with her for a while," Angel replied.

Chris nodded and answered his phone. Without wasting any time saying hello, he said, "I'm broke and homeless and I need some money. You still wanna be my friend?"

"The tornado hit y'all's house didn't it?" Harold asked.

"Yep. We just lost everything we worked years to get, including the Nova. I totaled it last night on my way back home when I heard the tornado touched down in Bryant. I just got out of the hospital a few hours ago."

"Man! Last night could've been your last day on earth," said Harold. "I know you're going to church tomorrow. Shoot, I'm going with you."

Chris answered Harold in a calm, low-toned voice, but his words rang in Harold's eardrums like a sonic boom from a jet breaking the speed of sound. "Too bad it wasn't. It'd be fine with me if God left me alone forever and stopped taking pleasure in torturing me. The so-called good Lord won't let me take care of my family. He curses my every move to live a good life."

Harold was speechless for a few seconds. He knew that Chris was crying out for help, but he didn't know how to respond to his suicidal thoughts. "Man, you've been beating the name of God down in the dirt lately," he said finally. "Pray, man."

"I'm scared to pray," Chris answered. "Every time I pray, some other burden always comes along with what I pray for. I'm tired of the games God plays when it comes to my prayers and my family's well-being. I can't ever get it right. God must be a politician—always tricking you with little words that make or don't make His statements true. Oh, he answers prayers. If he says no, then you can't say He didn't answer. I've been to college and sacrificed lots of things, and I still can't provide for my family and keep my wife happy because He won't let me. He has all the power to bless me to be like you and own my own business or let me have a good job. I'll be sure to thank Him for that when I pray tonight for the overload of the so-called blessings that I never asked him for."

"I'm going to pray for you, bro. I know you're hurting. Before you go doing something that your family and all your friends will regret that you did, I just want to tell I love you, man. Maybe He'll answer my prayer for you and deliver you and me both from the confusion we have about Him."

Chris paused a few seconds, rubbing his forehead and massaging his left temple. He immediately calmed down after Harold told him he loved him for the second time. But this time, it was ok.

"You're right Harold. I'm just upset and confused."

"That's the other reason I was calling. I've been asking around to try to find a good church for us to go to and this guy I talked to at the gas station said True Saints Baptist Church is the best church in Little Rock. You want to go with us Sunday to check it out?"

"I had planed on going to First Baptist over here close to Bryant. They're service starts at nine and I'm not sure when it ends."

"True Saints start at eleven. We'll come to First Baptist with ya'll and we can all get to True Saints a little late if they get out late.

"Alright. Is Bryan and Tony coming?" Chris asked.

"I'll run it by them and see, but more than likely you and I both know their not serious about trying to get back in church."

After he hung up with Harold, Chris got out of the car and immediately decided to call Detective Grant. He pulled the card from his pocket and dialed the number, staying outside so he could talk in private.

"Detective Grant speaking."

"My name is Chris Shoemaker and I got your card off of a tree in my front yard. I was calling to see what this was all about."

"First let me say that I'm sorry for your loss. Are all of your family members OK?"

"Yes, they're all OK. We weren't home at the time of the storm so we didn't go through it. That's mighty kind of you to ask."

"Unfortunately, another family that I had to talk to this morning was not so lucky."

Confused and having no idea what Detective Grant was implying, Chris braced himself for bad news. He concluded that the detective must have been trying to contact him to deliver bad news about a relative that didn't make it through the storm. *Who can it be?* Chris wondered. He leaned against the car to hold himself up.

"Who was it? Who was killed in the storm?" Chris asked.

"This isn't about someone who was killed in the storm, Mr. Shoemaker. It's about someone you killed."

Chris sighed with relief. He had nothing to worry about; he would know if he had killed someone. He took a deep breath and assured Detective Grant that he had the wrong man. "You really had me going for a minute. When did this killing take place?"

"Friday night, but—"

Chris cut him off. "I have an alibi and proof that I wasn't anywhere near wherever this murder took place."

"Let me explain, Mr. Shoemaker. I went to the hospital to get in touch with you after I left what's left of your house this morning. I had gotten a call saying that you had been checked in there."

"How did you know that?" Chris asked.

"Your car tags."

"My car tags?" Chris repeated.

"When we pulled your car out of the water we found a man dead under your car."

"What!"

"Apparently, the victim was walking down the street and jumped over the bridge into the water to avoid being hit by your car, which was spinning his way. The car rolled over the guardrails and landed on the victim, trapping him underneath. We need you to come in Monday for questioning. Accidents happen, but when alcohol is involved, it's no accident. I personally consider it to be murder."

Chris was silent, too shocked to speak.

"Are you still there?" asked Detective Grant after a moment.

"It was an accident. Are you threatening to arrest me?"

"If your test results come back OK, you won't be charged."

"What test results?" Chris asked.

"A group of men who helped you said that your breath smelled like you had been drinking. The hospital staff said the same thing and took blood tests to determine if you were over the limit. Mr. Shoemaker, if we find out that your alcohol level was over the legal limit during the time of this accident, you'll be facing manslaughter charges and jail time. Can you make it down here Monday, or do we need to come and pick you up?"

Chris did not respond immediately as he tried to grasp the seriousness of the troubles he was now facing. "What time Monday?" he asked finally.

"Whatever time is convenient for you. I'll be at the office all day." Detective Grant paused for a second. "I hope I didn't scare you or anything when asked you if you needed us to pick you up. I asked because I don't know whether the car you totaled was your only transportation."

"I had a 2004 Chevy truck, but it was destroyed. I'll be there though," answered Chris, feeling numb.

"Have a good evening, Mr. Shoemaker."

Chris closed the cell phone, so weary and burdened down that he forgot to say good-bye. Chris looked to the skies as he walked back into the house and thought about calling on God.

"No need in calling on you; I already know the answer," he said as he slammed his fist on the hood of Angel's car. After accomplishing nothing from beating on the hood of the car and kicking the front bumper, he calmed himself down and went inside.

"I fixed you some lunch," said Angel. "Yours is in the microwave."

"Thanks." Chris grabbed the deli-style turkey sandwich out of the microwave and sat down at the table in the eat in kitchen next to Angel.

"Did you call that detective yet to see what he wanted?" she asked.

"I'm taking off work Monday to take care of insurance stuff on the vehicles and the house," Chris answered. "Detective Grant wants me to come down sometime tomorrow to give a statement on what happened when I wrecked my car. We need a police report so we can file an insurance claim."

He glanced at Amanda, who was sitting in the den watching the news. Chris leaned over and whispered to Angel. "Let's go to the bedroom we need to talk. Something bad happened that I don't want to talk about in front of your mom."

"You've got me worried. What's this about?" Angel asked.

Before Chris could say anything, Angel heard the news reporter say his name on the news.

"A man was found dead under an over turned car around three thirty this morning. Police say the car is owned by twenty-nine-year-old Christopher John Shoemaker of Bryant," the reporter said. "Police are not releasing any other information because the accident is still under investigation."

"Oh, my God!" Angel and her mother said at the same time.

"What happened?" Angel asked.

"If you would've been at home with Angel, none of this would've happened. Did you ever think that these boy's need you at home and not in jail." Angel's mom, Amanda, said.

"We all might be dead if I had stayed home. Why can't I be thanked for something good for a change," replied Chris.

It was quiet in the room as they all thought about what Chris had said. Chris began breathing hard and taking deep breaths. He didn't know it, but he was having a panic attack.

"I didn't know the car had rolled over on anyone." He continued breathing heavily. "I'll be back. I got to get some air." He grabbed the keys and headed out the door.

Angel and her mother said nothing, thinking that he just didn't want to cry in front of them.

Outside, Chris felt woozy and leaned against the garage door to try and regain his balance. Five minutes later, he opened his eyes and found himself lying on his side. Seeing nothing but concrete and grass, he discovered that he had passed out and had landed safely on the concrete driveway.

Chris got into his wife's car and drove down to the dam site to hear the relaxing sound of the Arkansas River rushing through the floodgates. On one side of the dam, the water was as calm as the forest on a day with no wind. On the other side, the water was in a fiery rage. The floodgates seemed to have jet motors inside them. The dam reminded Chris of his own life. It seemed to him that God poured good things into his life only to create more energy and power for bad things to take over.

He backed the car into a parking spot that overlooked the dam, got out, and sat on the trunk of the car to watch and listen to the water rushing through the gates. As he sat there, he began to think about how all the water got there. His thoughts grew deeper as he thought about all the things God had created, the awesome power to create a universe in six days, with planets and stars that were far more bigger than earth. God's amazing Creations fascinated Chris, but it was the little things that he wanted God to do for him that would have fascinated him more. A magnificent and awesome but invisible God who loved him and answered his prayers would have been more amazing to him than anything.

Not many people were fishing. Chris climbed down from the trunk and searched the glove box for a piece of paper and a pen. After grabbing a map that was bound like a book from the side of the driver's seat so that he could have a surface to write on, he climbed back onto the trunk and wrote a thought to enter into his journal later on.

"Lord God. Please hear me. You have been quiet in my life for a number of years now. I haven't felt your presence nor have I been able to determine if you've been guiding me on the rough roads I've been traveling on. I'm tired of making the wrong turns for me and my family. I only talk like I've given up on you because I feel like you've given up on me. All the years of you being silent in my life have shown me one thing: I'll never be happy without you. I just want to feel your presence again, Lord. You don't have to answer any of my prayers; I've given up on them. I can't reach one dream or goal without you. If I don't have you, then I don't have anything. What good are a big house and a good job if I have no family to share them with?

"I don't know how many prayers it takes for you to answer just one, but I'm willing to pray every day for a week or a month if I have to. If you never answer another prayer of mine again, please answer this one. Please allow me to lead my family to you so that they can enter the kingdom of heaven.

Take care of them when I'm gone, hopefully to live with you forever. I'm not sure if you will forgive me for being angry with you for sending my father to hell. I'm not sure if you'll forgive me for all my sins because I've been told that my father's sin is one that You don't forgive anyone for.

"This is not an official suicide letter. Consider it an invitation to allow one last bad thing to happen to me because I'm tired and I have no more hope for my future or my life. If there is an angel in heaven that can hear my plea, please tell Jesus about my sorrows and my broken heart."

God sent angels to protect Chris as he drove back to their temporary home, but Chris didn't know it because he didn't see any around him. He finally made it back to his family at nine fifteen that night.

"Are you OK?" Angel asked.

"Yeah, I'm good," Chris replied as he walked over to play with Jacob and Heath, who were sitting on the floor watching cartoons. He poked them both with his finger on the back of the neck and tickled their sides as they laughed and moved around to try to block one of his fingers, only to be poked with another. They flinched like boxers taking hard blows and flopped around like freshly caught fish. He lifted Jacob up off the floor and kissed him all over his face and neck and then raised his shirt and made farting noises with his lips as he blew on Jacob's stomach. With Jacob still in his arms, he walked over to Angel and kissed her on her cheek.

"I love you," he said.

"Wow! What was that for?"

"What do you mean?" Chris asked.

"I haven't heard that in a while. I'm sorry for the way I've been acting lately."

"Lately being the past few months?" Chris answered sarcastically. "Or do you mean the last eight out of eight years we've been married?" Angel was silent, looking disappointed and angry.

"I'm just kidding," Chris said.

"No, you're not."

"Forgiven," Chris said quickly as he put Jacob down so he could finish watching cartoons. Deciding to work on his end of his bargain with God, he changed the subject. "Did you find anything clean and decent that you can wear to church tomorrow when we were at the house today?

"I'm kind of tired," Angel responded. "I don't really feel like going to church tomorrow."

"I really need to go tomorrow," Chris said. "I want you and the boys to go with me. God may be trying to tell us something. I know I've said that in the past and it ended up not being true, but this time I had a dream. How could I have dreamed about a Bible verse that I've never read unless it was a message from God? If we have to wear the clothes we have on right now; I want us to go to church tomorrow. I desperately need to go."

"OK."

"Thanks . . . You know, I've been thinking about all this. What if after all of these years of pain and suffering, God finally allows us not to suffer any more for the rest of our lives?"

"That would be great, but the thing is, we don't know if the rest of our lives will be fifty more years or one more year," Angel replied.

Chris knew what Angel said was true and that the likelihood of not suffering for fifty years was nonexistent. He started to ponder her comment and lost the optimism that he had felt after attempting to make peace with God.

"I guess your right. That little hope I had didn't last long. Kind of makes it hard to look forward to having something to live for." Chris and Angel both now had downed looks on their faces. "I'm going to take my medicine and go to bed. I'll set my alarm on my phone to wake us up. I'll get the kids in the bed."

He walked over to hug, kiss, and say good night to Jacob and Heath, but they had already fallen asleep. Chris picked them up and carried them one at a time to bed.

It was around ten thirty when Chris finally stopped surfing the internet with his phone and crawled into bed in the guess room located on the same end of the house as Jacob and Heath's room. The master bedroom where his mother in law slept was on the other side of the house. He didn't feel or hear Angel get into bed an hour later.

CHAPTER 8

Going to Church

At 2:30 A.M., Chris woke up as if the sun were out and lay awake in bed for hours. His hopes of falling back to sleep faded once he saw the dawn illuminating the windows of his mother-in-law's home. He managed to doze off thirty minutes before his cell phone alarm woke him up for church. Although very tired and sleepy, he got out of bed after getting only four hours of sleep and continued with his plans to attend church.

Eventually, all of them were up, breakfasted, and ready to go. The boys accepted the unusual decision to go to church without protest.

—

"This is different," Angel whispered as they entered the church.

"I'll say . . . Mostly everyone is wearing jeans and everyday clothes. I've never been to a church with Blacks, Whites, and other races all together." Chris paused. "Come to think of it, I haven't been to anybody's church in a while."

"I hope Jacob and Heath behave themselves in the kid classes," Angel said.

They sat down on a pew near the back of the church as the Praise and Worship Team were singing "Come unto Me" by Nicole C. Mullen. Symbony, an African American woman in her thirties led the song while Hanna, a plus sized Caucasian woman direct the choir. Although Chris and Angel entered the church close to the end of the song, what they heard gave them a feeling of comfort. Ushers came down each aisle, passing the offering baskets from row to row. Chris picked up an offering envelope from the back of the seat in front of him and placed twenty dollars inside as they waited for the basket to reach them.

"That was a different kind of church song," he whispered to Angel. "I like it. Kind of makes you feel like you're wrapped up safe in Jesus' arms . . . if he's nice enough to let you anyway."

"Yeah, it does," Angel whispered back. Chris influence still had Angel convinced that if God did indeed exist, He couldn't be trusted. He had given her good reason to go along with his theory by telling her that God who claimed to be the Truth but lied better than a politician, with contradiction after contradiction in His truth He called the Bible, couldn't be trusted.

Angel had never read the entire Bible. She was what regular church attendees called a CME church attendee. It was a title and abbreviation regular church attendees gave to people who only came to church on Christmas, Mother's Day, and Easter. All she knew was that what Chris said made a lot of sense and she couldn't prove him wrong. Her lack of biblical knowledge stunted her spiritual growth, causing her to grow just as confused about God as her husband.

"You got a pen?" Chris asked Angel.

"Hold on." Angel reached into her purse and pulled out a pen. "Here you go."

Chris filled in the appropriate information on the offering envelope and turned it over to read the back.

"They forgot to put a section on here for tithing," he whispered to Angel. Whenever I do make it to church, I always tithe. We definitely need a blessing right now."

"Make your own little box and mark it 'tithes,'" Angel whispered back. She watched him write in the amount he was giving and added, "That's not quite ten percent, but maybe God will have mercy and understand that right now, we don't even have a house to live in."

Chris put the envelope into the basket as it reached them and passed it on. Looking toward the front of the church, he recognized Pastor Larry Sanders, who was walking up to the podium on front of the stage. "I know him," he said softly. "He used to come by the house and talk to my dad. My dad stopped by his house a few times when I was little and took me with him."

Pastor Sanders made a few announcements before getting started with his sermon. One announcement in particular caught Angel's attention.

"I also would like to thank you all for your prayers and financial support in sending me to theology school. I'm very proud to announce that I will be graduating in May," said Pastor Sanders. Then Matthew 11:28 appeared on the projection screen that was mounted on the wall behind him and he began to preach.

"Come to me, all you who are weary and burdened, and I will give you rest. . . . Sounds like an awesome promise that we can hold God accountable for today, but there's only one problem: He promised in countless other verses something totally different that contradicts what he promised us here in Matthew. Turn, if you will, to Romans eight, verse seventeen."

Chris leaned over to Angel and said, "That's exactly what I've been saying all along about the Bible; see what I mean? It's too contradictory to be true."

Pastor Sanders continued teaching. "Now this promise here in Romans isn't as pleasant as the one in Matthew, so some of you may want to return this one to God and trade it in for the promise He made in Matthew." Pastor Sanders began reading Romans 8:17. "'Now if we are God's children, then we are heirs—heirs of God and co-heirs with Christ, if indeed we share in his sufferings in order that we may also share in his glory.' So, here we have one verse promising to give us rest from depression, weariness, and all of our burdens, and way over yonder we have a promise that we will see suffering in order to share heaven with Christ." Pastor Sanders walked around on the stage with his arms folded and his finger on his lips. "Who in here right now wants to get up and say God, you lied? Who can say that He has given you complete rest and you've never suffered here on earth? Anybody?"

Chris snatched his hand down quickly after realizing that he was the only person in the crowd who had raised his hand in answer to the first question.

Pastor Sanders continued. "If we never read the whole Bible, and we never read the entire context of a passage, we will always choose what looks to be a comforting promise from God and misinterpret our Creator's holy Word. If we had read everything God said in Matthew, we would find that He did not promise us rest while we live our lives here on earth."

Pastor Sanders returned to the podium, picked up his Bible, and read the verses following Matthew 11:28. "'Take my yoke upon you and learn from me, for I am gentle and humble in heart, and you will find rest for your souls.' Your souls! Our souls can only leave our bodies when we die.

The Bible promises eternal rest after death for the souls that have found Jesus. Jesus has prepared a way to give us rest for our souls."

Pastor Sanders paused and changed his tone, pretending to be a skeptical member of his own congregation. "'Well, Pastor Sanders, that's good, but I need a promise that I can hold on to today.'" He paused again, resuming his own voice. "God will give you rest from some of your burdens here on earth, but depending on what He's getting ready to do in your life, He may need to make you a little uncomfortable as He gives you the strength to handle that prayer you've been waiting for him to answer that you thought he forgot about years ago. Matthew 11:25 says that he made it so easy to get into heaven that even a child can understand how to do it. There is no excuse for not believing in Jesus Christ. Save your soul and come to Jesus. Jesus is the only way your soul can find rest. Whosoever will, Jesus has invited you to come to him. Just simply believe. I want to close with the very wise words of my dear friend Johnny Shoemaker, who has already gone before us."

Chris looked over at Angel and said in a surprised whisper, "He's talking about my dad."

"He used to tell me, 'The Bible is not a lie. We are.'"

Chris had known what was coming and repeated the familiar words along with Pastor Sanders. "My dad used to tell me that all the time when I was younger, but I still don't understand," Chris whispered to Angel as the pastor continued.

"I didn't understand what he was saying until I finally read the entire bible for myself. And then I realized that he was exactly right."

Pastor Sanders looked out over the congregation. "Before you hold God accountable and put words in His mouth that He didn't say, please read the whole Bible first. He may not have guaranteed us rest from all of our daily burdens and struggles, but if you ask Him, I guarantee you he'll lighten the load you carry just as He promised us rest for our souls when we die. But we will never find a promise in this sinful world better than the promise of eternal rest for our souls."

"The Praise and Worship Team is going to sing another great song before we dismiss," Pastor Sanders said, giving the team their cue to come on stage. "This next song should be our Christian anthem," he added before making his way to the front row to sit with the congregation. As Symbony sang "On My Knees" by Nicole C. Mullen, several people stood up and held their hands in the air. Some even shed a few tears.

Pastor Sanders said a short prayer and dismissed the congregation.

Chris had hoped to hear something a little more promising. He had been weary and burdened for years and his present situation was desperate. He had wanted to hear that he could somehow do something or give something to God that would end his suffering on this earth. Instead, Pastor Sanders had told him that he had to suffer and share Christ's burden so he could rest eternally with Christ Jesus.

"Go get the boys from class," he said to Angel. "I'm going to try to talk to the pastor real quick. Text me when you get to the front door."

"There was definitely a reason for us to be here today, huh? We need to start going to church more. Go ahead and catch him. I'll text you when we're headed to the car," Angel said.

CHAPTER 9

Lessons from Pastor Sanders

Chris made his way through the crowd of parishioners and finally caught up with the preacher.

"Pastor Sanders," Chris said as he tapped him on the shoulder. Pastor Sanders still looked the same to Chris after seventeen years except that his once sandy brown hair and beard had turned almost completely gray over the years and he now wore eyeglasses. The last time Chris had seen the pastor was at his father's funeral.

"That was a very good sermon," said Chris. "For a second there, I thought I was in a Devil-worshipping church or something. I thought, 'Wow, he's going against the Bible,' but I understood it as you went a little deeper at the end."

"Oh, no! I'm trying to teach only the true Word of God here at this church."

"You probably don't remember me. My name is Chris Shoemaker. I'm—"

"Johnny Shoemaker's son!" Pastor Sanders said, politely interrupting Chris. "You were about hip high when I saw you last; it's very good to see you again. Your father and I go way back. He was a very good man."

"I'd like to talk with you about him in private whenever you get some time," Chris said.

"Come with me to my office; I have a little time right now."

On their way to the office, Chris greeted and shook hands with dozens of people with pastor Sanders as he followed him to his office. When they reached the office, Pastor Sanders pushed the door open, turned around, and asked Chris, "How is your mom? Alive and well?"

"She's alive. If moving out of state to escape all memories of your husband and failing to do so by getting put in a mental hospital because you can't cope with how your husband left you is doing good, then she's doing excellent, thanks to my dad."

"I'm taking a wild guess here, but something tells me you're angry with your father?" Pastor Sanders asked as he walked over and stood in front of his desk.

"How would you feel if your father left you with a miserable memory of him to suffer and struggle with the rest of your life? Because of him, and what he did, my mother and I struggled in many ways. We couldn't get any insurance money to help pay for his funeral and all the bills. A few helpful neighbors reported to child services that we only had running water for half a month and electric the other half and got me taken away from my mother. After a year of struggling by herself and only getting to see me on the weekends, she finally got a job and was able to bring me back home. I was in a good foster home, but there's no place like home. She moved away after I left for college . . . I guess she couldn't stay in that house by herself. Too many memories of my dad. I feel like it's my fault she moved away and ended up having a mental breakdown because I was all she had left, and I left her, too. On top of that, all the years I spent going to college only got me a job as a janitor. If I hadn't tried to better myself, my mom might never have gotten so depressed."

Pastor Sanders sat down and turned on his computer. "Go ahead and have a seat. It sounds like you have a lot to talk about and I'd like to help. What is your e-mail address?"

Chris felt his eyes get as big as juicy red plums. Suddenly his cool user name, Sex Hulk, was embarrassing. It was definitely not an appropriate name to say in church. To say it to the preacher would've been even more embarrassing.

"I'm in—we're in—we were in the tornado that came through here Friday night and I'm going to have to change it when I get things set up where we're staying," he stammered. "What's yours so I can send you my new e-mail address when I get set up?"

Pastor Sanders opened his desk drawer and pulled out a card. "Here you go. All of my contact numbers and my e-mail address are on the card. We really need to talk and keep in touch. I know what chapter in life you're in, and I'd really like to help."

"'Chapter in life I'm in'?" Chris repeated as he took the card and put it in his pocket.

"That's another one of your dad's sayings. Whenever he counseled someone like you who was down in the gutter, he'd always encourage that person by saying, 'Wait until the page turns into tomorrow. All life stories have good endings for believers.' Your dad was a good man. I miss him, and I'm sure you do, too. What was it that you wanted to ask me about your dad?"

Chris felt confused and uncomfortable thinking about Pastor Sanders's reference to his father during the sermon. "You said something that I've never heard anyone say about my dad." He leaned forward and then back in his chair. "You do know what happened to him, right? I mean, you know what the police said was the cause of his death?" Chris couldn't figure out how he wanted to position his body to accept the answer he waited for Pastor Sanders to give. His father's suicide had haunted and tortured him since he was twelve years old.

"Yes, I know what happened," Pastor Sanders said.

"Then how can you say that he's going to heaven?" Chris asked.

"I didn't and can't say who is in heaven or who isn't," Pastor Sanders responded.

"Yes, you did. You said that my father had gone before us and you didn't mention hell."

Frustration and a familiar feeling of lost hope came down upon Chris. He began to feel as though he had made a mistake by coming to hear the sermon and asking about his father. He had loved his father deeply when he was alive, but after hearing several preachers tell him that his father was going to hell, he had started hating God and his father so that he could continue living without being extremely depressed. Thinking about how cruel God was and how his dad had hurt him and his mother was too much for him to bear. Every time he got excited about the possibility of God showing up again in his life, his excitement turned back into false hope. Pastor Sanders's words had shown him once again that everything that appeared to be good somehow worked more for the bad in his life.

He apologized to the pastor and chose not to argue about what he knew he heard Pastor Sanders say about his father not being in hell. He stood up and headed toward the door.

"Like I said, I didn't say your father was going to heaven," repeated Pastor Sanders.

"You're right, sir. I'm just crazy, and I already apologized," Chris said sarcastically.

"The Bible said it," said Pastor Sanders.

Chris froze and turned around slowly. "What did you say?" he asked as he turned and walked back toward Pastor Sander's desk.

"According to the Bible and what the Bible says, you'll be reunited with your father in heaven," Pastor Sanders said with a smile.

Chris sat back down in the chair.

"All my life I've been told that suicide is a sin that God doesn't forgive you for. Kids at school would say to me, 'I heard my momma tell my daddy that yo' daddy is in hell. She said all the people that believed in what he was preaching are in hell with him. And she said they gnash their teeth together so hard down there that it sounds like rocks being crushed at a quarry. That's where yo' dad's at.' They even had the nerve to ask me if I knew that. Since that day, I just haven't known if I could believe in a God that would do something so cruel. I loved my dad. If I loved him, then how could God not love him? As good a man as he was, preaching and telling others about God, he didn't deserve to go to hell! Off and on, I wanted to continue believing in God, but because of that one incident, I've been left in the dark for years, never hearing anyone tell me what you just said."

"You remind me of myself before your father helped Jesus set me free. Your father changed my life. He was a Bible teacher, not a preacher. There's a difference between the two. Motivation is always good, but when you want to get on another level with the God that created you, you'll need a Bible teacher to teach you exactly what the Bible says."

"Where does it say in the Bible that you can still go to heaven if you commit suicide?" Chris asked.

"The same place that it says that committing suicide is a sin that is unforgivable."

"Huh?"

"Nowhere." Pastor Sanders paused. "Nowhere in the Bible does it specifically say that suicide is one of a group of sins that God will not forgive you for. If suicide a sin then it falls under the category of all sins."

"But I was told that if you don't repent your sins, you'll go to hell," Chris answered. "Someone who commits suicide can't repent before they go through with—you know—the act of doing it."

Pastor Sanders started typing and clicking away on the computer, talking at the same time. "Interesting, but confusing, because, you see, the Bible says that we all have sinned and come short of God's glory. So to save ourselves from eternal punishment, we'd all need to know pretty much what day and time God will allow our souls to leave this world so that we can ask for forgiveness before that final hour that no one knows is coming. No one knows the day or the hour when God is going to call them home, which makes it impossible for anyone to confess every one of their daily sins. There is no way to repent at noon, the end of the day, or the end of the week if you die seconds after you've committed a sin and trust me, you will sin. God has promised that you will commit a sin; we all will. That's why Jesus died for us."

"OK," said Chris as he tried to understand all of what Pastor Sanders was saying.

"There are lots of ways to sin and not have time to ask forgiveness for your sins. Let's say you call your boss tomorrow and tell him or her that you're sick. Two minutes later, you hook a big fish. You stand up and lose your balance, fall out of the boat into the water, and drown. Do you think you'll be forgiven for that lie you just told to your boss?"

"I sure hope so. I've done that a time or two," Chris said with a laugh.

"God's Word tells you these things so that you can know so. The answer to your question about going to heaven is all over the Bible; it's not just in one place."

Pastor Sanders grabbed some papers off the printer and stapled them together. "Here is something your father gave me from his studies on sin. Jesus wouldn't have died on the Cross if you could save yourself by repenting and sacrificing animals like the Hebrews had to do in the Old Testament. He gave us salvation through believing in Him and that's the only way. He was the perfect sacrifice for our sins. No one needed to make animal sacrifices after His death. The one and only unforgivable sin is blasphemy against the Holy Spirit."

"Wait a minute; you just said that Jesus died for all our sins," Chris said. "Doesn't that include blasphemy? And why just blasphemy against the Holy Spirit and not God the Father or Jesus?"

"To believe in Him is to believe in the Holy Trinity. You can't believe in one part of God without the others because they are all the same. Not to believe in the Holy Spirit is not to believe in Jesus. The Holy Spirit is His gift for all who believe."

"I get it . . . I think." Chris's phone beeped, signaling a text message.

"My wife and kids are outside waiting on me; I have to run. I'd love to finish this conversation with you another time." Chris paused and stood up. "So my father isn't going to hell?" he asked, smiling like a kid playing with a new toy on Christmas morning. He instantly begin having a new feeling about life, his father, and God. It was the best feeling he had ever had in his life.

CHAPTER 10

True Saints of God Church

Outside on the parking lot, Angel and the kids were standing next to Harold's '69 Firebird talking to Audrey while Harold was deep in conversation with another antique car lover who was checking out the old Firebird. The weird weather had gone from a morning high of eighty-three degrees around nine o'clock to seventy-two degrees two hours later. It was the hot topic of conversation as parishioners walked to their cars. Angel waved to get Chris's attention, but he didn't see her. He was so deep in thought about the whole perception of God that he didn't even hear Harold honking his horn at him.

A teenage boy pointed in their direction and said to Chris, "Sir, I think they're trying to get your attention."

"Oh, OK, thanks," said Chris. He signaled to Angel that he'd drive the car over to where they were, but she couldn't understand him, so he called her on her cell phone. "I'm going to bring the car over there so y'all won't have to walk," he explained

"All right, we'll be here," said Angel. Chris drove the car around and parked a couple of cars away from Harold's Firebird. Just as he was getting ready to get out, Angel and the kids approached the passenger side and she opened the door.

"Harold said he'll see you at the other church. We'll go with you although you forgot to tell me about it." Angel told Chris. He's gonna stop and get some breakfast before they go. Y'all buckle up," she added to the kids as she closed the door.

"Where we going, Daddy?" asked Jacob.

"To church."

"Why we gotta go to church again, Daddy?"

"So we can hopefully get a blessing from God."

"Momma, Heath said we're hungry," said Jacob. "Can we get us something to eat, huh, Ma? Huh, Momma?"

"I did not," Heath replied.

"Didn't y'all just eat almost half a box worth of pancakes this morning?"

"But I want some more pannycakes. I'm hungry, and Heath ate more pannycakes than I did."

"We'll be out of church before you know it. I'm pretty sure it's not going to last that long."

"What kind a' clock is it gonna be, Momma?" Jacob asked.

"Probably twelve o'clock," Angel answered. She turned around and looked at them in the backseat. "Are y'all buckled up?"

"Yes, ma'am," they both replied.

"Speaking of God, Pastor Sanders taught me something that I've been misled on for years."

"How did that go? Did you find out if that was your dad he was talking about?" asked Angel.

Chris smiled at Angel and stared into her eyes like a young boy discovering that girls aren't yucky. "My father is in heaven," he said. God really is good." Hypnotized by the pure joy of his discovery, he forgot that he was driving.

Angel's mouth dropped open and her eyes swelled from a fearful site that she locked in her vision.

"Stop!" she yelled.

Chris slammed on the brakes and they all braced for impact with a midnight blue Toyota Tundra that had stopped in the middle of the interstate in front of them.

"Whoa!" Chris yelled as the tires screeched, leaving forty-foot-long tire marks and smoke behind them. They came to a stop about ten feet from rear-ending the parked truck. Chris checked the rearview mirror to make sure that no one was about to rear-end them and then looked forward again but couldn't see anything in front of the Toyota that could've caused the driver to stop suddenly in the middle of the interstate.

Suddenly, a medium build Black man got out and slammed the driver's side door as hard as he could, yelling at his wife, who was sitting on the passenger side of the car.

"You drive! You be the man! I'm so sick of you worrying me 'til I feel like jumping in front of this truck!" He pranced around in a circle, slowly moving out of the path of a freight truck coming toward him in the second lane of the interstate, and continued ranting and raving. "It's not my fault I got laid off. I'm doing the best I can," said the man, who looked to be in his mid forties.

"They almost got us all hurt over something that's probably not even worth arguing over," said Angel who had no idea what the argument was about. "It can't be that serious. Dang! Just ignorant, the way some couples act!"

"Humph," Chris mumbled.

The look on Angel's face said it all.

Chris quickly turned his sarcastic comment into noises by pretending that he was grunting and coughing. Out of the corner of his eye, he saw that Angel didn't have the pre-werewolf signs he had imagined on her face. His tactic appeared to have worked.

They both gathered the composure they had lost from the near-collision and continued their conversation as they got further down the road toward the church.

"As for your dad, how can he be in heaven when he . . . ?" Angel's voice trailed off. She never talked much about where she thought Chris's father had gone, but her small hesitation revealed the view on suicide that she had kept from Chris for all the years they had been together.

Knowing what she was about to say, Chris answered her with a touch of annoyance. "It's in the Bible!" he said.

Angel and Chris had never argued over their religious beliefs, and Angel declined the opportunity to argue now.

"Jacob! Jacob! Wake up! We're almost at church. Heath, wake Jacob up."

Heath shook Jacob and woke him up, but he went back to sleep seconds later.

"We're here, Jacob," said Angel. "Come on, we're fixing to go in and leave you by yourself. Come on, let's leave him."

Jacob woke up. "Can you carry me, Daddy?" he requested.

"You're getting too big for that now. You've got to be a big boy like Heath, OK?"

"Please, Daddy, I'm so tyrid."

Chris and Angel laughed at Jacob's cute mispronunciation of the word *tired*.

"I guess I can since your so tyrid," Chris said as he picked up Jacob and carried him to the front doors of True Saints of God Baptist Church. Chris opened the door one-handed and held it for Heath and Angel and they went inside. On a five foot long bench in the lobby area, an usher stood over one of the church members and fanned her with a hand held paper fan and rubbed her back as the parishioner moved her upper body up and down as if she had stomach pains and was on the verge of regurgitating her morning breakfast. On her downward motions, she double-clutched and stomped both her feet at the same time before throwing both hands in the air and shouting, "Glory! Thank you, Jesus!" on her upward motions as she sat on the bench.

Chris put Jacob down and reached out to open one of the double doors to the sanctuary. Just as Chris and his family were about to go inside, both doors burst open, barely missing Jacob, and a woman ran past them, screaming as if her soul had somehow been set on fire. Chris snatched Jacob out of her path just in time. Ushers tending to the woman in the lobby laid her down on the bench and ran to catch the other member, who had apparently been touched by a spirit of some kind after hearing one of the preachers speaking the powerful Word of God. As she jumped up and down, the ushers jumped with her as they tried to hold her still so they could fan and cool off her overheated soul. The ushers failed to cool her down fast enough, and she fainted. Chris and Angel found the shouts, the praises, and the Holy Ghost dance music, which had almost half of the members of the church on their feet jumping for joy, overwhelming.

"Hallelujah!" said the minister behind the pulpit into the microphone. "Praise God, Saints! He is worthy! There is no other God like him!" This church, which was packed with "saints," was obviously very different from the one they had just left.

"Daddy, I'm scared," Jacob said. I want to go home." Clearly, he had not gotten over the screaming lady who had almost run him over at the door.

"It's OK. It's OK. They're receiving blessings from God. That's why we're here," Chris said.

"I think we're in the right place for it," said Angel. "This pastor is laying it down in here. The pastor at the church we just left didn't give them anything to shout about. They praise God at *this* church."

All the seats were full, from the front to the back of the church, even though a few courteous young single members were standing along the back walls to allow families to sit down. One of the ushers approached

Chris and his family as they stood in the back scanning through the crowd for a place to sit.

"You all may sit here on the ushers' bench if you like," the usher said. "Follow me."

Fifteen minutes after the Shoemaker family sat down, the members of the church who had been touched by the Holy Ghost finally started to calm down. The ushers fanned as many of them as they could, but a few unattended men and women were lying out in the floor, crying and breathing heavily.

This bizarre behavior concerned Jacob very much. "Are they going to die, Daddy?" he asked.

"No, I don't think so," Chris replied.

Many people were yelling "Thank you, Lord Jesus!" while others chanted and spoke in tongues. One of the ushers walked down the aisle and approached a wooden podium in front of the stage to welcome all of their visitors. Evidently, no one had instructed the True Saints' members to say the welcome before the spiritually gifted tongue speakers stood up to give their message from God to visitors who spoke in languages other than English. Without any non believing visitors from other countries in their congregation, the people who spoke in tongues gave their messages to no one, and no translators were present to translate their messages to the rest of the congregation who believed in Jesus already. For all those reasons, their messages from God were lost in translation. The order for speaking in tongue wasn't being followed according to 1 Corinthians 14:27-28.

"Would all visitors please stand?" asked the usher who had seated them.

Every member of the congregation, including toddlers, was dressed in their Sunday best. Chris and Angel felt uncomfortable because of their casual clothes but they stood up anyway. Chris noticed Harold and his family standing on the other side of the church. For some reason, Tony and Bryan didn't make it. A few other guests stood, but the majority of the people there were already members.

"Would you like to have a word or give a testimony?" the usher asked. Another usher standing in the back of the church with a wireless microphone was prepared to give the mic to anyone who wanted to speak. As Chris looked around with the rest of the congregation to see if anyone had raised their hand, turning his head left and then right, he saw the usher walking forward holding up the cordless microphone. Chris looked directly at the usher. Somehow, there was a mix-up in body-language communications. The usher thought Chris was signaling to bring him the mic. Before Chris knew it, the whole church heard him breathing into the microphone that the usher held in front of him waiting for him to speak. He slowly took the microphone from the usher and scratched his head as he thought of something to say.

"My name is Chris Shoemaker. This is my wife and kids that I thank God for."

"Glory to God, praise Jesus," one of the members cried out.

"Uh, thank you, ma'am," Chris said. "I'd also—well, we're also thankful that we are alive today. The tornadoes that came through Friday night destroyed our home, but we were untouched."

Before Chris could finish his testimony, several members got out of their seats and began shouting. The organ player turned around and began playing another Holy Ghost dance tune. Right behind him with a hip-hop drum line of some kind was the drummer. He hopped on the drums and sent out a rapid pattern of beats as he caught up to the rhythm of the organ. Seconds later, when the drum and organ had gotten in sync, the church began to rock all over again. Unable to finish his testimony because of all the commotion he had caused, Chris gave the microphone back to the usher and sat down.

The usher handed Chris a guest and new member form to complete and pointed to a box on the back wall. "Put it in that box on the wall that says 'visitor's questionnaire,'" the usher said.

Five minutes later, the shouting finally ceased and the assistant pastor of the church stood up behind the glass podium in the pulpit area that overlooked the congregation.

"It's time to have church up in here!" yelled Bob Smith, the assistant pastor. "We're fixing to have church up in here! Are ya'll ready to have church?" he yelled and swung his fist around as if he were defending himself from an imaginary attacker. He rubbed his hands uncontrollably through his sandy brown hair as he stepped down from the stage.

The sound of strong winds began to blow and fill the sanctuary. Everyone stood up, and the lights slowly began to dim. Complete darkness filled the sanctuary, and a godlike voice spoke, saying, "Purify yourselves and prepare to hear a word from the Lord. The anointed one is here."

Lights on the edge of the stage beamed upward toward the baptismal pool enclosed ten-foot-high on the wall behind the pulpit, interrupting the darkness at three-second intervals. Another display of lights followed from lights in the ceilings that evaporated sections of darkness for three seconds as well. Chris could see smoke rising from the baptismal area, making a trail to the clear glass podium, which began to glow with special lighting inside it. A small stage light in the ceiling shone down directly onto the Holy Bible that lay open on the glass podium. Special effects from black lights and other stage lighting gave the smoke a glowing cloudlike appearance. The sound of thunder rumbled through the speakers and perfectly timed lights flashed on cue to simulate lightning. About seven seconds later, the stage lights aimed at the baptism area flickered off and then on. Rolls of thunder and displays of lightning started exploding out of control. Stage lights aimed at the baptismal pool flickered again and other stage lights mounted in the ceiling roamed all over the dark sanctuary, creating the illusion of a huge electrical storm. Suddenly, there was one huge, thunderous boom.

On the third flicker of the light aimed at the baptismal pool above the production-made clouds, the Reverend Apostle Prophet Joe Edgars appeared in a white robe and white gloves with his arms stretched out. The black lights made his all-white garments glow as if he were an angel from heaven. He slowly moved his hands in front of his face and bowed his head as if he were praying. With unseen cables connected to him, he slowly started to descend to the glass podium as if he were coming from heaven on a cloud to deliver a message from God. On his descent, he stretched out his right hand palm up toward the Bible that lay glowing on the podium. Complete darkness invaded the sanctuary of the church as soon as Reverend Apostle Prophet Joe Edgar's feet touched the floor. In complete darkness, two associate pastors who had been sitting near the glass podium helped the anointed Reverend out of his white robe and his wire harness and stored them in a hidden two-foot-deep by three-foot-wide storage compartment built into the floor eight feet behind the glass podium. When the lights came back on, Reverend Prophet Edgars was standing behind the glass podium that overlooked the congregation looking extremely handsome in a navy blue tailor-made suit that had only cost him forty-five hundred dollars. The stage stretched evenly across the front section of the sanctuary with fifteen rows of pews on each side surrounding the podium in a half-moon shape while the balcony stretched across the entire backside of the church. Once again, Reverend Apostle Prophet Edgars stretched out his hands and turned to his left, to his right, and then back to the middle before slowly dropping his hands to his sides, signaling to the congregation to be seated.

"It's offering time," said Reverend Apostle Prophet Edgars, "a time to give back a portion of what God has given to you. How else can we tell God thank you except through sacrifice? What can we offer God that He doesn't already have? — Our sacrifice. Part of being Christ like is to offer a sacrifice like Christ sacrificed His life. Malachi 3:8 tells us of a sacrificial offering we must make to show our love for Him and"—he paused dramatically—"to be blessed! How does a man rob God—through tithes and offerings? Give back to God and see if He won't open the floodgates of heaven and pour out blessings that will overflow your pockets! By tithing today, I guarantee you that whatever you're facing tomorrow, you can claim the victory right now! Name it and claim it and just wait on Him! He will keep his promises! Test Him and see! Ushers, please come forth," said Reverend Apostle Prophet Edgars who unintentionally misinformed his congregation of the meaning of everything he had quoted from Malachi 3:8.

After a quick prayer, the ushers grabbed the offering baskets and went from row to row, collecting money. The church grew quiet. No one talked or shouted during the offering. All Chris could hear was the sound of paper being put into the offering baskets. Ushers kept a tight eye on the baskets as they moved from row to row. Some of the baskets had gotten so full of money that they had to be escorted back to the offering table by deacons to be emptied out and returned to circulation two to three times. As the ushers went from row to row. Chris and Angel discussed in a low voice how much they were going to put in the offering basket. After the short lecture about sacrifice that Reverend Apostle Prophet Edgars had given, they felt obligated to give, but they didn't have much money after giving a tithe offering at Pastor Sander's church earlier that morning.

Ushers and the offering basket had made it to their pew. Reverend Apostle Prophet Joe Edgars must have sensed the unwilling spirits of several people in the congregation that wanted to hold back part of the tenth that they were required to give because he provided more motivation by paraphrasing another Bible verse, emphasizing the word *Lord* by saying it loudly.

"Let us not forget what the Scripture says about the leaders of the church. The Bible says that the *Lord* has commanded that those who preach the Gospel should receive their living from the Gospel. Don't forget about your leader today as the baskets come around. It may hurt, but sometimes you have to give until it hurts. They whipped him all night long. Jesus gave 'til it hurt. Let us be Christ like and give until it hurts. Amen."

"Hand me the checkbook," Chris said, stirred by this motivational doctrine. "Let's just write another check."

"We need to check the balance before we write any more checks," said Angel.

"When you tithe, you don't worry about that young man, this is the one time I wouldn't listen to my wife if I were you," said Mother Idella Banks, an older Black woman with graying hair who was seated next to them. "God will mysteriously put money into your bank account. Test him and see. A heap see, but a few knows about the blessings behind the promise of tithing."

Mother Idella was the wife of Deacon Eddie Banks. They were both in their late fifties and had been faithful members of True Saints for over forty years. Idella served faithfully on both the usher board and on the mothers' board. She and Eddie lived the traditional life of many older Christian couples. They read their Bibles every night after watching the news. They never read the New Testament, because they believed it to be added to the bible as a government scheme to brain wash their minds. Then they'd fall asleep with the good old spirituals playing all night long to keep evil spirits out of their home and holiness in.

A word from the wise, Chris thought, turning around to look at her. If anyone should know about being blessed, it would be an older Christian like her. But then he remembered that both young and mature Christians had been misinforming him for years that his father would spend an eternity in hell for committing suicide. He decided to listen to his wife instead of Mother Banks. He gave the checkbook back to Angel and pulled two ten-dollar bills out of his pocket. When the offering basket came past them, he put one of the ten-dollar bills in the basket and the other back into his pocket.

"I know that ain't ten percent," said Mother Banks, who was secretly watching. "Good luck if you want to be blessed."

"We just lost almost everything we had in a tornado," Chris replied. "I'm sure God will understand."

"Did you pay your tithes before the tornado came?"

"Well," Chris hesitated. "No. I've been working on Sundays for years and we haven't been able to go to church."

"You ever heard of a mailbox? Humph, if you'd put God first, then you still might have your house. I tell young folks all the time, put God first; put God first."

Minutes later, Chris looked over at Angel, who seemed a little uncomfortable.

"Are you ready to go?" Angel asked.

"Let's stay. Give me the checkbook."

"If we don't have it, then we don't have it," said Angel

"Let's—" Chris paused and looked around to make sure that neither Mother Banks nor anyone else was listening. Then he leaned over close to Angel and whispered in her ear. "Let's just try it. Write a check for one hundred dollars."

"A hundred dollars! We don't have it to give!" said Angel in a loud whisper.

"Give me a pen," he insisted.

Realizing that he wasn't going to write a check since she still had the checkbook, Angel found a pen and looked on as Chris completed the visitor's questionnaire.

"They want a copy of our W-2's!" said Angel, reading over his shoulder. "Uh-uh! You can give 'em yours, but I'm not giving them mine. What kind of church is this? They goin' t' pay some of our bills or something?"

"It won't hurt to try this tithe promise thing, Angel," Chris replied in a low whisper. "Calm down, now. You know we need some blessings."

"Wise choice, young man. A blessing is coming your way," said Mother Banks whose hearing was apparently still as good as it had been when she was twenty years old.

Chris was in shock that she'd heard every word he had said.

The time came for Reverend Apostle Prophet Edgars to share a new revelation he claimed to receive from God. New revelations were always recorded and entered into the Bible so that all believers in God could read it. In this case, the message from God might have been meant specifically for True Saints Baptist Church members only. It seemed rather odd to Chris that the good Reverend was claiming that God kept secrets and revealed new things to believers other than what He had already stated in the bible as His true and perfect word.

After a two-and-a-half-hour sermon on how to bring prosperity into your life, the church service finally ended and Chris felt as if things were going to start turning around for him and his family. Angel, however, had fallen asleep in the middle of the sermon and hadn't gotten anything out of it. Harold and his family had left an hour and a half into the sermon.

Tired and hungry, Chris and his family rushed out to their car and headed home.

Maybe this is why life has been so hard, Chris thought as he drove to his mother-in-law's house. *God's gonna make everything all right.*

Out of motherly instinct, Angel turned around to make sure that Jacob and Heath had strapped themselves in and noticed they both had disappointed looks on their faces.

"What's wrong with y'all? Who hit who first?" asked Angel.

"We're not fighting, Momma. We're tryin' to figure out if God is good like people say because we went to church and He didn't give us no blessing," Heath explained.

"I don't think it works like that, baby. Blessings aren't something we can buy or pick up from the store. You think we didn't get a blessing because we didn't carry something out of the church, sweetheart?"

"No, ma'am. You and Daddy didn't scream and shout like the other people did, and Daddy said we were there to get a blessing like them, so me and Jacob were wondering about what kinda person God is."

Angel and Chris looked at each other, not knowing exactly what to say. Neither of them had ever studied the Bible for themselves so they did what most Christians have done for centuries: believed in what preachers said that sounded good even if it contradicted other things in the Bible.

"We have to wait for his spirit to enter our bodies," said Angel. "We'll get the Holy Ghost, too, if we continue to go to church."

"Are we going to keep coming to church, Momma?"

"For you and Jacob's sake, yes, we're going to start going to church more often." Angel looked at Chris and asked, "Did I tell him right about the spirit thing? That is how it works, isn't it?"

"I don't know, but I think I'm going to do better and start reading the Bible for myself to find out. For years, I thought my father had no chance to be forgiven, because I was listening to someone else's interpretation on suicide. All of this has got me desperately wanting to learn more about the Bible."

CHAPTER 11

Testing God

After getting a good night's sleep, Chris woke up Monday morning ready to set aside his years of anger against God and to test Him by naming and claiming the blessings that he thought he had earned through the tithe covenant. First on his agenda was going to the police station to conquer the possible manslaughter charges from the accident. Next, he claimed that God was going to bless him with a new automobile, which he could surely buy with his insurance money and not add to his tithe promise name it and claim it list. He had proclaimed in the name of Jesus that he would get the CCSA aircraft sales position he had tried several times to land as well. In fact, he had such strong faith and confidence in the tithe promise that he expected the rest of his life to be full of nothing but blessings and prosperity.

Everything was great; life was wonderful. Chris thought he could now hold God accountable for the promises He had made in the Bible, but had not kept, but first he needed to be blessed with some wheels so he could go out and get everything he claimed would be his through the promise he believed God made to all Christians who believed in Him.

"Are you taking your mother to work or is she taking you and the boys? Chris asked Angel as he sat down to breakfast.

"We're riding with her."

"You know, the tornado may have worked things out for the best. Our insurance check should be enough for us to build a new house that we shouldn't owe that much on. We can finally get a brand-new car for you, and I can get the car of my dreams . . . a '69 Camaro.

"That's what I've been thinking," said Angel. "I'll start calling around for a builder and looking on the Internet for some house plans for us to choose from. I'm excited."

"I'm going to hug and kiss Heath and Jacob good-bye and hop in the shower. I'll see you this evening," Chris said, kissing Angel on the cheek.

After a quick shower, Chris put the same clothes he was wearing back on, shaved, and brushed his teeth before calling his boss to explain about the tornado and the accident and ask for a vacation day.

Chris said a prayer before leaving to go to the police station. "Keep your promise, Lord. Lord, please keep your promises to me." His first stop would be the most important. He knew he hadn't been drunk the night of the accident, but his word alone was not enough to save him. Just as he backed out of the driveway, his phone rang. Chris pulled back into the driveway and answered the phone.

"Hello."

"May I speak to Chris Shoemaker, please?"

"This is him. I mean, this is he," Chris answered.

"This is Detective Grant. I was trying to catch you before you headed this way to save you a trip. According to the test result, you were under the legal limit. You can just email me a statement of what happened when you get some time. You have a good one, hear," said Detective Grant before hanging up the phone.

The tithe covenant was working. God was immediately answering his prayers and protecting him just as He had promised. He pulled back into the driveway and thanked God all the way to the front door.

"Where is the key?" he said out loud to himself as he remembered that he was homeless and living at his mother-in-law's house, a situation that he believed was going to change. Sickness, poverty, homelessness, or any kind of suffering was no longer a problem—not because Chris faithfully kept the Ten Commandments but because he faithfully sacrificed ten percent of his income.

Taking his cell phone out of his pocket, he called Angel.

"What's up?" she asked after checking the caller ID.

"Do you have a key to your mom's house?"

"Look in the ashtray. I meant to text you that I put her spare key there this morning before we left," said Angel.

"How is everything going on your job?" asked Chris.

"Fine, why do you ask?"

"Just wondering if the tithe promise has been working for you," Chris said, smiling proudly.

"Chris, I don't know about this covenant stuff. Look around the world. Why does poverty still exist? I'm sure the ghetto is full of people who tithe. As a matter of fact, I saw Brenda at the True Saints Baptist Church yesterday. I know she's been tithing because she's a member there. About a month ago, I ran into her at the grocery store and she said she still lives in the ghetto and still struggling to try to make it. Why is that?"

"Maybe she doesn't give from her heart," Chris replied.

"My boss is coming; I'll call you later. Bye," Angel said and quickly hung up the phone.

Chris thought about Angel's doubts because of her friend's situation, but he refused to surrender to his own doubts about the tithe covenant. The only thing on his agenda was his big plan to get the getting while the getting was good. God was now answering his prayers after many years of silence. After getting the key from the ashtray, Chris went inside and prepared a very long tithing prosperity list. He still had lots more tests to perform as if he were enabling God to show him that He was worthy of Chris's praise. After all, the Reverend Apostle Prophet Joe Edgars had said that the Bible says to test God with tithes and offerings. So Chris intended to do as he thought the Bible said.

Patience was not part of his life right now; it was harvest time. He had sown his seeds and had been patient for years. Chris felt no shame in telling God all the things his heart desired. He had no sympathy for people like Angel's friend Brenda who still lived in the ghetto because, for some reason, she wasn't protected under the tithe covenant. He looked around at what was going to be his family's home for the next year or longer and decided that it was time to claim a new house in the name of Jesus. Chris grabbed the insurance card out of his wallet and sat down on the couch, grabbing the phone on the end table next to him to call his insurance agent.

"Yes, ma'am, I have insurance on my house and cars with you guys and I need to file a claim," said Chris. After a disappointing forty-minute conversation with his insurance agent, Chris was doubtful that his insurance company was going to change their policy because he had made a tithe covenant with God. They informed him that they were only obligated to pay him what his home was worth when it had been built in 1977. No one had provided Chris with any information on GAP coverage for his insurance policy. Chris immediately assumed that his lack of knowledge would not over power the covenant he made with God. He had faith that not even the toughest situations were too hard for the tithe covenant to fix. Despite the disappointingly small amount that they were to receive from the insurance company, Chris was sure that everything would work out fine. God, Chris's father in heaven, would never lie, and God had made a promise to all who paid their tithes. It was in the Bible. At least Chris thought it was.

He got their laptop from the bedroom that Angel had taken with her to her mom's house on the night of the tornadic storm and spent hours trying to figure out how much they could afford to spend on a new house. After working on a scenario of what their entire financial outlook would look like after they had paid off some of their debt with the insurance check they were due to receive, Chris addressed another problem that he had been meaning to take care of. He pulled out Pastor Sanders card and sent him an e-mail after changing his inappropriate Internet username. He then sent Detective Grant the statement he requested to complete his accident report.

Angel, her mother, and the kids had finally made it home after stopping by their storm-damaged home to check the mail and salvage anything else they could find that hadn't been stolen.

"Did you request an address change from the post office?" asked Angel.

"I forgot to do that; I'll do it tomorrow," said Chris.

"So when will we be getting our insurance check? Did they say?" Angel asked excitedly. "I've been looking at house plans all day, and I've found several I like. Here." She handed Chris a stack of house plans. "I also have a list of several builders we can talk to. Did you know that some builders are building houses for less than it costs to buy one already built just to keep from laying their workers off? Don't get me wrong, they're doing it to make something instead of nothing, but it's their loss, our gain."

"Yeah. Um, about that, I've been calculating all the costs, and we could just buy a house and not have to wait a year or however long it takes to have one built," Chris said.

"It will only take four to five months. One builder I talked to said he'd even put that in the contract; he guaranteed it."

"Let me show you something on the computer in the bedroom." Chris grabbed the laptop and headed down the hallway. The rest of their conversation required privacy.

"We're kinda not getting as much as I thought we were getting from the insurance company," he said when they were alone.

"So what's the problem? What are you saying?"

"We're only getting 65,000 dollars for the house and personal property. The insurance agent never said anything about gap insurance."

"So what are you saying?" Angel repeated.

"The home owner's policy only covered what the house was worth when we bought it. If we were to rebuild the same house today—the same way, the same size—it would cost about 135,000 dollars. In other words, we're about 70,000 dollars shy of what it would cost to rebuild our house or any house the same size it was. GAP insurance would've covered the 70,000 dollar difference for what it would cost to rebuild it at today's price. If we decide not to rebuild in the same spot, they'll give us twelve thousand dollars for our lot."

"What! We're going to have to take out a loan and get further in debt than we already are! Even if the house was paid for we'd have to get another loan and start over? We've worked too hard for everything to keep getting taken away from us."

"We can give a bigger tithe and . . . ."

"I don't want to hear about paying no tithes right now. God owes us, and He hasn't kept his word. All of our hard work and sacrifice . . ." Angel started crying. "I'm tired of being a slave to this world. It just seems as if God doesn't love us anymore and we've done nothing wrong. I don't understand why He makes us suffer so much. I look at all the people who lie, cheat, steal, and kill, and sometimes I want to be like them. They're blessed. But look at us. Constantly trying to be honest and forgiving, constantly trying to do right. A few blessings sprinkle on us. People who don't try to do right swim in the blessings that rain down on them. Blessings just overflow. I'm tired of breaking my neck to live right. What's the use? Where's our reward?" Angel was now fully engulfed in tears.

Angel's mother Amanda was on her way to the bathroom when she heard Angel crying. She stood outside the door and she began to cry silently as she listened to her daughter talk about how she and Chris had been struggling.

Jacob, who was left all alone, decided to investigate the whereabouts of all the grown-ups. As he walked toward his grandmother, she put her finger in front of her lips and signaled for him to be quiet.

"What's wrong, Grandma?" Jacob asked. "Grandmomma, Grandma, whatchoo doing?"

She tiptoed past Jacob and hurried back into the living room, sitting on the couch before answering Jacob so that her voice could be heard coming from the living room instead of the hallway.

"Getting ready to watch the news," she said. "Come over here and talk to Grandma."

Chris and Angel heard Jacob in the hallway answering his grandmother but thought nothing of it.

Chris continued explaining his new game plan. "For some reason, I still believe God's going to see us through this. I've decided to take the insurance money for my car and put it toward getting a house. We're getting thirty-five thousand for the Nova, which will leave us needing a thirty-five-thousand-dollar loan to buy or build."

"Are you serious? They gave you thirty-five thousand for that raggedy old car?" Angel asked, not realizing that Chris had invested forty thousand dollars of his own money into the car.

"No, I'm just trying to get you to stop crying," said Chris.

Angel balled up her fists and eased them up toward her eyes. She screeched louder and louder as she began to cry from a level of sadness stored deep down in her soul. She rubbed her eyes with the inside of her fists like a helpless child who didn't know which way to turn for help.

"Just kidding," Chris said as he walked over and sat on the bed next to her and gave her a hug. "I can find a Camaro that needs to be restored for about three thousand dollars and save some money by doing it myself. It'll take a year to finish it if I work hard, but that's OK." After a short pause, Chris rubbed Angel's back and hugged her tightly again. "I have an interview for that sales position tomorrow. If I get it, then most of our financial problems will be solved."

CHAPTER 12

It's Harvest Time

The next day at work, Chris was interviewed for the third time for the CCSA aircraft sales associate position. He had all the qualifications each time he applied, but he had always been overlooked. Chris had almost finished college on his first attempt at the sales position, but he was turned down because he hadn't completed his degree. Weeks later, Chris had found out that the candidate who landed the position didn't have a degree of any kind. On his second attempt, he had completed his finance/marketing degree but was told that he needed more experience. The following week, his coworker Bill Select, who had also interviewed for the position, received the news that the sales position was his. Bill had been with the company for only two years and had one year left to complete his degree, yet he got the job that Chris had been striving toward for seven of the eight years of his employment. After Bill got the position, he quit school. But now Chris had a failure-proof secret weapon for his third and final attempt: the tithe covenant.

To Chris's surprise, Bill Select was sitting behind the desk waiting to interview him. Through the course of a few years of sitting behind a desk, Bill had moved up in the company and in his clothing size as well. He had been promoted to manager of the sales department. Since they had worked together in the janitorial department for a few years, Chris was sure that the position was finally going to be his. The old who-you-know-not-what-you -know policy was sure to be in effect. After several minutes of small talk and catching up on each other's lives, they began the interview.

"So are you still married?" asked Bill.

"I sure am, are you?"

"Yeah, but not to the same woman." There was a pause. "Are you still married to the same . . . biracial woman you brought to the company picnic?"

"Color gives us false identities, don't you think? We all look different from one another, but we're still the same. What color am I, Bill?"

"I've never really figured that out," Bill said. "Your wife has a lot of Black, but you . . . you have features of both colored people and White people; your skin color could go either way."

"Let me help you figure out what color I am," Chris replied. "I'm both, neither, other, and all of the above. I may not sound too sure of what color I am, but the one thing I do know is that I was, am, and will always be a child of God. Created in his image . . . colorless," Chris replied.

Three minutes after the interview started, it was over and they both stood up to shake hands. Just as Chris was about to ask Bill what his chances looked like as far as getting the job, there was a knock on the door.

All the high-ranking executives, presidents and CEOs of the company were showing the new owner, Mr. Willie Stewart, around his newly purchased aircraft company. They apologized for interrupting and introduced Mr. Stewart to Bill.

"No need to apologize," said Bill. "This interview was just ending."

Mr. Stewart walked over to Bill and shook his hand. "The sales department is the backbone of any company. I want you to provide me with a list of all of your sales strategies and whatever else you can provide for my advisement team meeting in two weeks," he said.

"Yes, sir," said Bill.

"Excuse me, Mr. Stewart. But do you remember me?" Chris asked.

The look on Mr. Stewart's face had changed from summer to winter in an instant.

"I-I—" He hesitated and stuttered before finally finishing his sentence. "I think so. You look very familiar."

"Chris. Johnny Shoemaker's son," said Chris as he tried to jog his memory. Mr. Stewart's behavior was noticeably weird. It took a couple of seconds for the ice to melt off his face. He was seconds away from needing a defibrillator to get his heart beating again.

"Whoo! You scared me for a minute there. I thought you were going to say you were my long-lost son," said Mr. Stewart as they all laughed.

One of the executives said something that turned Chris's facial expression as stiff as concrete.

"When you're rich like we are, people come from everywhere looking for a handout and claiming to be kin," he said as everyone laughed except Chris.

I'm just like them, Chris thought. *The fatherless young men who looked for a handout by pretending to be somebody's son. Not a handout of money but a handout of love and an understanding of a difficult thing called manhood.* A fatherless young man was no laughing matter to him.

On their way out of Bill's office, they patted each other on their shoulders and on their backs and laughed all the way down the hall. Something had come to Mr. Stewart's mind after making it two corners away from Bill's office.

"Pardon me, gentlemen. I forgot to tell Mr. Select something," said Mr. Stewart. Some type of vision played in his mind as he grabbed the doorknob to Bill's office. He paused for a couple of seconds, turned his back against the wall, took a deep breath, and shook his head. After picking his chin up off his chest, he reentered Bill's office. "Chris, do you mind if I have a word with Bill in private?" he asked.

"No, sir. I was just leaving. It was good seeing you again," Chris replied.

After Chris left the office, Mr. Stewart asked, "How long has Chris been here and what is his job title?"

"He's been here about eight years as a janitor. And . . . ." Bill held onto the word as if it were a musical note. "He has a degree, but he has no experience in aircraft sales."

"Hire him."

"With all due respect, sir, I know how important the sales department is to you and this company which is why I feel the need to inform you that he has zero experience in aircraft sales," said Bill.

"How much experience in aircraft sales did you have before you started working here?" Mr. Stewart asked.

"Well, I did have experience selling cars, sir," Bill explained, "but I realize it's not the same thing."

Later that day as it came close to quitting time, Chris's boss, Henry, a snuff-chewing, country-talking Black man, approached Chris with the results of his interview.

"Congratulations, Chris. I'm no longer your boss. You got tha' job."

Chris entered his mother-in-law's house that evening with a sad look on his face.

Through the years, Angel had gotten used to seeing her husband coming home sad and thought nothing of it.

He sat down on the couch next to Angel. "Aren't you going to ask me what's wrong?"

"Let's go to the room so we can talk," Angel said in a low voice, not wanting to discuss anything in front of her mother, who was sitting on the loveseat talking on the phone.

"We can talk about this in front of your mom. She's going to find out, anyway." Amanda quickly got off the phone and took advantage of the invitation by pretending to be totally concentrated on the program that was on television.

"Are you going to jail?" Angel asked. "Did they change their minds? What's going on?"

"No, no. Nothing like that," he replied.

"What is it?" Angel repeated with a note of desperation in her voice.

"Y'all are going to have to suffer some consequences with me. Before you get hysterical, let me say that I don't think it's fair that God forced my whole family to suffer consequences for being under my leadership," said Chris.

"Consequences for what?" asked Angel as she braced herself for some sort of painful news.

"Consequences for my obedience to God. Now my whole family, my prize possession, is going to reap the consequences of the tithe covenant that you didn't want me to be a part of," Chris said with a smile.

"I don't get it. I thought the tithe covenant was supposed to be a good thing, with good consequences?"

"It is," said Chris. "That's why we're fixing to prosper and get our part of the inheritance that God promised Abraham and everything else, such as protection from evil and sickness, that the tithe covenant brings. I tithed on Sunday and I was immediately blessed on Monday and Tuesday, I got the job! I got the job, Angel!" He hugged Angel as she cried tears of joy. *All it took to be blessed was to tithe from the heart*, Chris thought. This was the answer to everything. In the past when they had tithed, their hearts must not have been right or maybe they weren't living right. Sin had somehow blocked them for many years from God's tithe covenant. But, magically, through tithing a few hundred bucks, their storm was finally over.

"Baby, it's harvest time. With this new job, we can go out to any neighborhood in the state and buy a house. Guess where we going tomorrow to look for one?" Chris asked.

"Deer Creek," Angel replied.

"Naw. Those houses are too small. We deserve better than a twenty-four-hundred-square-foot home. We're tithers. We're going to Cane Lake Estates. I won't be too far from work. A ten-minute drive and I'm at work making that bill money. We both are fixing to get new automobiles this weekend."

"God is good. He really is good," said Angel.

"Did you get a chance to go by and check the mail?"

"Yeah. All the mail is on the dresser in the bedroom."

"I just want to look at all the bills we used to have one more time before we pay 'em all off," said Chris. On the way to the bedroom to retrieve the bills, Chris looked up toward heaven, winked his eye, and smiled. He grabbed the three bills off the dresser and sat down on the bed.

"Mr. Light Bill, well, we will never be able to pay you off, but, you, Mr. Department Store Bill, our debt to you is about to be paid in full . . . . What's this?" he asked himself out loud. It was a letter from First Baptist Church in Bryant where Pastor Sanders preached. The letter read:

Dear Mr. Shoemaker:

Enclosed is our pastor's business card and the check you requested to be put into our tithe offering. Unfortunately, we cannot grant you this request because of the curse. We, the members of First Baptist, do not practice tithing. Those who tithe are under a curse. Believers in Christ who continue to follow one part of the law must follow all parts of the law or be cursed. Please read Galatians chapter three. For more information on tithing under the old and new law, please contact our pastor, Larry Sanders.

Sincerely,

Patsy Brewster

Church Secretary

Angel walked into the bedroom to discuss a game plan for keeping the blessings rolling in at the end of each month.

"Which church are we going to pay our tithes to, both churches or one? I was thinking, what if we went to both churches and tithe? Would our blessings be doubled? What do you think? Maybe we can just go to one church and double it there. A church is a church. The one in Bryant gets out early, and they don't have all that screaming and hollering. Plus with gas costing the same monthly as a house note, we can save a little somethin' on gas. We can go there, can't we?"

Chris sat on the bed, unresponsive, with a zombielike expression.

"What's wrong?" Angel asked.

"Uh, well. Let's just slow down," said Chris.

"Put those bills down," Angel said. "Don't worry about those bills. They're going to be paid off, right? They're God's problem now. Let Him worry about how they're going to get paid."

"You're right. I've got an even better idea. I'm going to put them in my Bible after I pray and hand them over to God. I'm going to the bathroom and pray over them."

Chris went into the bathroom, sat down on the closed toilet seat, and turned his Bible to Galatians chapter three. He read the entire chapter and read verse ten several times to get a good understanding. "All who rely on observing the law are under a curse, for it is written: Cursed is everyone who does not continue doing everything written in the Book of the Law."

"I don't need to hear this right now," he said to himself. "There's probably some explanation. All I know is I'm finally getting blessed. I'll talk to Pastor Sanders after I finish harvesting my blessings."

—

Pastor Sanders had taught Chris more biblical truth and explained more important biblical contradictions in one hour than he had learned from listening to other preachers for more than twenty years. Yet, for some reason, Chris chose to make his family's place of worship the True Saints Baptist Church instead of the First Baptist Church where Pastor Sanders taught the Bible.

After attending church there every Sunday for three months, Chris and his family had gotten to know lots of people at the True Saints Baptist Church. Threats of a layoff had become a part of the everyday talk around both Chris's and Angel's places of employment. News stations reported new layoffs every week. The economy was not improving. Chris figured that the only thing he could do was to give more money to the church so that God would protect his family from layoffs.

One evening in August, Chris and his family arrived home from church. Almost immediately, he decided to look over their bills. After hearing the Sunday morning sermon, Chris contemplated on giving a little more for his tithes and offering in hopes of guaranteeing the seeds he sowed for financial prosperity and protection. As he sat at the computer, he thought back on all the problems he had been having in the past and realized that he had gotten into trouble because he thought God was leading him in the direction that He had wanted him to go. Finally, he relieved himself by blaming himself instead of God. *Somehow, this must be my fault,* he thought. *Maybe I'm not specific enough in my prayers,* he thought. As he thought about all of his problems, he looked into the computer screen as if God were inside it and questioned God as he had done many times before.

"How many prayers does it take?" he asked. "What's the magic number to get one prayer answered?" As Chris starred into the computer questioning God on what he thought was a slow track record for answering prayers, Chris had somehow failed to realize that several important prayers he prayed about had already been answered. He begged God to protect his wife on the night of the tornado, and He did. He prayed that he'd be found innocent of drunk driving and vehicular homicide, and he was. He also prayed for the aircraft sales position and finally got it after several tries. They had also prayed for a bigger home seven years prior and they were now in the process of getting that prayer answered.

—

After six months of going back and forth wondering rather or not he should trust in the covenant or believe what Pastor Sanders had said in the letter from his church about tithing, Chris finally set forth to trust God and claim everything he claimed would be his through the covenant he made with God at True Saints Baptist Church. He replaced nearly half of the things he lost in the tornado from bicycles, lawnmower and yard tools to tools for working on cars. Chris and Angel traded in her Ford Escort for a 2010 charcoal gray SRX Cadillac for Angel, a black 2010 Toyota Tundra truck for Chris, and a new thirty-six-hundred-square-foot house on the lake in Cane Lake Estates in west Little Rock. It had a three-car bay and a separate double-car garage that Chris planned to use as a shop to work on the '69 Camaro project car he was on his way to pick up on a sunny Saturday afternoon.

Four months after becoming a member, he had accepted an offer to go through a three month long trial period to become a deacon at the True Saints Baptist church. Reverend Apostle Prophet Edgars had directed Deacon Banks to recruit Chris for deaconship one Sunday evening after seeing how much money Chris was sacrificing for his tithes and offerings. He felt a huge obligation to give more money than normal during the two months he had been on trail to become a deacon. Despite his new six-figure salary, he couldn't afford to spend forty thousand dollars it would've taken to purchase a fully restored '69 Camaro. He had settled for a rusty '69 Camaro in need of major work instead of one that was already restored. But giving up his dream car to be able to tithe was a small price to pay for a new house for his family, and the rusty Camaro was better than no Camaro at all. She was a beauty in Chris's eyes. All he could see when he looked at the rusty, dented car with her faded paint job was a vision of how beautiful she would look when she was restored.

He called Harold, Bryan, and Tony on his way home and invited them to come and see his dream car he had just bought. They all showed up in their hot rods shortly after Chris unloaded the Camaro off the car hauler he had borrowed from Tony.

"She just has a few small flaws is all," said Chris with a proud smile as he showed her off to Angel and the guys.

"Wow! A few flaws!" began Tony. "This here is a piece of—"

All the guys gave Tony the look and he stopped and changed his wording. "This is— wow!" he said.

"She's unique, that's for sure," Bryan said in an attempt to keep the sparkle in Chris's eyes after Tony's innocent near insult. "Y'all know Melvin will be home in May?" Bryan added.

"Naw. How'd you find that out?" Tony asked.

"I ran into Sasha at the grocery store the other day and she told me." Sasha and Melvin had been married for four years. She was a Russian model Melvin had met while he was stationed in Germany. Melvin had been gone for a year to serve a second tour of duty in Afghanistan?

"How much did we spend on this—car thing?" Angel asked. Chris looked at Angel with a weird looking smile on his face. "Never mind. I know that look. I'm going back inside to check on the kids," said Angel before Chris could respond. Chris saw beauty and worth in the Camaro and paid three-thousand dollars for it. All Angel saw was the rustiest, most raggedy, most beat-up shape of metal she had ever seen.

Later that evening, after the guys had left, Chris went out into the garage to make a list of things he would need to replace on what he refused to call a piece of junk. He sat and stared at the Camaro and reminisced about the days when he and his father had worked on what was supposed to have been his first car when he was old enough to drive. It had hurt his father badly when he'd had to sell the '69 Camaro after unexpectedly getting laid off because of the bad economy at the time. Chris went into a daydreaming trance and replayed one of many precious memories he had of himself and his father working on that old car.

"You got a girlfriend?" his dad had asked the eleven-year-old Chris who was standing next to him as he was adjusting the hood latch on the gray primed Camaro parked backwards in the garage. The garage door was up and the Arkansas heat was down due to the overcast skies that shield the sunlight away.

"Yes, sir. I got three of 'em," Chris had answered.

"Why do you need three girlfriends son?"

"Because all of my friends have more than one."

"I think it's time for us to have the old cars and new cars talk," his father had said as he stood up and leaned over and pulled another lowboy stool from the corner of the garage next to his forty inch, twenty three drawer tool chest and rolled it next to the stool where he was sitting and motioned for Chris to sit down. "You aren't even old enough to drive yet and you're trying to drive three cars at the same time. The only thing that's going to happen with that is a big wreck," his father said as he took one step toward his tool box; opened the drawer and pulled out a *Hot Rod* magazine with a beautiful, midnight blue '69 Camaro on the front cover and sat down next to Chris. "You have a lot to learn about girls. The first thing you need to learn is that we males really don't deserve them… and to have one is like having a precious jewel like this car. Almighty God was gracious enough to allow them to be apart of our lives, so respect them as the greatest of all of His creations that they are." His father handed him the magazine, and Chris flipped through some of the pages to see what the car looked like before its fascinating transformation.

"It looks new." Chris paused. "It looks better than most of the brand-new cars," said Chris.

"Jesus loves and restores us this same way," his father said. "God the Father sees us shiny and brand-new because of his son Jesus, who restores us. Jesus saved us from the metal scrapping yard called hell. You're at the age now when you need to decide if you want to sign the title of your soul over to Jesus and let him own you completely."

The memory faded, and Chris sighed. He loved and missed his father. Although he no longer feared that his father was burning in hell, his father's suicide still affected him. The problem now wasn't whether God was cruel; it was whether his father really loved him and his mother. Only one person that he knew of other than his mother could tell him things about his father that could help him answer that question.

CHAPTER 13

Curse or Blessing?

It had been six months since he'd talked to Pastor Sanders. After the letter he'd received from Pastor Sanders church about tithing being part of a curse, Chris had stopped talking to Pastor Sanders out of fear that the pastor might've been right about tithing. Wanting to know more about his father, Chris decided he'd send Pastor Sanders an e-mail message.

Pastor Sanders responded by asking Chris to talk to him face-to-face about personal matters that dealt with his father. Chris agreed to meet in Pastor Sanders office on Wednesday evening one hour before Bible study.

Several people were still at the church that Wednesday evening. Some of the parents had not yet picked up their children who attended the church's learning academy school. Pastor Sanders was sitting at his computer working on that night's Bible study lesson when Chris knocked on the open door.

"Jesus, is that you?" Pastor Sanders said with a smile. "You've been gone a good long while."

"Oh, no! I hope He doesn't come today, I'm not sure if I'd be ready to go."

A concerned expression passed over Pastor Sanders's face.

"Have you ever read the whole Bible?" asked Pastor Sanders.

"No, sir, I haven't," Chris replied.

"Have you accepted Jesus and believe that He died for *all* of your sins?"

"Yes," Chris responded.

"Do you believe that He's the only way you can make it to heaven?"

"Yes, I do."

"You've got no problem, then. You're a fast learner. Sounds like you're absolutely sure about heaven now. What else can I help you with today?"

"Just that easy, huh?" Chris said as he sat down.

"It's that easy," Pastor Sanders responded.

"If only it were that easy to understand the Bible so I can stay saved and not get confused about everything it says."

"Once you're truly saved, you're saved forever. Don't let the hypocrisy of the deceivers who say that they're saved fool you. And don't let the way you see some Christians who are truly saved fool you either. At certain times in all Christians' life's your going to see them step out of line, but rest assure—the Holy Spirit will correct them rather it be one month, or five years later."

"Hymph," said Chris.

"Some people read the Bible with their minds desperately focused on reading something to give them instant hope that they can hold on to during difficult times. If you go grocery shopping when you're hungry, you'll buy lots of food you won't be able to eat. Buy only what you need. Read the Bible every day because it's our daily bread and will keep us from getting hungry for non nourishing food that does our body no good. If you read it only when you're in trouble or hungry, your hunger will cause you to gather up a bunch of foods that you can't eat. Foods with a lot of salt and sugar are not good for people with high blood pressure or diabetes, but they can eat those types of foods if they properly—I said *properly*—prepare those same cakes, pies, and other harmful foods without the salt and sugar that's not good for them to eat. We have to learn how to apply bible scriptures to our daily bread," said Pastor Sanders.

Chris's listening skills had improved dramatically. He had become very hungry and passionate when it came to learning about God. "So, in other words, when we get desperate for answers, we make the Bible say what we want it to say and miss what the Bible really says. It sounds like your saying that us New Testament believers are like people who have diabetes and high blood pressure and can't use all the ingredients from the Old Testament to prepare our daily bread and we can't have every promise that's written in the Bible," said Chris.

"That's right. You can't eat all of the food in your refrigerator," Pastor Sanders said as he held up a Bible and pointed at it. "You've got to share some of it with the rest of your family who live far away from the Promised Land. Our share is on the top shelf labeled prayer and salvation. It's fresh and appropriate for the time we live in. Tithing is in the freezer with freezer burn on it because it's so old. It was for the people who lived under the law. You can take it out and unthaw it if you want to, but when it thaws out, you'll see that it's no good for you to eat."

"Just to make sure I'm with you, the food represents Bible verses, right?" asked Chris.

"You're a fast learner. God can definitely use you," Pastor Sanders answered.

"What about these two curses that are cursing the same thing?" asked Chris as he reached into his pocket and pulled out the letter he had received on tithing six months earlier from Pastor Sander's secretary. He unfolded the letter and laid it on Pastor Sander's desk. "Why would there be so many contradictions in the Bible like this one in Galatians chapter three about the laws?"

"It depends on what you want to believe, but the truth is written right in front of you. It's been there and has never changed since the Bible was written," Pastor Sanders said as he picked up the letter and read it. "Oh!" he laughed. "Do you still want to tithe and command God to bless you by keeping His promise now that you know what you know?"

"I want Him to bless me, yeah, but I'm not commanding Him to keep His promise."

"You would if you didn't know the truth and the seeds you had sown from tithing weren't growing," said Pastor Sanders. You'd curse God to His face for not keeping what you thought He had promised you. I've seen it too many times from people who I couldn't convince that tithing and other promises that they believed in were never a part of what God wanted from his New Testament believers."

"How can I determine what promises were for me and which ones weren't?" Chris asked. "How do I know when the Bible is talking to me or when it's not talking to me or to us Americans, what's the point of reading the whole Bible if some of it isn't referring to us?"

"Think of your relationship with God as a marriage. This life on earth is the courtship. We get to learn all about God's character, integrity, personality, and a lot of things about him before He comes to marry us. It's only right to get to know someone before you promise to marry him or her forever. We never would've known what we were doing wrong and what was unpleasing to God if it weren't for the Old Testament. It's called 'old' for a reason: the old way of living to make it to heaven which required obeying over six hundred laws versus the new way of living to make it to heaven which only requires the believe in the name of Jesus. Both the Old and New Testament tells us about our future and God's love, but we can't claim specific promises that were made to Old Testament believers."

"What in the world are we supposed to learn from the promise of tithing if it wasn't promised to us?" Chris asked.

"How to give to the poor, how to share your wealth and worldly goods with people who are going through hard times like you were after the tornado struck. How to give and support your church in it's efforts to reach out to people and teach them about God. Everyone who was ever created will suffer or not have enough money at some time in their lives. God has promised that if He loves you and you claim to love Him, you will see some type of suffering one day. This is a promise from God no one wants to hold onto like they do other promises that they think benefit them. Where are the tithes of today going, do you know?" Pastor Sanders asked.

"To God, aren't they?" Chris replied.

"Are all the tithes from every church in the world being given to the people God commanded them to be given to today or are some churches cutting off God's hand once the money is put in the tithe basket? What did the Lord God tell the Levite priest—oh! I'm sorry. I meant to say, what did God tell the New Testament leaders who are receiving tithes today to do with the tithes? Surely, He gave them instructions in the New Testament on what to do with the tithes just as he gave instructions for the Old Testament saints who lived under these laws he died for?" Pastor Sanders looked at his watch. "It's getting close to Bible study time. Do you fish?"

"Yes, sir," said Chris.

"Let's finish this conversation Saturday morning at Cedar Tree Lake if you're not busy. Your dad and I used to fish there and have Bible discussions all day."

"OK, but what's the answer? Where are we supposed to put the tithes today?" replied Chris while they both got up and began to walk out the door.

"Since tithing never dealt with money. I suggest putting it in the love God command us to have for one another. To find the definition of love, you'll need to read the entire bible. If you don't feel obligated to give anything after reading the bible, then you might not really be a Christian," Pastor Sanders smile was almost a smirk. "Read Galatians chapters three and four and we'll discuss it on Saturday. Pay very close attention to verse sixteen in chapter three. It tells you what part of God's promise to Abraham we Gentiles received and how the promise is not about Abraham's seeds, plural. We Gentiles are seeds of Jesus, not Abraham. The part of the promise that we receive through Abraham is from Abraham's seed, singular, one person. That person is Jesus. Verse fourteen says that Jesus redeemed us so that the blessing of Abraham might come to the Gentiles; in other words, we Gentiles were going to receive the promise of the Holy Spirit by faith." Pastor Sanders snapped his finger and pointed. "Right there! You see that totally different method to make it to heaven and the totally different group of people being spoken about right there? A lot of us New Testament believers reject this promise and try to infringe on God's promises to other people when the promises we have are the best by far: salvation and the power of prayer."

"So you're saying that all we get is the Holy Spirit part of the promise?" Chris asked.

"No, *I* didn't say it; that's what the Bible says," answered Pastor Sanders. "That's what God told Paul to tell us, and He meant what He said. The Holy Spirit is the anointing we receive as a mark inside our hearts when we accept Jesus. The Old Testament saints didn't get this kind of promising assurance. They had to continue to sacrifice animals for their sins. 2 Corinthians 1:21-22 says now it is God who makes both us and you stand firm in Christ. He anointed us, set his seal of ownership on us, and put his Spirit in our hearts as a deposit, guaranteeing what is to come. You see Chris, once we've been anointed, we're anointed forever. Without the mark of the Holy Spirit, no one can enter heaven. And we receive this one time anointing by believing Christ died for all of our sins."

"If Jesus is Abraham's seed, then so are we, aren't we?" asked Chris.

"Galatians three, verses twenty-eight and twenty-nine, says that we are all one in Christ and heirs to the promise—not promises, but promise. As heirs, we share some of the food in the refrigerator. Abraham and the Jews get all the other promises. Let me just sum this up because I need to get set up to teach Bible study in a minute. God knows everything. We can't put words into God's mouth and say that this means we're now Jews instead of Gentiles and this is what God meant to say. Nowhere in the Bible did he convert us and change us to Jews. Most of the Bible controversies and contradictions come from arguments over the Old Testament law and how we interpret one or two small, important words that get overlooked in a lot of verses. One way to determine whether someone is teaching you incorrectly or your understanding something incorrectly is to ask yourself,

Is what I'm reading or what I'm being told restricting my freedom and requiring me to do something besides believing in Jesus to receive blessings and salvation from God? Question any information that goes against freedom. God the Father said whom ever the son sets free is free indeed. Free is free. That's what the Cross did for us." Pastor Sanders paused. "If we break manmade laws, can we avoid going to prison?" he asked.

"No," Chris responded.

"In the same way, God said that the punishment for breaking His law is eternal, never-ending, ever-lasting torture." Pastor Sanders then said uncontrollably. "But because of Jesus—" Pastor Sanders took off his glasses, pulled his handkerchief from his pocket, and wiped his eyes as his face began to turn red.

Chris felt tears in his eyes, but he somehow held them back as he had done many times throughout his life.

Pastor Sanders who was now teary eyed finished teaching Chris about Jesus. "Our sovereign hero. He set us free from the law that promised us a free one-way ticket to the lake of fire. Salvation offers us a free ticket as well, a ticket to heaven and everything in it, free of charge, if we believe in Jesus."

"It's been over seventeen years since I've cried," Chris said. "It's been so long that I've forgotten how to cry and what it feels like to shed tears. But what you're telling me . . . ." Chris put the inside of his fist against his lips and held back the tears that were ready to erupt from his eyes.

"When you start understanding God's Word and realize in your own personal way how good God is through your personal Christian relationship with him, you just might cry every day for the rest of your life," answered Pastor Sanders. "When you get to the point where you understand the Bible and believe that every word of the Bible is God's true Word—" Pastor Sanders choked up again. "Excuse me. I just can't seem to get it together." He cleared his throat and continued. "How can you truly believe someone who has been known to tell a lie? If you believe that the Word of God is controversial and self-contradicting, you need to study more and learn how to read the Bible because God's Word is true and He has never lied. He's being lied about still today, and it just hurts when you're a true child of God and you hear your father's name being . . . shoveled and thrown around like it's something that came from cleaning an elephant's pen at the zoo. The abolishment of the law in the New Testament fixed every controversy and misunderstood contradiction you can find in the Bible that fell under the law. I'll show you some other things on Saturday that will help you understand anything that looks or sounds like a contradiction."

"I'd appreciate that a lot," said Chris. "I'm very interested in knowing that. That's valuable, pure gold information. I'll see you Saturday." They shook hands and went their separate ways.

—

That Friday before his fishing trip with Pastor Sanders was a rough one. Tim Nugget, the root of all his problems at work was a childish coworker who loved causing problems for Chris and would do anything he could to make himself appear to be the department's hardest worker. At age sixty, Tim had somehow missed the stage in his life called adulthood. He had never grown out of tattling, whining, throwing temper tantrums and complaining. Chris thought of him as a three-times-divorced, lonely, bald, overweight, overage grown kid with lots of health problems. After suffering two heart attacks, Tim was still a bitter, jealous old white man who didn't appreciate the life he had been given. He was more thankful for the government and politics than he was for God. His trust was in man and man alone. No one including Tim's own dog, could get along with him.

"Hey, Chris?"

"Yeah, Tim," Chris answered.

"Bill called and asked me to tell you to come over to his office for your yearly eval."

"All right, thanks, Tim."

"Wow, time flies, doesn't it? It's already been, what, six months, has it?"

"You seem to keep up with my time pretty well, Tim." Chris turned around to make sure that Tim wasn't standing behind him before mumbling under his breath, "Keep up with my business better than a married man keeps up with his wife's most personal business."

DaFrenchy James, a young Black man in his mid-twenties whose desk was close to Chris's, heard the mumbled comment and snickered. "Ooh. Now that's something nosey right there," he said too softly for Tim to hear.

"Well, I hope you get a good eval," said Tim. "Thumbs up, buddy." Tim grinned devilishly through his staggered teeth. "And good luck."

"Mm-hm," Chris mumbled as he struggled to return the old thumbs-up sign back to Tim after his Oscar-winning performance. He had a feeling that his fake buddy Tim had graciously helped him get the bad marks he'd received on his three-month job performance evaluation, and he hoped that the same thing wouldn't happen this time. *Surely a supervisor wouldn't take a known liar's word about another employee and put it in his file*, he thought as he walked toward Bill's office.

Bill's door was wide open. Chris walked in and peeked over the computer monitor to find Bill hunched over with his elbow on his desk and his head resting on the back of his right hand, obviously dozing.

"You wanted to see me?" Chris said loudly.

Bill flinched and jumped up with a flabbergasted expression, knocking over a cup with a small sip of coffee left in it as he moved around in hopes of convincing Chris that he had not been asleep.

"Yes, come on in and have a seat while I get your file; it's evaluation time." Bill grabbed a napkin and cleaned the coffee spill. "Are you excited?" he asked.

"Oh, I'm ecstatic," Chris said nonchalantly.

Bill pulled his file and began silently reading a few notes he had written to himself.

"Just a few things we need to talk about here. Since you guys are in a remote office, I got a little input from your coworkers on your job performance."

"Yeah, I figured that out after my last evaluation."

"Yeah, it's just input; it's not like I'm letting them do your evaluation. That wouldn't be fair. I know that's what it seems like, but, anyway—"

"It does seem like my coworkers are the ones who gave me the last bad evaluation I got, but not this one, right?" Chris asked.

"No. They gave input only," Bill replied.

"You've never asked me for input on their evaluations. Just out of curiosity, why haven't you?" Chris asked.

Bill looked at his watch and started gathering up his things. "Um, well, I didn't realize what time it was when you came over. I have a meeting to go to, so I need to make this quick so I can prepare for it," Bill said, blowing off the question. "One of your coworkers told me that you've been taking extended breaks, about fifteen extra minutes per break almost every day. Now, I don't mind any of my employees eating at their workstations, but if you're going to eat for fifteen minutes past your break, you'll need to start clocking out," said Bill.

"You can't be serious. Everyone in the department eats at their desk all day long. What makes me any different? If that old lying Tim told you that, then you need to ask him if doing his bills and ordering everything that's for sale on the Internet is a part of his work description. I look through my work-related paperwork while I'm eating. Tim sits right next to me, and I know he eats a full-course breakfast, second breakfast, lunch, and second lunch and then spends thirty minutes after each of his unscheduled breaks in the bathroom. He's never finished eating either breakfast or lunch before me."

Bill slid the evaluation form over to Chris without giving a response.

"Read this over and sign at the bottom, I'm going to start gathering up information for my meeting. Let me know when you're done."

Chris took a few minutes to read over the comments and then said, "You wrote here in the comments the same thing you just told me was just input from my coworkers and worded it as if you said it yourself. I'm not signing this."

"Why not?" Bill asked.

"For one thing, it's totally false."

"That's fine; do whatever you feel like you need to do. I don't care one way or the other. I just need to prepare for my meeting," said Bill. He kept on working as if he were extremely busy and deeply involved in his work.

Without saying a word, Chris stood up and headed back to his office.

Tim and DaFrenchy were not in the office when Chris got back. Unable to wait for DaFrenchy's return, Chris called him on his cell phone and questioned him about the input Bill said that Chris's coworkers had given him for his evaluation.

DaFrenchy's answer was just as Chris had expected: DaFrenchy told Chris that Bill had never asked him anything about Chris's work performance.

"I knew he was lying. I'm putting in for the senior CCSA position in the jet repair center. I'm tired of Bill and his fits,"

"You'll be protected from the layoff if you get it. From what I hear the layoff won't affect them because they're separate from us. I heard it's supposed to go down real soon." said DaFrenchy who spoke on the other end of the phone.

"Lay off? I'm not worried about this layoff rumor. God's going to protect me," said Chris.

On the other end of the line, DaFrenchy rolled his eyes and laughed before saying good-bye. To him, the name of God was number one above Santa Claus on the list of made-up characters.

CHAPTER 14

No Weapons Formed Shall Prosper?

Cold beer or whiskey all day long on Saturday was what Chris really wanted after the way his week went at the office, but instead, he kept his appointment with Pastor Sanders and continued on with his goal to stop drinking and learning more about God for his kids' sake.

Pastor Sanders and Chris arrived at the same time at the lake that morning. They gathered their fishing supplies and loaded them onto a green wagon with tubeless rubber tires and wooden side rails that Pastor Sanders had brought with him. After Chris helped him unload his wagon from his truck, Pastor Sanders snapped his fingers and opened the passenger side door as he remembered that he had something for Chris.

"Before I forget, let me give you these books, essays, and other reading material I borrowed from your dad," said Pastor Sanders. Chris opened the rear drivers side door of his truck, took them from Pastor Sanders and sat them on the floor. Pastor Sanders got his homemade walking stick off the back of his white 2009 Dodge Ram 1500 Big Horn truck and they headed down a wooded trail that led to the lake with Chris pulling the wagon in front of Pastor Sanders. After setting everything up, they took their portable folding chairs out of the wagon, unfolded them, and sat down.

"Did you get a chance to study the passages I told you about?" Pastor Sanders asked while casting his fishing lure into the lake.

"Yeah, I did. That reading opened my eyes to a lot of things that I've misunderstood for years," Chris replied.

"The book of Galatians was written by Paul to teach confused Judaizers that the Gentiles could go to heaven without obeying the Jewish laws. You and I are non-Jews, so what does that make us?" Pastor Sanders asked.

"Gentiles," Chris replied as he put a bobber onto his fishing line.

"That's right. What applies to us is what was written for us. I highly recommend that you get a NIV Life Application Study Bible if you want to easily understand the Bible in English." Pastor Sanders held up a copy so that Chris could see what he was referring to. "The Word of God is so important that all Christians should read it as many times as possible and have as many versions on their bookshelves as they can get. Knowing who God is talking to in the Bible is critical. The vital statistics at the beginning of most books in the New Testament study Bibles will tell you the purpose, when and for whom the book was written. You won't find the words written for *the Gentiles, believers everywhere, Christians everywhere*, or any words related to Christians in the vital statistics of any Old Testament book. They focused on God's people, the Jews. The only books written to help us Gentiles make it to heaven are in the New Testament starting in Acts."

"Were any new laws given to us?" asked Chris before finally casting his lure into the water.

"God gave six hundred and thirteen laws to the Old Testament believers to make it to heaven, so you can only imagine how many He gave to the New Testament believers."

"Bad as we are today; with all the new technology and way more opportunities to sin than the people in the Old Testament had, I can't imagine how many thousands of new laws were written for us," said Chris.

While Chris was talking, Pastor Sanders laid his pole beside him and positioned his tackle bag under the center of his of pole. He then grabbed a pen and a spiral notepad from his backpack, along with a small pocket Bible. "Let me write them all down for you," he said.

"You don't have to go through all that trouble right now, Pastor; we're fishing. It'll take all day to write all the laws for us to obey. Whenever you have some time, just fax or e-mail them to me."

"Oh, I'm done," said Pastor Sanders. He tore out the page from his notepad and handed it to Chris. Six hundred and twenty-three commandments all summed up in one command. "Let me know what you think about our awesome God when you're done examining all the new laws."

"God is good is what I think," Chris said with a smile. He read the note out loud. "'Galatians 5:14. The entire law is summed up in a single commandment: love your neighbor as yourself.' That's definitely not happening today. It must have gotten misunderstood and misinterpreted like the verse that I misunderstood about all sins, past, present and future."

"In John 13:34, Jesus asked us to love one another even more than He commanded us to love our neighbors and ourselves in Galatians 5:14. He asked us to love one another the way he loves us. Every one of us has failed at keeping the one commandment He gave us all to obey. He asked us to love each other unconditionally the way He loves us."

"Since there's a curse on obeying the law, what happens to those of us who try to obey the law today? Excuse me, I meant to say 'obey the old law today'?"

"Well, they're safe," Pastor Sanders said with a grin. "You see, a Gentile who was never under the law could never receive the benefits of obeying the law. So if a Gentile today obeys the law that was never written for him, he's just wasting time doing someone else's job. He'll never reap any benefits promised to Jews or make it to heaven for obeying the old laws. Tithing was a law that was never in us Gentiles job description."

Pastor Sanders opened his Bible to Galatians 3:10 and gave it to Chris, who was sitting on his left. Chris propped his pole up against his tackle bag and held the bible in both of his hands. "Verse ten says, '*All* who rely on observing the law are under a curse. For it is written: "Cursed is *everyone* who does not continue to do everything written in the Book of the Law."' I know you know what 'all' means. That small word *all* caused you to hate God for many years, didn't it?"

Chris nodded his head in agreement.

"'All' is different in this passage," continued Pastor Sanders. "It takes time and studying to discern when 'all' means everyone and when 'all' means every member of a certain group, you see. In Galatians 3:14, Paul was talking to the Galatians who were trying to put themselves under the Jewish law. Even if there were thousands of Gentiles there to hear Paul speak, they would've known that the curse didn't apply to them because they knew they weren't included in the 'all' that the verse was talking about. The context of the passages will help you to discern the meaning of what is being said."

Chris felt confused. "That little word *all* caused me to live in the darkest days of my life," he said. "I couldn't see myself in heaven because

I was angry with God. I couldn't see myself in hell because I'm not stupid enough to want to go there. I know there's no in between, but I sure wanted one to be. And I was sure that God didn't love me. Now, I want God's love more than all the treasures in heaven and earth. I'm tired of living in darkness. But it seems to me that you're contradicting the Bible just to tell me what I want to hear and make me feel good about my father's fate. Now you're saying that *all* doesn't mean 'all.'"

"You've just learned a valuable lesson. If something sounds like a contradiction, pray to God and ask for understanding. If you keep reading, God will always reveal the answer to you. In regards to salvation, we all were included. Verse fourteen declares that Jesus included the Gentiles in the blessing of Abraham through faith in his name. Jesus' death was for all people who believe in Him. No contradiction there; your father was and still is included forever in the promise of salvation."

"Oh," Chris said with a sigh of relief.

"You know, it's a great insult to God even for us Gentiles who accept his gift of salvation to turn right back around and do the same things that He said He had set us free from. 'Thank you but no thank you for your son, Jesus' is what we tell God when we try to put ourselves back under the laws that Jesus died to free us from." Pastor Sanders looked in his backpack again and pulled out a typewritten copy of the laws, with notes typed beside each of them, and handed them to Chris.

Chris returned the Bible to him as he took the copy of the laws and Pastor Sanders placed the bible back into his backpack. There were about ten pages front and back stapled together.

"Your dad gave these to me. He and I were very good friends. I owe it to him, because he was such a loving friend to me, to teach you what he taught me about the Bible. You have no idea how your father helped me. I was lost like a million-dollar ring at the bottom of the ocean floor. He believed that knowing these laws was one of the most important steps in understanding and teaching others about the Bible. One of these days, I'll have to sit down and tell you how your father and I became good friends."

Chris picked up the papers and read the title out loud. "'The Six Hundred and Thirteen Commandments of the Mosaic Law.'"

"Plus ten; here you go," Pastor Sanders said as he handed another page to Chris.

" 'The Ten Commandments,'" Chris read.

"Six hundred and twenty-three reasons why Jesus died on the Cross, along with countless other reasons," said Pastor Sanders. "Would you say He's our hero?" said Pastor Sanders.

"Indeed," Chris replied.

"Read and study all of this information. The more you read and gain true knowledge of God, the closer you and God move toward each other. He's waiting to show you more, but you have to want him to. He's been trying to get your attention all these years through the storms he allowed to pop up in your life."

"I feel like He succeeded," said Chris. "I'm falling deeper and deeper in love with Him the more I learn of all these new things about Him that I never knew. I feel like He purposely put me through some storms that He knew would cause me to hate Him because He knew that, in the end, all the bad things He allowed to happen to me would only cause me to love Him more than I did before."

"He allowed you to hate Him . . . so that you could love Him more. Humph. That reminds me of how God operates and teaches us things. He works backwards. He always has a good reason behind every lesson he teaches us: to love and trust Him more. You might've just summed up one of the reasons He allows us to suffer hard times and difficulties—they cause us to seek Him and love Him more."

Somewhere on the other side of the woods, a gunshot rang out. They both flinched and ducked.

"What was that?" asked Chris.

Pastor Sanders gathered his composure. Pretending that the shot hadn't scared him, he picked up his pole and continued fishing and said calmly, "Sounded like a gunshot to me. Haven't you ever heard a gunshot before?"

"Of course, I have. I can tell you're well aware of what a gunshot sounds like, too. You flinched like I did," Chris replied.

"If you call jumping to catch you from running on top of that water being scared, then next time I'll just let you skip across that water and find out your name isn't Jesus," Pastor Sanders snickered. He managed to get a chuckle or two out of Chris despite still feeling nervous from the sound of the gunshot. About seventy yards away, he spotted the perpetrators through a small patch of woods on the other side of the lake as more shots rang out. Three teenage boys were shooting empty beer bottles after they had emptied them into their stomachs.

"Don't you know God promised us in the Bible that no weapon formed against you will prosper?" Pastor Sanders asked.

"Oh, yeah, I heard that one before lots of times," replied Chris.

"Well, do you believe it?"

"I'd have to read it first to see who that verse was talking to, I guess. It may not be a promise that we can apply to our lives today."

"Now, you're learning," Pastor Sanders replied as he propped his pole back over his tackle bag and grabbed his Bible out of his backpack again. "Here it is. Read Isaiah 54:17 and tell me if we can apply it to our lives today."

He picked up the homemade walking stick that he liked to carry with him for protection.

Chris handed the Bible back to Pastor Sanders and then reeled in his fishing line to recast it into a different spot.

"Well, do you believe it?" asked Pastor Sanders.

"Yeah, I believe it. It said it right there in the Bible. Isaiah 54:17. No weapons formed against you shall prevail. I'm going to try to memorize that one." responded Chris.

"Wow! That's a powerful verse, definitely being a promise coming straight from God." Pastor Sanders paused. "We should've brought some worms with us. Hey, Chris, look under that rock over there and see if you can find any worms. Maybe I'm old school, but I think nothing really works like using worms."

Chris walked over to the cantaloupe-sized rocks and began to look under them for worms. "You know, I wish that verse had applied to me when I was a kid."

Still holding his stick, Pastor Sanders looked at it and then said, "Maybe that weapon called a whipping stick wouldn't have prospered against me when my father used it on me as if I were his disobedient dog that bit the hand that fed him. When my dad used to whip me, I was hoping God would do for me what he did for Shadrach, Meshach, and Abednego when they got thrown into the furnace."

They looked at each other and said at the same time, "Put out the burning fire." They both laughed as they thought back on the days when they had both received what felt like lightning strikes from their fathers when they failed to spare their rods.

When they had stopped laughing, Pastor Sanders asked, "So now you've been introduced to a new promise from Isaiah's Book of Life?"

"I didn't say it was in the Book of Life. You turned to it in the Bible, don't you remember? We may need to get you under a shade tree or something; you're getting too much heat."

"Wouldn't it be safe to say that the book of Isaiah is a book in the Bible of Isaiah's life experience as a messenger for God?"

"I guess you could say that," said Chris. "It's not Isaiah's whole life story, but it does tell of some chapters in Isaiah's life, so to speak."

Pastor Sanders's veins began to swell up on the back of his hand as he gripped his homemade stick tightly. He had made the strong stick from a quarter-inch-thick metal rod and a one-inch-thick piece of solid oak approximately four feet long. He didn't want it to break if he ever had to use it on a wild animal or someone who gave him a little trouble while he fished. Slowly, he lifted the stick tiptoed behind Chris, who was bent over with his back turned to him searching for worms under the rocks.

"If you've never studied that verse, how do you know that it was a promise that... *God!*" Chris let out a very loud, delayed yell of God's name almost as loud as the gunshots that rang out from across the lake after he felt a sharp, hot, burning pain strike his rear end like lightning. He could have set a new world record for the vertical standing high jump that day. When his feet returned to the ground, he continued to yell God's name several times while he hopped around like a kangaroo with his hands glued to his butt.

"I missed," said Pastor Sanders.

"You hit me!" said Chris, shocked and angry. "You don't know me like that. What did you hit me for?"

"That horse fly was about to attack you with its vicious bite. Turn around and let me get him."

Chris took his hands off his butt and turned around to try to hit the horse fly himself and avoid another lightning strike from Pastor Sanders. "I don't see any horse flies around here," Chris said with pain in his voice.

Pastor Sanders swung again, hitting Chris on the first swing and missing him on the second. "Be still and let my weapon prosper against this horse fly," he said.

Chris hopped around, tripping over his own feet and landing on his butt. He squirmed around close to the edge of the lake, getting his feet and the seat of his pants wet.

"Let him bite me! Let him bite me! His bite can't be any worse than you hitting me with that stick."

"I'm sorry; I didn't mean to hurt you. Those swings were meant for the horse fly. I guess that verse applies to the horse fly, too. My weapon didn't harm him at all. As a matter of fact, there is no horse fly. I formed this weapon against you to see if it would prosper." He paused. "Can you tell me why my weapon prospered against you?"

"I don't know," replied Chris as he sat on his hands trying to get some relief.

"The Bible says, "No weapon that is formed against you shall prosper." Maybe my weapon prospered because you didn't have enough faith that it wouldn't prosper. Get up and have a little faith, and let's see if God will prevent this weapon from prospering against you. Let me help you up so we can test God again."

Chris looked and felt confused. He didn't know if he wanted to risk getting hit again with the lightning rod or prove that he had faith in God, and he was still shocked that an old man he didn't know very well had hit him with a stick for no reason. "You're not my enemy," he said. "Maybe that's why it prospered."

"Yeah, but a weapon doesn't know who's the enemy and who's not. It says, 'No weapon formed against you,' right?" Pastor Sanders extended his hand. "Let me help you up and try to explain this." Chris accepted the offer, and he and Pastor Sanders sat down in their chairs.

Pastor Sanders laughed. "You know, your father did this exact same thing to me in this very spot."

"He did?" Chris always perked up when someone reminisced about his father.

"Yeah. He had a strange way of teaching the Bible. Everything that you've learned from me I learned from your father. If you learn how to determine who God is talking to in the Bible, you'll get a better understanding of God's Word. The reason any weapon can prosper against you today is that God was talking to his servants in that verse."

"Aren't we His servants?" Chris asked.

"In the context of the Book of Isaiah, God's servants are His chosen people, Israel. Every weapon formed against them and us will prosper today. This doesn't mean that we found a lie that God told. You have to pay attention to the particular time period that the Scriptures are referring to as well as who God is talking to. When the appointed time comes for our Lord and Savior to return to the earth and rule it for a thousand years, His chosen people will build the Temple for him to return to. While this Temple is being built in his chosen people's holy land, no laws, artillery, or any other kind of weapon will prosper against his people because He's coming back and no one or anything will be able to stop Him or His servants from carrying out what has already been written by God. They will live in their land and be His people. Then and only then will weapons formed against them fail to prosper. Machine guns used on them will be as harmless as water guns. Nothing will be able to stop them from receiving what God has promised them. When Jesus gets ready to come all the way to the earth for his second return, this verse will be fulfilled. And it'll be after He raptures us believers up."

Chris picked up his pole and bobbed his bobber to attract any fish that may have been swimming by.

"That makes a lot of sense. Christians, God's people, His servants; they all die every day from sickness, weapons of many kinds, and everything else that falls under what that verse said God would protect us from. I mean protect His servants from. We can't say He lied or forgot to include us in that verse because he didn't make that promise to us."

Suddenly, a loud, wind-slicing whir startled Pastor Sanders and scared all the fish in the lake as Chris snatched his pole back to set the hook on a fish that had taken a good bite on his bait.

"My goodness!" said Pastor Sanders. "You're trying to snatch his bones out of his flesh. The meat is what you want to keep, not the bones. Fishing is like basketball; it's in the wrist."

"That was a big one; I felt it. I didn't want him to get away," Chris replied.

"Looks like it got away, anyway. As you study the Bible, don't be so quick to set the hook on what appears to be a good bite or promise. Take your time and make sure it's a good bite before setting your hook of understanding into it. Don't try to snatch everything out of the Bible so quickly." Pastor Sanders laughed and Chris joined in with him.

"I did snatch at that bite kind of hard, huh?" said Chris.

Pastor Sanders reeled his line in and they both cast their lines back into the water and continued fishing and discussing the Bible.

"So my Dad taught you all this stuff?" Chris asked.

"Life-changing, isn't it? It gave me a whole new respect for God." Pastor Sanders looked at his watch. "Doesn't look like they want to bite today. I apologize for hitting you with the stick. It may have hurt you for a little while, but that painful lesson is nowhere near as painful as someone deceiving you about God's Word. I'd rather take a swat on the butt to learn a lesson anytime than a hot, eternal lesson."

"That's OK. I learned something," said Chris.

"He didn't bless us with a full cooler today, but if He had, what would you have done with a cooler full of fish?" asked Pastor Sanders.

"I'm kinda scared to say," answered Chris. "This might be another stick question. Let me hold your stick and I'll answer it." They both laughed. "Seriously, though, I'd probably give half of them away and keep the other half."

"Your father's would be proud of you, but don't you think you'd be putting yourself back under a curse by giving any portion of those fish away? They paid tithes with food and animal sacrifices in the Bible, you know."

"Now, you're asking me all of these heavy questions about the Bible like I've been studying it for years. Give me a month or twelve and I can find the answer."

"You already know the answer. There is a pattern, an order in understanding the Bible. Once your eyes have been opened from studying it faithfully, you'll see what I mean. The answer is the new way we tithe, so to speak. You didn't say you'd trade half the fish or sell them. You said you'd give a portion of them away. When you give something away, you don't expect anything in return. We've learned from the Old Testament the same lesson that God was teaching the Hebrews. God loves a cheerful giver. He just may open the floodgates of heaven and pour you out a blessing that you won't have room enough to receive."

Chris paused as he stored all the new information into his own way of understanding things. "So the Old Testament is like a transmission and the New Testament is like a motor. Neither one can do its job without the other in transporting the car body, which represents the body of believers, to their destination, which is heaven."

"Yes. That's a good analogy. You could make a good teacher of God's Word," said Pastor Sanders as they packed up and prepared to leave.

CHAPTER 15

Bad News for Reverend Edgars

After talking with Angel about everything he learned from Pastor Sanders on their fishing trip, Angel was convinced and agreed with Chris to move their membership to Pastor Sander's church. After putting the kids to bed, Chris went into his office where he read for hours some of his dad's essays and dissertation before falling asleep in his chair. Early Sunday morning before church; Chris typed up an informational document that summed up everything he had read the night before regarding tithing with the intentions of giving it to Reverend Apostle Prophet Edgars. The next evening after church, Chris barged into Reverend Apostle Prophet Joe Edgar's office and gave him the bad news. He placed his document on Reverend Apostle Prophet Edgar's desk and sat down.

"What's this?" asked Reverend Apostle Prophet Edgars.

"A summarization of something I've been reading on why we shouldn't tithe and why we should give what we want from our hearts," Chris replied.

"What!"

"My wife and I talked it over last night, and we think it's best for our family to move our membership over to Pastor Sanders's church," said Chris.

"I heard about that church. They don't believe in tithing over there. How do you think you your going to be blessed on a higher level than you are now if you go over there? I can't believe you'll choose to go to some White church and let them steal you away from here. You gonna listen to

106

a school-taught preacher over one who's been called by God? Preaching is just a job to preachers who get a degree to preach."

"First of all, my Black dad taught Pastor Sanders everything he knows about the Bible. He only went to school to gain more knowledge, which isn't a bad idea for all pastors to do. People of all races who love God attend that church, so it's not a White church. God's not going to make a Black heaven and a White heaven. If he did, then he'd have to split me in half. My mother is White and my father was Black. I've learned more in just two visits at that church than I have in the going on a year that I've been attending church here. I'm tired of being taught wrong. I've been in the dark about God's amazing love way too long because of improper teachings."

Reverend Apostle Prophet Joe Edgars sat as still as a rock for a few seconds, staring angrily at Chris. In the twinkling of an eye, he slammed his fist down on his desk and yelled at Chris.

"Get out of my office with that blasphemy!"

Startled by the sudden outburst from the good Reverend, Chris jumped up quickly, tripped on his chair, and almost fell over backwards but caught his balance.

"Get out before we have a physical discussion up in here, you hear me! You goin't' criticize my preaching in my face!" Reverend Apostle Prophet Edgars stood up, picked up his Bible from his desk, slammed it in his chair, and turned his desk over in a holy rage. He grabbed his Bible and lifted his left foot to climb over the overturned desk. "I'm a' beat you upside the head with this Bible and knock that evil spirit back where the hell it came from."

Chris walked fast toward the door.

Pastor Edgars laid his Bible back in the chair, picked up a stapler off the floor, and threw it at Chris, hitting him on his right thigh as he turned to the side to dodge it.

Chris picked the stapler up and drew back to throw it back at Reverend Edgars, but Reverend Edgars bounced from side to side, making it almost impossible for Chris to aim and hit him.

"Be still, man of God. Don't you believe that no weapon formed against you will prosper? Practice what you preach. Be still and test God," said Chris as he tried to zero in on Reverend Edgars, who moved from side to side like a kid playing dodge ball at recess. Chris tossed the stapler onto the floor. "This makes absolutely no sense to fight over interpretations of the Bible," he said, tossing up one arm at a time as he explained himself.

"If you believe I'm wrong, then you should be satisfied that I'm going to hell and not you. I'm only trying to help. What good is fighting about it going to do? It's not going to make your version true. All I've ever heard you preach about is being blessed and prospering. I've been leaving here thinking that every time something doesn't go right for me it's been my fault because I'm doing something wrong or not living right. It's not fair to use God to mislead people like you're doing here at this church!" At that moment, Deacon Terry Wright and Deacon Banks came into the office to see what the commotion was all about.

"I honestly didn't think this would offend you," Chris continued, "but I guess your pride is blinding you from seeing the truth because you've been teaching it differently for so long."

"What's uh, what's going on in here?" asked Deacon Wright.

"Get him out o' here! Let him go to that other church and follow them to hell if he wants to. You'll never be a deacon or a blessed member of this church. Take yo' money and leave. Come in here lying on God in His house. He come in here chastising, ridiculing, and persecuting against me with some stuff he learned from some store-bought preacher from some storefront church. Let him gone on!"

"Is this true, Chris?" Deacon Wright asked.

"Now, this is what happens when you church hop," interrupted Deacon Banks. "You get too many differ'nt opinions 'bout the Word. You in a good church, so what's the poir'nt in leaving? It's a scanus and a shame that you can't see you being taught right, right here at True Saints. Stay at one church so you won't get all confused from hearing so many different interpretations."

"Every church I've been to says that exact same thing. Which one's right and which one's wrong is what I want to know, don't you? I apologize for thinking you'd be interested in what could mean that you're contradicting the Bible. No preacher should want to do that." Chris paused and looked at Reverend Apostle Prophet Edgars. "You'd better check to see where I come from before you huff up to me next time." Chris picked up his report on tithing from the floor, laid it in a chair next to the door, and left.

"Don't leave that trash in my office. Take it to burn with you!" Reverend Apostle Prophet Edgars yelled after him.

"One man's trash is another man's treasure," said Chris in the hallway as he continued on his way.

"He gon' mess around and make me—I feel like going out there and bouncing my fist off of his lips and head, but I'm a' let God handle it this time, but next time—I'm a' help," said Reverend Apostle Prophet Edgars to the Deacons.

CHAPTER 16

DaFrenchy's Salvation

The next day at work, Chris couldn't stop thinking about how he had been deceived for years by the many different interpretations of the Bible. He knew that his coworker DaFrenchy was a nonbeliever and thought it would make DaFrenchy happy to know that whatever had kept him from believing in God could possibly be a misinterpretation of God's truth.

"DaFrenchy?"

"'S up?" DaFrenchy answered.

"I know we're not supposed to talk religion here at work, but this I have to say is more important to me than anything. It's even worth me losing my job over. I know God will provide for me. You won't report me for talking religion, will you?" Chris asked.

"Free country," DaFrenchy replied. "Freedom of speech and religion. Go ahead."

"I went online and read up on that new religion I heard you talking about to someone on the phone a couple of weeks ago. Y'all might want to consider a few things that they don't believe in. I mean, what do they offer that's better than what God offers? I'm just curious to know, because I recently learned that the bible is true and it's us that are confused."

"This book we're being taught from is based on facts about life that we can see and do every day," DaFrenchy explained. "Not the same old boring do's and don'ts of an invisible philosopher called God. All those so-called facts in your Bible are coincidences and myths, and all those so-called prophecies have happened a million times. Wars and rumors of war, earthquakes; Come on, Chris; think about it. Those predictions ain't nothing but global warming and politics. *I* could've predicted those signs. There's always going to be wars, earthquakes, and storms. How long is too long to continue believing in that book?"

"You don't have to change religions just because you don't understand the bible. Christianity has everything we need. It's part of God's perfect plan. And it's not a religion; it's a personal relationship with God." DaFrenchy shook his head and rolled his eyes.

"Have you ever prayed and asked God for understanding of his Word?" Chris asked.

"Don't you think I'd need to understand Him before I asked Him to help me understand His Word?"

A thought inside Chris's head was so loud that he looked up at the ceiling and turned toward the door to pinpoint where the voice had come from.

"What's wrong with you, man?" DaFrenchy asked.

"You didn't hear that?"

DaFrenchy shook his head.

"Someone said, 'This is why I need you.' it sounded like he was sitting right here next to us."

"I can tell you how to beat the drug test, but you'll still need to work on quitting," said DaFrenchy, grinning.

Chris remarked DaFrenchy's implication. "Anyway, back to what I was saying, when you understand His Word, you understand Him. At least, that's the feeling I'm starting to get. Don't miss out on a gift from God because of someone else's misinterpretation of the Bible. Accept Jesus and be free. Do me a favor when you go on the test flight today. Look deeper into all the beautiful scenery. Don't take the beautiful things we see for granted this time. Study everything you see and ask yourself who made these things. Look at how the light holds back the darkness of space." Chris opened his desk drawer, pulled out his pocket Bible, and gave it to DaFrenchy. "Read the beginning of Genesis and look out the window when y'all reach the edge of space. Look out of your window and remember that yo' boy said there is a God. His creation of everything from nothing says so."

DaFrenchy hesitated but took the Bible. "I guess I can do that. I'm not sure whether God exists, but I can keep an open mind. I really never thought about it until just now when you mentioned the outer layer of space, but all my life I've believed in many things that I've never seen. Humph . . . how weird." DaFrenchy put the Bible inside his flight bag.

"I've believed in outer space for years, but I've never really seen any signs with my own eyes that it exists until I got this job and was able to fly high enough to see the outer layer of it for myself. I'll read this when we get close to the darkness of space and remember that my boy said there's a God." He paused. "What made you decide to get so holy all of a sudden?" he asked.

"I've been reading and learning a lot about the Bible lately. Every day, to be exact. When you learn how to read it, you'll realize that it's not a lie and there are no contradictions in it. Some kind of change that I can't explain has come over me. It's like I need to hear more and more of the truth daily so I can breathe. The Bible really is our daily bread. I'm beginning to know what that means now. It's a love story that can be read over and over. The more you read it, the sweeter the story gets. We just so happen to be the characters that the love story is about. I probably won't be here when you leave for your flight; I'm fixing to go to lunch. When you get back on the ground, tell me what you think about God's creation." Chris stood up and stretched. "Y'all have a good flight, man. I'll be praying for y'all."

"All right, man. I'm a' think about it for real. I'm a' read it." DaFrenchy paused and scratched his head. "You know what makes my head itch?"

"What?"

"On a clear day, we can fly to the top of earth's atmosphere and look into the darkness of space," said DaFrenchy. "Flying at the top of daylight, we can literally see it push back the darkness of space. But when we look up there from the ground, we can look up through the blue sky and see the moon that sits in the darkness of space, but we can't see the darkness. Why is that?"

"I don't know. I still can't figure out how astronauts in the space can see sixteen sunsets in one day. The moon doesn't disappear and reappear more than once a day in our eyes. Neither does the sun when you're standing on earth. On top of that, the stars sit in total darkness and we can see them with our naked eyes sometimes in the daytime, but we can't see the darkness that surrounds them. How can stars so far away be visible but not the darkness? All I can say is that He's a God of awesome wonders." Chris stood up and left the office.

When Chris was gone, DaFrenchy put his lunch, along with the CDs, DVDs, IPod, laptop, and binoculars he had collected for the six-hour test flight into his flight bag. His responsibility as the sales associate aboard the plane was to pretend to be its owner during the test flight to assure quality and alleviate as many problems as possible before the real customer took possession of the airplane.

The flight line crew was on their way to taxi the aircraft out of the hangar and out to the runway to fuel up and perform preflight engine test. Just before takeoff, DaFrenchy and the rest of the test flight crew called their wives as they always did. They all knew that every test flight was extremely dangerous and every flight could be their last. DaFrenchy didn't get an answer from his wife's cell phone, so he left her a message telling her that he loved her.

Very thorough preflight test and checks gave the test pilots great confidence that the plane would fly without any complications. The engine runs was the last preflight check before the plane hurtled into the lower level of the heavens. For about twenty minutes, the three powerful jet engines made a sharp, whistling sound so loud that it would pierce the eardrums of those around it even with their fingers plugged in them. The ground crew signaled to the pilots that they were ready for takeoff. Wing walkers stood on the end of each wing to assure that no planes or other obstacles were in the jet's path as it taxied to the runway. Once the wing walkers gave the clearance signal, the flight crew headed off to the runway for takeoff.

Flying with certain pilots was no different from riding with them in their cars. Pilots who drove their cars fast liked to take off as fast as they could down the runway. Pilots who drove recklessly liked to take off as straight in the air as possible. Some pilots liked to hit every cloud in the sky while others liked to dodge as many clouds as they could. Even their landings were all different, but whether the pilot hit the air brakes as soon as the front wheels touched the runway or applied the brakes three quarters of the way down the runway, a safe landing was a safe landing.

Aircraft sales were at a record high. With so many planes needing test flights performed, Raven Jet had to rent a few extra pilots to meet aircraft completion dates. All the regular pilots were busy flying other planes, which gave DaFrenchy and the others on board a chance to take note, observe, and poke fun at the flying style of the new rental pilots. Gerald, who was better known as the Bullet, was a Black pilot in his mid fifties who was piloting the plane in front of them. He guided it onto the runway and stopped for about thirty seconds before applying a small burst of power for takeoff. Gerald's takeoffs always seemed to be below the minimum speed required to fly. Every crewmember who flew with Gerald gripped his seat and yelled at him to give the plane more power. As soon as Gerald took off, he'd turn left or right after rising only one hundred feet off the ground, which caused his nervous crew to think they were falling out of the sky. Flying with Gerald took guts.

As Gerald took off, Dustin, the rental pilot who was flying DaFrenchy and his crew, grabbed the copilot's arm and yelled, "Oh, my God! More power, more power!"

Randy, the copilot, had watched Gerald fly before both from the ground and from the cockpit. Knowing that Gerald had the airplane under control, he said calmly, "Old Bullet. That's just how he flies. Nice and slow. My grandmother can drive to Texas faster than he can fly there. They'll reach the clouds sooner or later."

"What kind of nickname is 'Bullet' for a slow-flying pilot?" asked Dustin as he released Randy's arm. "What does he think they call it flying for?"

They watched and waited for Gerard to fly a safe distance away before they took off. "Looks like it's our turn," Dustin said to Randy. The sat parked forty feet off the top side of the runway. Before Dustin could line up the nose of the plane and aim it straight down the runway, he gave the engines a dose of nitrogen, whipping the plane along the runway as if ten cops were in hot pursuit of the plane with a bank robbery suspect on board. In six to eight seconds, Dustin sent the jet jumping into the air as close to a ninety-degree angle as he could.

"If we weren't ready, that's just too bad. Dang!" said Mike, a member of the flight crew who was on board to train Jim and test, program, and fix any avionic problems that might fail to work during flight.

"He probably runs all the stop signs and whips out in traffic the same way when he drives a car," DaFrenchy said. "I can tell this is going to be a long flight."

In the cockpit, Randy stared Dustin down with a look that showed Dustin that he was not impressed. "I didn't know we were shooting for a movie. Should I radio them on the ground and see if we need to re shoot the stealing of a fighter jet scene again?"

Dustin laughed at what he thought was a joke until he looked over at Randy and discovered that Randy wasn't laughing and his laughter slowly faded way.

Randy wasn't impressed with Dustin's takeoff, but after a brief moment of silence, it was back to business as usual.

"What test do you feel like performing first?" Dustin asked.

"Since our nerves are already stimulated and you got us going straight to outer space, we might as well climb up high enough to do the wing vibration and strength test, fighter jet cowboy," Randy suggested.

Fifteen minutes after takeoff, they had already made it out of Arkansas and were sailing over Texas skies. Ben, the flight test engineer, peeked his head into the cockpit and informed the pilots that all of his recording devices were set up and ready for all noise tests. After reaching approximately forty-five thousand feet, Dustin aimed the nose of the jet down toward the ground and made a sharp left turn, sending the plane spiraling toward the earth. The wings flapped violently and everyone on board struggled not to vomit or pass out. The G forces were so strong that the crew felt as if their heads would explode or be pulled off their neck bones. Zero gravity caused all the lightweight items inside the aircraft to float around. DaFrenchy closed his eyes tightly and struggled to keep his mouth closed. When the plane hit an air pocket, DaFrenchy's mouth flew open, snatching the gum he was chewing out of his mouth and sending it floating across the fuselage like a rock in space. With the jet still speeding toward the earth faster than the speed of sound, Dustin leveled the nose of the plane and went right into the airbrake test, causing the plane to shake and vibrate violently. After a successful testing of the airbrakes, they cruised smoothly in the sky giving the rest of the crew time to perform a few of their minor test. Jim put in his Third Day CD and played their version of the song God of Wonders and walked through out the plane checking the quality of the surround sound system and volume level of each speaker.

"How about engine stalls next?" Dustin asked Randy.

"Sounds good," said Randy. "Let's take her back up. I'm going to use the restroom real quick. I'll be right back."

"Look in the storage area of the vanity; I put some air freshener in there. You know there's no ventilation up here, so take it easy on us, bud."

"That's not what I have to do," said Randy whose face was glowing red with embarrassment.

"Loosen up, bubba; I'm just kidding with you," said Dustin.

Randy walked past DaFrenchy and Mike, who were laid back watching a movie with headphones on testing the headphone jacks of each seat. DaFrenchy took one side of his headphones off as Randy got close to him.

"What test are we doing next, Randy?" DaFrenchy asked.

"Engine stalls." Randy looked at Jim who was standing in the middle of the aircraft. He knew that he was a first timer who had no idea how dangerous the engine stall test were and patted him on his right shoulder when he approached him. It was tradition to break in a rookie by taking turns seeing who could scare him the most.

"Say your prayers for the next test," Randy told Jim. "Say them until you sweat." Randy snickered and grinned before he continued on his way to the restroom, knowing that the game of making Jim nervous had begun.

As soon as Randy closed the lavatory door, Jim walked over towards Mike and DaFrenchy and asked, "What do we do during the engine stall test?"

Mike and DaFrenchy looked at each other for a few seconds and then looked at Jim. They both said at the same time, "You mean you don't know?"

"Naw, I don't know. What should I know? Tell me!" Jim sat down and gave his full attention to them while they explained.

"Oh, it's nothing to worry about, really," Mike said." That's why we signed that waiver before we got on the plane, remember?"

"I thought that was so we could get paid for flight time," Jim said.

"Oh, no, that was more than a just a time sheet," DaFrenchy said. "That was to get life insurance money for your family in case the engine stall test fails."

"What! Fails! What can happen during the engine stall test?" Jim asked.

"Let me give you a little comforting news," Mike said. "The wing vibration test was the worst test we'll do today. If the wings had broken off, we'd have crashed for sure. But with the engine stall test, when they cut the engines off and we start plummeting toward the ground, we'll know we have some kind of chance to survive if they get the engines back running before we . . . ." Mike moved his face in front of Jim's, stopping half an inch away before saying loudly, "Boom!"

Jim flinched. "Ahhh!" he screamed, looking like a little kid getting ready to cry.

Randy had finished using the restroom and headed back to the cockpit. "Hope you're all prayed up, Jim. It looks like we're almost there," he said as he passed them on his way back to the cockpit.

"I'm going to say my prayers and read my Bible before we make it to the top of the blue sky," DaFrenchy said. "This is why we bring our Bibles on these types of test flights. I'm surprised nobody told you about this risk Jim?"

Jim sat still and shook his head no.

"All we can do for this test is remain very quiet and pray," DaFrenchy said.

"We don't even believe in God, but we pray during this test just in case," Said Mike.

"When you hear the engines come back on, that means that we passed."

"They're going to cut the engines off? Are you serious?" said Jim.

"Yeah, man. We're adrenaline junkies. This is the most exciting part of the flight. Lean over toward the window and look up. Notice anything?"

"It's completely dark. We're not going up there, are we?"

"If we do, we'll never come out. That's the outer edge of space. If we get too close, this plane will ball up like a soda can, and boom!"

"Ahhh!" Jim flinched and yelled again. DaFrenchy continued.

"No more you and no more me."

Jim fell back into his seat and took a deep breath.

"What's the matter?" Mike asked. "Don't you believe in God?"

"Yeah, but I've always wanted to die in my sleep. I don't want to know when I'm going to die."

"He'll come get you if you believe. That's what I hear, anyway. Me and DaFrenchy are what church folks call nonbelievers and proud of it. Ain't that right, Frenchy? Isn't that right, Frenchy?"

DaFrenchy was so involved in reading Genesis chapter one that he had completely blocked out what Mike was saying.

Mike spoke a bit louder, but he didn't get a response until he touched DaFrenchy on his shoulder. "DaFrenchy!"

"Yeah, Mike."

"I said,' isn't that right?'"

"Right, right," DaFrenchy said absently, not knowing what he was agreeing to.

"Have you ever noticed that the sky is blue, but when we fly into the blue sky, we never fly into anything blue? It's just as clear up here as it is on the ground."

"What are you doing reading that Bible?" Mike asked. "You're scaring me, French. I thought we saw eye to eye on that subject."

"You know, I've never really read the Bible because I couldn't understand any part of it that I read. Take for instance here in the beginning where

God says, 'Let there be light,' and He separates the light from the darkness and calls the darkness 'night' and the light 'day.' I can see that happening because up here we can see the light being separated from the darkness of space. But then it goes on with some outrageous incomplete story about how He separates water from water and puts the sky in between. Tell me, where did all that water go? You see what I mean. There's just too many things in here that don't make sense. It's negative seventy degree up here. Why in the world aren't we seeing blocks of ice up here if there's water above the sky? We're almost in outer space right now."

"That's easy," Jim said. "I asked my Sunday school teacher that question when I was ten. She asked the pastor, and the pastor said that when you keep on reading, Genesis tells what happened to that large amount of water that was up there since the beginning of time. It all came raining down for forty days and forty nights when the earth was flooded in the days of Noah."

"Oh!" DaFrenchy said in amazement as he started to wonder how many other things that he had wondered about in the Bible had simple explanations.

Before DaFrenchy could say anything more, Ben, the flight test engineer, walked out of the galley, area of the aircraft and sat down in the seat across the isle next to Jim and put on his seatbelt. "Might want to buckle up just in case if we have to glide this thing to the ground," he said. "We're getting ready to stall the engines."

—

Sixty thousand feet below and one state away from Texas, Chris sat alone in the office catching up on paperwork when DaFrenchy's office phone rang. Chris and DaFrenchy always answered each other's phone when one or the other was out flying.

"Chris speaking. How may I help you?"

"Hey, Chris. This is Renita," said DaFrenchy's wife. "I was returning my husband's call, but since you've answered his phone, I know he must be flying. What time are they expected back?"

"Probably around five something. They left around eleven, and it's a six-hour flight. I can call him in the plane and tell him to call you if you'd like."

"That's OK. I can wait two more hours."

"He normally calls to test the phones before they come down, so I'll tell him to give you a call."

"OK. I'll talk to you later, Chris."

—

Back in the air at sixty five thousand feet, Dustin had killed the power to the engines. Everyone sat quietly as the plane coasted for several miles before it's nose started to rise slowly toward the darkness of space.

Jim covered one ear with his hand and cupped the other hand around his other ear to try and hear the sound of the engines. With a pale face, he sat back in his seat and remained stiffer than red clay mud baked on work boots by the sun.

"The engines are off," he said. "They—are—really—off. Oh, my God!"

The slower the plane coasted, the farther up the nose pointed toward the empty darkness of space that hovered above the light of the world. Suddenly, Jim's organs began to function normally as he heard the low buzz of the engines as they were automatically turned back on by switches on the wings. "Whew!" he breathed. "Thank you. Oh, thank you. I need to use the bathroom. Can I get up and go now?"

"We're done, but you may want to wait a few minutes before you use the restroom. We're about to take a quick dive down to forty-five thousand feet. It'd probably be hard to use the restroom while you're floating like an astronaut."

"I think I'll wait," said Jim.

Suddenly, they heard a loud noise that sounded like a car crashing into a light pole. "What was that?" exclaimed DaFrenchy, Mike, and Jim all at the same time.

"Oh, God!" Randy yelled.

"What happened?" Ben yelled in a panic.

"I pulled the wrong handle. I pulled the flap slats handle. I think they're jammed out of place."

At sixty thousand feet, the hard tug had created small holes on both sides of the wings where they connected to the fuselage. Mike and DaFrenchy went to the sides of the plane, looking out the window to see if they could see any structural damage on the wings.

"Try pulling it again; maybe they'll automatically go back in place like they're designed to," Dustin said frantically.

They could all hear a loud screech coming from the wings. Mike, DaFrenchy, Jim, and Ben all looked at each other with their eyes so wide open that it looked as if their irises had shrunk to the size of their pupils leaving most of their eyeballs white. Dustin's idea of pulling the handle again to make the flap slats on the wings reengage had only worsened the already bad situation.

"I think we'd better buckle up; both wings are crimped and the fuselage is wrinkled," said DaFrenchy. He and Mike sat down across the aisle from each other and put on their seat belts.

High winds and the flap slats that the pilots had tried to get back in place were causing a heavy drag on the plane. The high winds moaned like ghosts as the plane moved steadily upward toward outer space, the wings stuck at an angle that made descent ion impossible. Everyone sat still and took deep, hard breaths. But something more than fear was making it hard to get enough oxygen.

"I can't breathe," said DaFrenchy.

"Me, neither," said Mike.

As if the airplane had heard and understood what they were saying, the oxygen masks dropped from the valance panels, and the plane started bouncing and shaking violently. Jim fainted and sat slumped over in his seat.

"Were losing cabin pressure," Ben said, sounding frantic. "Hurry and put your masks on."

Struggling to put on his mask, DaFrenchy feared the worst. His conversation with Chris about God started playing in his mind. He remembered what Chris had said about not taking a chance with his salvation. The logical explanation of where all the water had gone after God created the earth was enough evidence for DaFrenchy that Chris could've been right about the Bible and God.

Maybe it's all just a huge misunderstanding and God really is good to those who believe in him, he thought. *Maybe I've misunderstood the Bible my whole life.* Images of Chris telling him to remember that there is a God kept replaying in his head. Then, words from countless people who had tried to witness to DaFrenchy throughout the years about God took over his thoughts. "Believe that Jesus died for our sins"; "Creation, is His prove that He exist"; "Avoiding hell is only one prayer away"; "It's easy to get to heaven"; "All you've got to do is believe, believe, believe." The word *believe* seemed to echo forever in DaFrenchy's mind, and he started to pray what he thought could possibly be his last prayer.

"I believe you died for my sins, Jesus," DaFrenchy said as loudly as he could with the oxygen mask attached to his mouth. He started feeling cold. He took off his oxygen mask and leaned over to Mike and with what strength he had left, he pleaded with Mike to accept Jesus just in case if they didn't survive. "Say you believe in Jesus. Mike, please. Say you believe."

Tears started flowing down DaFrenchy's face. Mike had already passed out, along with the rest of the crew. DaFrenchy realized that God had spared his life just long enough for him to accept Jesus. He put his oxygen mask back on and lay back in the seat. He could see the light fog of his breath through the clear oxygen mask as he struggled to breathe.

"I believe, I believe." DaFrenchy repeated over and over until the cold high altitude temperatures froze up the fuel and water lines, completely paralyzing everything else on the plane, leaving it a piece of floating metal caught in the earth's orbit. Unable to move any part of his body except his eyes, DaFrenchy sat alone in the plane freezing to death, taking what he knew were his last breaths of life.

DaFrenchy looked up into the darkness of space and saw a charcoal-colored object approximately half a mile in circumference. Quietly and smoothly, it floated down from space, stopping when it was level with the plane before moving into and through the right side of the plane like a ghost passing through a wall. For a brief moment, the spaceship seemed to swallow up the plane. Then the spacecraft moved upward and hovered about a hundred feet above the plane and released ultraviolet energy waves that made the top of the plane invisible.

As five bright lights, each the size of a compact car, appeared out of the darkness of space, the spacecraft hid itself by becoming invisible. One of the bright lights entered the plane and then dimmed. The other four remained outside.

Still unable to move his body and taking short breathes; DaFrenchy turned his eyes to the light as it entered through the top of the plane and stood at the aft end of the galley. Through the still-bright halo of light surrounding the humanlike figure, DaFrenchy saw what appeared to be six wings fold down on the being's back. He knew that the beings inside the bright lights had to be angels from heaven, but he wondered about the beings he thought were aliens in the spacecraft.

The Bible passage he had just read had said nothing about the creation of aliens. Since he had never studied the Bible, he had no way of knowing that Satan was the prince of the air, living in the second heaven, and his army of fallen angels were demons who were out to deceive mankind into thinking that they were aliens from other worlds somewhere in outer space.

DaFrenchy was dying. Because he had accepted Jesus and the Holy Spirit had instantly marked him as a child of God, his confusion about the Bible and aliens couldn't erase his name from the Book of Life. Because he believed in Jesus, DaFrenchy experienced the beautiful magic of death.

The angel inside the plane held out the palm of his right hand toward Mike's heart. A beam of light came from the palm of the angel's hand, seeming to X-ray Mike's chest. The angel shook his head in sorrow and let his chin drop to the base of his neck. He didn't see the mark of the Holy Spirit inside Mike's heart. Out of desperation, the angel got closer to Mike's chest and tried again to find the mark of the Holy Spirit. Bluish white light beams flowed in rotation from Mike's body to the palm of the angel's hand. The angel scanned Mike's head, neck, and even his hands trying to find the mark of the Holy Spirit. Backing away with what appeared to be tears on his face, the angel left Mike's soul for death to hold.

Before DaFrenchy could blink his eyes, he saw the angel's glow coming from the cockpit as he moved on to search for more believers in Christ on board the plane. Another light that wasn't beautiful and bright like the other lights appeared outside the aircraft. The other four lights outside the plane glowed as bright as stars. The Angel inside the aircraft went through the walls and joined the four angels outside the aircraft as they chased the imitating angel away. A cluster of what appeared to be stars appeared in the darkness of space. The stars were really thousands of angels watching and waiting for the five angels near the plane to take the souls of the believers on board the plane to heaven. They gleamed brightly as they watched the five angels chase the counterfeit angel away. A dark, shadowy figure hovered over Mike's body and then disappeared. Not half a second later, the five heavenly angels all appeared inside the plane. The angels couldn't take Mike's soul because they couldn't find the mark of the Holy Spirit inside of his heart.

The heavenly angels gathered the souls that belonged to Jesus, including DaFrenchy's, and temporarily took them away from earth until their time would come to reign with Christ on earth during His thousand year reign. They left Mike's soul for the dark angels to deliver to Death's home in Hades. As soon as the heavenly angels left, three alien like creatures appeared. At the same time, each of them put their hands inside of Mike's body and snatched his soul out of his body. A beam of light came through the top of the aircraft. It was five miles long and at the top of it was the spacecraft that disappeared and now hid itself five miles above the aircraft in the darkness of space. Mikes soul looked liked his body, but in a ghostly image. The aliens who had a tight grip on Mike's soul transformed into who they really were and the three dark angels ascended through the long five mile tunnel of light that beamed from the spacecraft with Mike's soul.

—

No one on earth ever knew that DaFrenchy had given his life to Christ just before the airplane began to crumble like a soda can being smashed. The explosion from the plane entering space pushed one of its wings back into the earth's atmosphere, leaving behind the only evidence that the recovery workers would later find of the disaster.

CHAPTER 17

Surviving the Layoff

Sixty thousand feet below and one state away, control tower operators at the Dallas, Texas, airport lost radar contact with the airplane and radio contact with the pilots. Texas tower operators contacted tower three at the Little Rock Airport where the pilots had reported departing from. One of the airport tower workers telephoned Bill, who called everyone together for a meeting to inform them of what was going on.

"We've just received news that tower control has lost contact with—" Bill's cell phone rang, cutting him off. He quickly looked at the caller ID and saw that it was someone from the control tower before answering the phone.

"Hello." He paused for what seemed like forever as all the employees who had gathered for the meeting stared at him.

"Are there any survivors?" Bill asked the person on the phone. "Are you one hundred percent sure?" Bill hung up the phone and explained to the rest of the sales department that DaFrenchy and five others who were on board with him, including the pilot and copilot, had perished in a mysterious crash. Bill offered anyone who wanted it the opportunity to take the rest of the day off.

DaFrenchy's wife was expecting him to come home late, but, instead, he was never coming home again. Because he had never made a public statement of his faith by getting baptized, his friends and loved ones didn't want to think or talk about what they thought were heartbreaking facts of his death. They never found out he gave his life to Christ—just as the aircraft entered into the outer layer of the second heaven; The temporary home of the fallen angels.

—

Three months after the unexplainable accident that killed DaFrenchy and five others, Raven Jet began laying off employees, including Chris, giving the bad economy and the unexplainable disappearance of one of its planes into space as the reason for the layoffs. At about the same time, the auto manufacturing plant where Tony had worked since he had graduated from high school laid him off. Like Raven Jet, the manufacturing plant used the economy as an excuse to save money.

Being laid off confused Chris a little, but it didn't change the deep love he now felt for God. After his semi physical discussion with Reverend Apostle Prophet Edgars, Chris church-hopped back to Pastor Sanders's church where they gave him money to attend seminary school. DaFrenchy's death became one of two driving force that lead Chris into wanting to become a Pastor. Helping teach the Word of God to confused Christians and non believers was his other driving force. Chris looked at DaFrenchy's death as his first lost in ministering. He was the first person Chris had ever tried to lead to Christ. Chris never knew that DaFrenchy listened to him that day and put his life in the hands of Jesus, right before he died— at the outer edge of space.

Chris believed that God wouldn't let him fall, but some days he had his doubts. He felt that God allowed him to be laid off from his job and he didn't know why. His doubt soon diminished after three months of being unemployed when he noticed that he hadn't struggled or had fallen behind on any of their bills. Eight months after the layoff, there was still more food in the cabinets and the refrigerator and more money in their savings account than there had been when he had a job. All this was happening even after Chris had stopped tithing. He gave what he could which was sometimes over ten percent and wanted to give more, but tough economic times had forced him into giving a little less than he wanted to give. Chris read the Bible every day in search of a promise he could hold on to. Often, he read the Bible all day and all night. He read and studied the entire Bible three times using his dad's notes. Everyday when Angel came home from work, he shared something interesting that he'd learned from his Bible studies with her. Instead of the layoff driving Chris and Angel apart, it brought them closer together. Through Chris; the faith in God that Angel had been confused on for so many years was now being restored. Angel's strong support and encouraging words enabled Chris to passionately study the bible and drove him to be the best husband that he could be for her, an their family. They both prayed several times a day and believed that God was going to continue blessing them during the time they needed him the most.

Chris had gotten used to being home alone. On the Friday before Memorial Day weekend, Jacob and Heath both had dental and doctor's appointments. After finishing their last appointment around lunchtime, Chris decided to let the boys skip school and spend the rest of the day with him at home. While the kids played in the great room, Chris sat in his office studying the Bible and different Bible interpretations of religions after he searched the Internet for a job.

"Jacob and Heath, y'all are too loud," Chris repeated every five minutes as he sat at his desk. Unable to concentrate because Jacob and Heath were too loud, he decided to search the web for a song he had heard the last half of on the radio earlier that morning. He typed in several possible names from the chorus of the song until he finally found it. He turned the volume up on his computer and clicked on "Hallelujah" by Heather Williams. After the song was over, quietness rang in Chris's ears for five long minutes as he asked himself repeatedly whether he wanted to go through the suffering he expected to come once his unemployment benefits had expired. To Chris, the thought of Jesus coming back to rescue everyone began to look like the only fix to the situation the world, and he was in.

Jacob and Heath began to play sneaking ninja. They quietly slithered on their bellies under cover of the edge of the desk that blocked Chris's view of everything lower than two foot above the floor of the doorway. Chris felt something lightly stroke the tops of his bare feet and rubbed the top of each one with the bottom of the other foot. After the third time he felt something touching his feet, he heard snickering under his desk, rolled his chair back, and looked under the desk to find Jacob and Heath giggling.

"We snuck up on you like ninjas, Daddy. We got you," said Heath.

"Now you got to fight us since you caught us. Hyah!" said Jacob, throwing a karate chop to Chris's foot.

"Ouch! Now wait a minute. That hurt! I'm busy right now. We'll have to play later. Daddy's trying to find a job and study my school lesson. OK?"

"What kinda clock is it gonna be when you can play with us, nighttime o'clock or daytime o'clock?" asked Jacob.

"Daytime o'clock after Momma comes home," Chris answered.

Standing in a karate stance with a smile and his fist balled up, Jacob said slowly, "If you don't . . . we gonna have a pa prize for you." Chris knew that Jacob was mispronunciation the word surprise and assured him that they'd play later.

"I promise, I'll play with ya'll later on," said Chris.

Five minutes later, Jacob and Heath came back into Chris's office and stood together on his left side.

"Um, Dad?" Heath asked.

"Yes, sir, Mr. Shoemaker."

"Me and Jacob were wondering something about God,"

"Something like what?" asked Chris.

"We see you reading the Bible all the time, and me and Jacob was wanting to know. Why, um, why God hide heaven from us and why do we have to die to see Him?"

Chris looked at them with his eyes opened wide and scratched his head. "Whoo! How in the world do you keep coming up with hard questions that the Bible doesn't answer? Uh, well, it probably has something to do with Adam and Eve eating from the Tree of Knowledge of Good and Evil. We're here on earth to learn knowledge of good and evil because of the curse that came with eating from the forbidden tree. And, um, all the years we spend on earth learning are not long at all. This whole world has only been in existence for a few days in God's eyes, but billions of years in our eyes. This life is a short learning period. God probably allowed human life to exist so we could know how much He loves us and what He saved us from and remember it forever. Death is part of knowing good and evil. This earth is like your school. When heaven comes, we're going to graduate from this earth. We'll eat from the Tree of Life and live forever. Getting to eat from The Tree of Life is like a graduation present from God. We'll be cursed to live forever with Him when we get to eat from the right tree… which is a good curse."

Apparently, Jacob and Heath didn't fully understand his answer to their question. "So why does He hide in heaven and why do we have to die to get there?" Jacob asked.

Chris tried again, keeping it simple this time. "He's not hiding. He's only left for a moment that seems like forever to us, but He'll be back real soon," Chris explained.

He pulled them both in close to him and hugged them tightly. "When I was y'all's age, I wasn't as interested in God as you guys are. I'm proud of you guys." Before Chris could say anything else, the alarm beeped twice, signaling that a door had been opened. Jacob and Heath ran toward the door in the kitchen that led to the garage. It never dawned on Chris that God was answering yet another prayer right up under his nose. His entire family was being led to Christ, just as he had cried out and asked when he wrote his unofficial suicide letter.

"Mommy," they both said, running toward Angel with their arms held out to give her a hug.

"Hey, boys! Were y'all good for Daddy today?" she said as she got down on her knees to hug them.

Chris followed behind them and laughed when he heard the answer Jacob gave Angel.

"Yes, ma'am. We were real good for Daddy. Can we go to the toy store and get a toy for being good?"

"We have to cut back on our spending," Angel answered. "Remember, me and Daddy talked about how you can't be picky eaters and we can't buy you stuff like we used to because Daddy doesn't have a job right now."

Chris's happy mood evaporated. He dropped his head, sank down on the couch and fought the slight discouragement he had due to still being unemployed for almost a year.

All of the energy suddenly left the children's little bodies and their faces grew long. After a moment of sadness, Heath's face lit up with excitement as he turned toward Chris. "Hey, I know, Daddy! You can ask God to give you another job. Right, Dad?" Heath asked.

For a long moment, Chris didn't answer. He saw history repeating itself as he thought back to his childhood when God had allowed his father to be laid off from work. Chris remembered saying a prayer for his dad to get another job, but it hadn't happened. Instead of God blessing his father to get another job, he'd lost his father to suicide. Knowing that God answered prayers if He chose and when He chose to made Chris afraid that he and his family were about to be tested as he and his mother had been when his father died. Although his faith was strong, his past experiences from when he used to hate God always haunted him and caused him to fear that God would one day retaliate for the sins he committed against Him. But instead of causing Heath to worry about God not answering prayers and putting mixed emotions about God into Heath's innocent heart, Chris decided not to go into details about how God sometimes lets people suffer and see hard times for different reasons. "I sure hope so, Heath," he said. "Daddy sure hopes so."

Angel walked back into the room. "Heath, go get the milk and cookies out of my car and put them in the fridge, please. I almost forgot they were in there," Angel said.

"You know," Chris said to Angel when Heath had gone, followed by Jacob, "When I was in the hospital and had that dream, God must have been trying to let me know I was about to be laid off so I could work for Him. When I woke up, the newscaster was talking about Raven Jet's financial troubles. Then after I got the sales rep position and tried to transfer as a senior sales rep in the jet repair center, I was denied the job even though I was qualified and already working as a sales rep."

"Yeah," Angel said, sitting beside Chris on the couch.

"Well, I'm just speculating, but I believe that low down cross eyed rat faced hog, Bill blocked me from getting that position. Why would they have given it to a maintenance guy with no experience," Chris explained.

Angel seemed to miss the signs of Chris's dejection. "I know it's not the end of the day yet," she said," but tell me again what you said to me the other night. It really makes me feel good. I don't mind getting up in the morning and going to work for my family when you say those words." Angel eased over and sat on Chris's lap. "You make me feel like a queen when you consider me and my feelings at the end of the day," said Angel.

"I don't feel like I deserve to ask you that anymore. I should be the one working, not you. What can I do for you and our family with no job? I just don't feel like a man anymore, Angel; I'm sorry. This layoff has taken my manhood away from me. You're the only one working. It's like you're the man of the house and I don't like it, but I can't do anything about it 'cause no one is hiring. I just can't proudly ask you if your servant has served you well at the end of the day when I haven't gone out and worked for you!"

"Stop trying to figure out why you got laid off. You should hear how mentally unstable you sound. You still deserve to call yourself my servant. You've served me and the boys in many ways that don't require having a job and lots of money. You're a wonderful father and an excellent husband." Angel put her hand to her right ear. "Now let me hear it."

Chris folded his arms and sighed. "Has your servant served you well today?" he asked in an emotionless monotone.

"Yes, you have. I'm well pleased," Angel said with a smile before quickly changing the subject. "If I could get your car sold for five thousand dollars, would you sell it?"

"I don't really have a choice. I don't have a job," Chris replied.

"Why don't you take a field trip and get out of the house? Go fishing or jogging. I'll watch the kids. Take your mind off the negatives and focus on the positives of being laid off. Greater opportunities may come our way."

"I guess a light jog wouldn't hurt. I'll be back," said Chris.

—

While he jogged approximately two miles through his neighborhood, Chris thought about God and his family. It was a beautiful evening. The wind blew steadily, which kept him cool in the ninety-plus heat from the sun. After he finished jogging, he walked around to his backyard and stood by the lake while he caught his breath. With God still heavily on his mind, he kneeled down to put his hand in the water. When he reached out to touch it, a hand-shaped wave landed on the back of his hand and slowly slid down. A finger on the hand shaped out of water touched the tip of his finger for two seconds before leveling off with the rest of the waves. Chris put his hand into the water and tried to catch it so he could hold it a little longer. Instead of pulling the hand that had touched him out of the water, Chris pulled out a handful of water and released it with a gasp of wonder after he saw an image of Jesus face with a crown of thorns on His head in its reflection. He stood up and looked at the trees surrounding him. For two seconds as he looked at each tree, he saw images of Jesus face looking at him. In every direction he turned, he saw the face of the Lord God and many angels in the wind watching his every move. Before walking away from the edge of the lake, he saw an image of Jesus, whose body was made of water, walking on water and Chris began to smile. A sense of peace had calmed his mixed emotions and his faith had been recharged through the amazing wonders of the Lord God's creations.

He went inside and took a shower, ate dinner, and went through his entire nightly routine with his family before putting his kids to bed and ending another page in his life. But before going to bed, he looked out the window into the beautiful night sky, staring at the Lord God's creation and talking to Him while kneeling in front of the window. The last thing he said to the Lord God as he gazed at the moon and the stars was, "I see you." He immediately closed the blinds as if he were playing peek-a-boo with the Lord God. What made it a funny game to Chris was that he knew he couldn't hide from God behind an eighth-inch thick set of plantation blinds or even a wall as tall and thick as Mount Everest. He was just letting the Lord God know that he admired his great works of creation and that he could see him, and he knew that He was beautiful just by the things he saw that He created.

CHAPTER 18

Angel's Secret

The next morning, a Saturday, Angel left home around nine thirty, telling Chris that she was going out to buy a new pair of shoes. As she drove past all the shopping plazas and shoe stores, Angel still felt just as excited as she had on Friday evening when she began acting strangely. She blushed heavily as she turned her signal light on and turned into the parking lot of her secret destination, a hotel on the other side of town from their home. She was so excited when she parked the car that she forgot to turn off the ignition before she got out of the car. After walking past the front of the car and hearing the motor running, she quickly turned around and switched the ignition off, retrieved her keys, locked the car doors, and continued on her way.

"Oh, I can't wait!" she said to herself as she walked toward the entrance of the hotel. "Calm down, Angel; calm down." She already knew the room number her special guest had reserved, so she walked right past the front desk and went straight to the elevator. As the elevator doors opened, Angel was surprised to see her friend Sasha getting off. Sasha was the wife of Melvin Phillips, the fifth member of the gang of hot-rodders', who had joined the army two years after graduating from high school. She was a tall blonde who used to work as a Russian model.

"Hey, Sasha. I didn't expect to see you here," said Angel.

"Me, neither," Sasha said with her Russian accent. "I mean, I didn't expect to see you here, either.

"I heard Melvin was coming home sometime this month."

"Yes, today, I'm picking him up from the airport in a few hours."

"Oh, OK, girl, I'm not going to hold you up," Angel said. "I know you missed him dearly and you can't wait to see him. Hey! We're having a get-together on Monday for Memorial Day. Why don't you and Melvin come by? You don't have to bring anything," asked Angel.

"OK. What time?"

"Three o'clock. Oh! I'm going to tell Chris I ran into you at the shoe store and invited you guys. Don't mention that you saw me here at the hotel. It'll spoil a big surprise that I'm trying to keep from him."

"Don't mention to Melvin that you saw me here, either; it'll spoil my surprise, too," said Sasha. "I'm here looking at the size of their banquet hall. I'm thinking about renting it and having welcome home party for Melvin, but it's expensive."

"Looks like both of our husbands are going to be in for what my five year-old calls a big pa prize. I'll see you Monday."

Angel and Sasha hugged and parted ways.

Angel got off on the second floor and walked to room 210. Just before her knuckles hit the door she pulled back and decided to call the man she was there to meet to make sure she remembered the room number correctly. She placed the call and put her cell phone on speaker. She had forgotten her blue tooth and was subconscious about getting cancer from holding her cell phone directly to her ear.

"Hey, it's Angel. I'm standing outside of room 210. Am I at the right room?"

Coincidently, Bryan was two doors down in room 214 preparing to leave his room when he heard Angel in the hallway talking on the phone. He quickly closed the door almost completely, leaving a crack so that he could see and hear Angel without Angel seeing him. When he heard a man's voice answer the phone he gasped and put his hand over his mouth to keep himself quiet.

Angel looked toward his door at the sound but thought nothing of it and continued talking. She was still so excited that she couldn't think straight.

"No," the man's voice said. "I'm glad you called. I told you wrong; we're in 310, not 210. Two ten was the departure time for our flight yesterday. I have so many deadlines and numbers running through my head that I gave you the wrong number."

"That's OK," said Angel. "I just thank you guys so much for coming here to do this. Oh! I left the pictures in my car. It wasn't easy with my husband being laid off and at home all the time, but I managed to take close-up body shots without him seeing me from different angles. Maybe you can use the pictures I took for the magazine, too. I'm going to go get them and I'll be right up."

"OK, great, the photographers are here in the room with me. They can pick out the best photo's you have while we go over everything else. The camera crew will be here Monday night— set up Tuesday— and that's when all the action starts."

By this time, Bryan was so shocked that his tongue felt like 80 grit sandpaper and his mouth was as dry as brown grass in a midsummer drought.

Later that afternoon, Bryan nervously went over to Tony's house to help prep a 1977 Dodge Good Times van for paint. Tony had started restoring and painting cars full time to help cope with the mental anguish that came after losing a job that he had held for twelve-years. All the guys had agreed to give Tony a hand with the van. The owner, a retired fighter pilot, wanted to have an airbrush mural on both sides of the van depicting an F-14 fighter jet taking off from a navy ship with fire coming from the engines. Tony and Harold had just started working on the van when Bryan got there.

After thirty minutes of Bryan's strangely quiet behavior, Tony and Harold had had enough.

"What's going on, man?" asked Harold. "You've been too quiet. We know something's up, so you might as well get it off your chest."

Bryan hesitated. "Y'all told me Chris said he'd be here a little later after Angel gets back from shoe shopping so she can watch the kids, right?"

"Yeah," they both answered.

"Well, pretty soon she'll be able to buy a whole lot of shoes."

"How's that?" Tony asked.

"Well, I saw her this morning getting ready to do community service work at the hotel for video stores and magazines if you know what I mean?"

"I'm still in the dark," said Tony. "Turn some mo' light on this subject so I can see."

"She was talking to some dude on her cell phone who had photographers in his room and they were waiting for her to come up there to their room. I overheard her say something about body pictures being put in a magazine."

"Man! You done turned on the bright lights and exposed some stuff," said Tony.

"I can't believe this," said Harold. "This has got to be some sort of terrible mix-up, man. Most people get real religious when hard times hit 'em. It just doesn't make sense that she'd do whatever it is she's doing."

"Maybe that's why Chris got laid off," said Tony. "God must be punishing her whole family for how she's living."

"Y'all think I should tell Chris?" Bryan asked.

"No!" Harold said. "Not yet. He's got enough on him right now. Going to school to become a preacher and dealing with being laid off. Plus we're all going over there for Memorial Day. It'd be best to tell him after the get-together if we decide to tell him at all. It might make him suicidal again."

CHAPTER 19

The Memorial Day Barbecue

At nine o' clock that Memorial Day morning; aroma from barbecue smoke was stronger than all of nature's natural air fresheners in the air. Chris had just finished mowing the lawn with his riding lawnmower and was about to put the finishing touches on his yard work with his weed wacker when his IPhone rang.

"Hey, how you doing Deacon Banks," Chris answered.

"Hey what you say now. I didn't catch you at a bad time did I?"

"Not really, I'm just doing a little yard work. It's starting to get hot so I don't mind taking a break."

"Don't let me stop you from working. I'll just holla at you when you done."

"OK." Chris paused. "Hey, if you're not doing anything today why don't you and Mother Banks stop by and have dinner with us? We only have a few friends coming over," Asked Chris.

"Yeah, we're not doing nothin'."

"Well I'll see ya'll at three o'clock then."

"OK. We'll see you da reckly," said Deacon Banks.

Chris finished his yard work and took a shower. Later that afternoon at one o' clock, he fired up his grill and began grilling.

Deacon Banks and Mother Idella Banks we're the first guest to arrive. At the last minute, Tony, Harold, and Bryan phoned Chris one after the other giving different reasons why they couldn't make it to the Memorial Day dinner. Truth was, none of them felt comfortable enough to talk to Chris and pretend as if they didn't know anything about his wife Angel's mysterious behavior so they all lied and blamed their wives as the reason that they couldn't make the dinner.

"My wife told me this is the worst time to try to open up a business and chase after a dream that requires people to spend money and it was time for a divorce. She just doesn't have any confidence in me and wants me to find a real job. I'll catch up with you another time cause right now with no job—I don't even feel like a man and I'm kind of depressed," said Tony. It was true that he and Tina had gotten into an argument and were planning to divorce. But he failed to mention that they'd had the argument a week earlier and he and Tina were sleeping in separate beds until she found somewhere else to live.

Harold called next. "Audrey and I got into a senseless argument last night over the kids. Basically, I didn't get her permission or approval to spank the kids; like I need help being a father or something. I'm not trading clothes with her, man. I'm a' be a man and wear what I'm supposed to wear. I'm tempted to divorce her and find a woman who wants a man and who'll let me be the man. I'm not going to be able to make it."

Bryan's excuse was slightly different. "Cynthia got called in to work today and she wants me to have lunch with her, but I'll stop by a little later and pick us up a plate on my way to meet her."

"I understand," Chris said to each of them before hanging up. The doorbell rang just as Chris got off the phone with Bryan.

Melvin and Sasha had managed to make it without running into any problems like the rest of the gang. Melvin and Chris silently embraced each other. It had been a little over two and a half years since they had seen each other. Melvin had spent his leave time with Sasha in Germany where he'd been stationed before he was sent to fight in Afghanistan. With both parents in prison on drug-related charges, Melvin had decided that it wasn't worth spending his leave time in Arkansas just to see his parents for a few hours on the weekends. Besides, the last time he'd flown halfway around the world to visit them, it had turned out to be a wasted trip. Melvin's dad, who knew he was coming, got into trouble and lost his visitation privileges two days before his visitation date. At the same time, the prison where his mom was incarcerated had cancelled all visitations for reasons unknown.

Melvin and Chris exchanged small talk as they walked to the great room. In the middle of the conversation, Chris excused himself to go and check on the ribs and chicken he was cooking on the grill.

Deacon Banks, who was in the kitchen with his wife, Idella, and Angel, followed Chris outside to help him.

"I didn't see dem boy'z where they at?" asked Deacon Banks.

"Upstairs in the game room playing," said Chris while opening the grill.

"Boy, I tell you, only in Arkansas can you barbecue without using charcoal one day then have to wear a sweater the next day. They say it's sposed ta be sixty-five degrees tomorrow, which I'm OK with 'cause my air stopped playing in my Caddy. This is the first thing to go wrong with it since I bought in 1970," said Deacon Banks.

"You sho' right. It's a different kind of hot out here today," Chris said as he fanned the smoke away to see which pieces of chicken and ribs were ready to turn.

"You got any hickory wood in that fire?"

"I don't grill without it," Chris responded.

"Aw. You might know a little something 'bout 'cueing. I can't wait to taste it and find out." Deacon Banks leaned against the back left corner of Melvin's shiny black '68 Chevelle, which was parked in the driveway.

"It seem like you might know a little something 'bout the Bible, too like you do 'bout cueing. That paper you wrote discussing tithing and how we misinterpreted many things in the Bible was purty interesting. I picked it up and made a copy that day you and Reverend Apostle Prophet Edgars had that disagreement. You know we had to let Joe go not too long ago for stealing money and running around with the women of the church?"

"No, I didn't know that," Chris responded.

"He had a couple women in the church 'pregnated. Some more than once. He'd pay for 'em to get a 'bortion on Wednesday and preach on not get'n a 'bortion the very next Sunday. On top of that, I don't know how true it is, but it's a rumor goin' around the church that he kept male secrets, if you know what I mean." Deacon Banks twitched his eyes and twisted his lips to the right and the left.

"Oh!" Chris said after decoding the message. In other words he was secretly using women's' antiperspirants and perfume?"

In a big up-and-down motion, Deacon Banks nodded his head to indicate that Chris had correctly read between the lines of his hidden message. After a brief pause, Deacon Banks changed the subject to address a more serious issue.

"What you wrote on how we need to re sturdy everything we've heard about the Bible a little mo' deeper," he began. Deacon Banks pointed his right index finger and shook it a couple of times before folding his arms and going into deep thought. "You know, it turched me. A lot of that makes so much sense and explains many confusing questions I had that Reverend— oh, his title is just too long—Edgars—you know who I'm talking 'bout. He couldn't answer a lot of those questions and would never preach from Revelations. Told me to stop reading and asking him questions 'bout that book 'cause it makes God look mean and it shouldn't be in the Bible. All the answers he did give me kept contradicting one thing after another."

"Actually, my dad wrote it. I rewrote and summed up a lot of things he wrote about in his dissertation and in his essays when he was getting his doctorate in theology. The truth should make sense, but a lot of people don't want to accept it because of pride when they learn that they've misunderstood the bible. I was lost for years until I learned the truth about God and how to read His poem of love that we call the Bible. The truth about God's love really will set you free—free for eternity," Chris said.

Deacon Banks paused before responding. "Pride is the reason why I never mentioned to you that I read your paper. I've been too proud to tell you that I've learned a lot from that paper 'cause I didn't want you to think I was ignorant and hadn't read the Bible. I may talk country, but I'm not ignorant. I been a Christian serving the Lord all my life. How it look for me not to know all this new stuff and start over at my age relearning the Word? On top of that, I done read the whole Bible and, according to yo' daddy's paper, I hadn't learned nothing. There's a right way and a wrong way to read it like yo' daddy said and I read it the wrong way. It's embarrassing to know that everything I thought was so ain't so."

"When dealing with religion, there's no easy way to discuss any misunderstood passage someone has believed for years. My father's paper isn't really insulting your intelligence at all. Satan's deceptive lies of God's word aren't easy to correct and re teach. He's been watching us every moment since the days of Adam and Eve. We've been deceived in countless ways during our lifetimes just like them. Satan knows exactly what to do to fool us and make God look as if he's a liar. That' why it's important to know who you are in the bible and when the bible is talking to us. Which time period is being talked about is also vitally important."

"I know your father was just trying to hope people. The first shock of finding this stuff out just hurts so bad when you're my age and you thought you been serving the good Lord the way He wants you to then somebody come along and tell you what yo' momma and daddy taught you ain't right."

"Well, it's not your fault that we've all been taught a lot of things about the Bible incorrectly. The deceiver and creator of all lies and contradictions isn't living in hell yet. Nothing God made is ignorant except for falling angels and people who choose to be evil. We, and me included may not ever get it all right, but there's one thing God made clear for sure. Believe in Jesus. Whether we misunderstand some parts of the Bible or most of the Bible, we get a free ticket to His eternal heaven if we simply believe in Jesus. But getting to know and understand Him through his word while we're here makes this life on earth extremely beautiful."

"Speaking of misunderstandings, I know something you don't know and you might not agree with me on this one, but when our loved ones die, friends comfort us by telling us they're in a better place and they wouldn't wanna come back down here to earth and leave where they're at for nothing."

"Yeah," Chris replied.

"Well, I don't know if that's in the Bible or not, but I have proof that that ain't true," explained deacon Banks.

"I'm a' have to study up on that one, Deacon," said Chris. "I believe that myself."

"Sturdy it and let me know 'bout that one 'cause I seen a ghost in my house some years back," Deacon Banks said. "Do you bleeve in ghosts?"

"I don't believe in ghosts because I've never seen any. I've never seen God either for that matter but some dreams I've had about Him sure seemed to be real. But the difference between ghost that I've never seen and God whom I've never seen is that He left all kinds of evidence through creation that He exists. I've never seen any hard evidence that ghosts exist. It amazes me that some people believe in ghosts and aliens that they've never seen, but they don't believe in God."

"Yeah, maybe they don't exist, but I still like that TV show *The Ghost Whisperer.*"

"Yeah, me, too. I love that show. You just have to understand that it's just entertainment," said Chris.

"Do you bleeve in aliens?" Deacon Banks asked.

"If that's another name you want to use for demons, I do. It seems like I read somewhere in the Bible that Satin is the Prince of the air and the fallen angels live with him or something like that. They're not living in hell yet, because Judgment Day hasn't happened. Therefore I believe there are billions of fallen angels living in outer space," said Chris.

"Wow! That's interesting . . . ." Deacon Banks paused. "What about that part you wrote about being absent from the body and present with the Lord being Paul's opinion and not a promise made for anyone including Paul. Did you get that from your dad's whatchamacallit . . . his, uh . . . dessert—dessertation? You didn't give his final answer on that; you just mentioned it. If that weren't true, then that would mean that ghosts may really exist, don't you think?"

"I'm still studying that question. I haven't found in the Bible where it says our souls go straight to the third heaven yet, but that's not to say it's not in there. I'm still learning. I'll never know it all, but we've learned in my theology classes that we can't be in the presence of God the Father without being made brand-new. We'll be made new with new bodies after the Rapture when the dead believers in Christ and the believers who are still living are transformed. That kind of makes it seem like we won't be with Him right away until everyone is raptured up." Chris thought for a moment and then added, "Let me finish studying that one and get back to you, because I could be missing something."

"OK, but hurry up. I'm an old man. I'd like to know what to 'spect before my time comes."

"OK, I got you," Chris answered with a smile.

"You can bleeve whatever you wanna bleeve about ghosts, but maybe you'll change your mind after I tell you this story." Deacon Banks paused dramatically. "I was barbecuing some chicken and ribs just like you doing right now. They wanted me to hope 'em out cooking the food for the dinner after my uncle's funeral."

"They wanted you to help them out," Chris said as he tried to correct Deacon Banks's pronunciation of the word help.

"Let me finish now before you go asking questions. This was years ago, but I 'member it like it was this mawning. I used a right smart of my secret sauce and ingredients. That hickory smoke come a rolling out dat grill like smoke outta a steam engine train, and I knew it was goin' t' be good. Later that night, I lied down after sampling it to make sho' I didn't need to do nuttin' else to it." Deacon Banks put on his most animated expression as he moved within eight inches of Chris's face and continued, "I heard something in da kitchen keeping up a fuss, so I got up to look-see what it was. The 'frigerator doh was wide opum, and I thought maybe something fell and knocked it opum." Deacon Banks backed away from Chris's face to a comfortable distance and continued, "I rayched my hand out to grab the doh and it start ta closing by itself, and a man was sittin' there smacking on my ribs and chicken."

"Aw, man! What did you do?" Chris asked.

"Well, I couldn't kill him 'cause he was already dead," Deacon Banks explained.

"Huh?"

"It was my uncle. That's why I don't bleeve it when they say our relatives don't wanna come back down here with us once they gone. My uncle said he smelled my ribs and chicken all the way up in heabum' and begged God to give him a temporary leave so he could come back to earth and eat some of his nephew's cueing one last time."

Deacon Banks and Chris laughed as they walked through the garage on their way to take enough meat inside to start the feast, leaving the rest on the grill to finish cooking.

"I'm just kidding with you. Ain't nothing down here worth coming back for," said Deacon Banks.

Chris stuck a fork in a small piece of rib and gave it to Deacon Banks. "Here. Here's a sample. You had me going for a minute. I'm a' have to try some of yo' ribs if they're that good."

"Yes sir. My 'cueing is so good it'll make yo' dead relatives wanna leave heaven to get some. If yo' ribs can't make a saved soul leave heabum, then you need to let me learn you how to cook there, young'un." Deacon Banks cut into the sample rib with his teeth and dumped it down his throat with his tongue. "Emph, emph, emph," he said.

"It's good, ain't it?" asked Chris. Deacon Banks stopped Chris before they went inside.

"You put some English on them ribs. Can you come and feed us some good food for our faith and our brains like these ribs? That's why I called you this morning to discuss a dilemma the church is in right now. We need a pastor." He licked his fingers, smacked his lips, and continued, "Put some English on God's word like yo' daddy did. We waitin' on God to send us another leader. In the meanwhile, we got differ'nt guest preachers preaching one contradictionary message after the other ever' Sunday. Why don't you come preach a few Sundays to get some practice on leading a church?"

Chris started to correct Deacon Bank's mispronunciation of the word *contradictory* but changed his mind as he considered the deacon's offer. "Contra—never mind."

"Contract? No, no contract, but we'll give you a generous love offering after church," said Deacon Banks.

"I'm not an ordained pastor yet," Chris answered.

"Neither was Reverend Apostle Prophet Edgars. You don't have to be licensed to preach, but you have to be licensed to be a doctor or a lawyer. Neither one of those professions can save your eternal life or keep you from being sentenced to eternal damnation. Ain't that something?"

"I forgot about that. I'll do it. I'm laid off and nobody's hiring. I plan on making this my new career, anyway. Plus, I could always use a few extra dollars."

"Thanks, Chris. Let me get this doh for you," said Deacon Banks, opening the door that lead to the kitchen from the garage.

Chris went inside and placed the 12x16 inch pan of meat next to the cooktop.

"The rest of the meat will be ready in about ten more minutes. Harold, Bryan, and Tony cancelled out on us at the last minute and won't be able to make it," Chris said to Angel, who was standing in front of the cooktop preparing brewed tea, talking to Sasha and Mother Banks as they were arranging different dishes on the table. He leaned over and whispered to Angel, "I'll tell you why later on."

"Might as well tell her now," put in Idella. "We may be able to pray over their situation and get "em healed and over here in time for supper. My God can make a way."

Angel and Chris both dropped their mouths open in amazement over how incredibly nosy Idella was.

"Oxtails! Boy ya'll be eating good and hearty up in here. Where yo' forks, hot sauce and other eating artillery at?" asked Deacon Banks who had opened up their refrigerator and took a peak inside.

"Whoa, slow down. That ain't on today's menu," replied Chris. He looked at Angel and said. "I'm about to gather everyone around so we can say grace and eat before Deacon Banks eats all my oxtails." Chris looked back at Deacon Banks and said, "Cursed be the stomachs of anyone who eats anything in the refrigerator that's not on today's menu."

Deacon Banks continued to stare at the oxtails in the refrigerator after Chris had left the kitchen and deemed them cursed. "I done been cursed before. That don't scare me," said Deacon Banks as he pinched off a piece of the forbidden oxtails and rubbed his stomach. Chris walked over and stood at the bottom of the stairwell and yelled. "Jacob, Heath, come on down, it's time to eat." After hearing the pitter pattering sound of their feet running down the upstairs hallway, Chris walked to the great room to gather Melvin and Sasha so he could say grace over the food.

They all gathered in the dining room and Chris blessed the food. "God we thank you this evening for allowing us to gather here safely for this celebration for millions of soldiers who sacrificed their lives for our freedom. We thank you for Melvin's safe return and for the millions of soldiers throughout the centuries who fought to protect our freedom. I'd like to honor one special soldier whose name can't be found on any military enlistment list, but was present in every war that has ever been fought. One who protects millions of both believing and non believing soldiers at the same time and gathers up the souls of the ones who are killed and takes them to a place of peace where they can rest while He continues to fight for centuries and centuries to come. One who died and did what millions of soldiers and other people could never do, pay the ultimate sacrifice for our everlasting, eternal freedom. Thank you, Lord of lords, King of kings, and hero of all heroes for traveling into the end of time, defeating our enemy, and coming back to what is the past to you to give your children the good news that our victory has already been won. Amen."

CHAPTER 20

Three Conversations

After dinner, Heath and Jacob went back upstairs to play in their play room. Deacon Banks fell asleep on the couch while Angel, Sasha, and Idella cleaned the kitchen. Chris took out the trash and was met by Melvin in front of the garage on his way back inside.

"There's an appropriate time and place for everything don't you think," said Melvin.

Seeing that Melvin wasn't smiling, Chris felt puzzled. "Like what?" he asked.

"Like drawing all the attention to your fantasy hero of all heroes on a day like this."

"Dude, you gotta be kidding me! It's good to be patriotic, but are you going to be prouder to be in the U.S. army or the army of heaven? I'm a soldier just like you. I'm in God's army now. I show my patriotism for two armies. That's why I acknowledged both armies of heaven and of earth when I prayed."

"I've been on two tours of duty. My fellow soldiers saved me each time I was in danger and I saved some of them. I believe in Him, but what makes him a hero? A lot of good men were killed over there, he didn't save them."

"He saved us and our loved ones who have died. He guaranteed our freedom forever. No man can fight and win a war like that. Man's army will only be able to watch when the final war of all wars begins."

"Yeah. That's all your big hero has ever done was watch as we fought."

145

Chris frowned.

"Do you need some counseling?" Chris asked. "What happened to you over there?"

"Counsel me Chris. Impress me. Tell me something about this hero to make me consider him one," Melvin said sarcastically.

"This hero loves us and made us," Chris explained. "We are His greatest creation. We may be a part of His army, but all we're going to do is watch the war for the two seconds that it's going to last. God the Father and Jesus are gonna kick some serious butt for us. Do you hear them saying our eternal freedom is worth fighting and dying for? Angels have been with God before Jesus created the heavens and the earth. I don't know about you, but it amazes me that He loves us so much, that He's going to rank us above all the mightiest of angels in heaven. They've been with Him since the beginning of our time, yet God said we are His greatest creation. Not the angels in heaven who've never sinned, but us who have lived a life of sin. Us nasty, filthy, maggot humans are his greatest creation. There's no salvation plan for angels. His love, grace, and mercy are deeper than I can understand. His love is amazing. It's time to start getting uncomfortable with the ways of this world. It won't be ours to fight over pretty soon."

Melvin was speechless for a moment. "He really loves us that much? That's in the Bible?" Melvin asked.

"You bet your life savior it's in there. That's just a taste of how much He loves us.

Before Chris and Melvin had finished their conversation, Willie Stewart pulled up in front of Chris's house, honked his horn, and signaled for Chris to come to his car.

"That's the owner of the company I used to work for. Let me see what he wants," Chris said to Melvin as he walked toward Mr. Stewart's car.

"Hey, Mr. Stewart. I hadn't seen you driving through in a while. Are you feeling alright?" asked Chris.

Mr. Stewart seemed to be in a daze with something weighing heavily on his mind. His head was shaved bald, and his body was weak from chemotherapy treatments.

"I've been in and out of a hospital overseas for the past nine months, I'm OK, but I'm just tired.

"I was wondering why I hadn't seen you driving through in a while." Mr. Stewart got quite again as Chris waited on a response.

"Stop by the house when you get a chance," Mr. Stewart said. "I have some very important things to tell you and give you. I'm going to get you your job back for one. Word got back to me that Bill and Tim had something to do with you being laid off. Bill only hired you because I made him hire you. He knew I was going to be in the hospital and away from work for at least six months and he got busy doing dirty work. Tim didn't know Bill had already put your name in the hat to be laid off and filed a false report behind your back. He said you were badmouthing the company, saying you wished they would lay you off and that he heard you threaten to find Bill if you got laid off."

"I never said that, Tim lied!" Chris explained.

"I didn't believe it when I heard it."

"It doesn't surprise me one bit that Tim lied behind my back like that. That's all he ever did was lie to put himself above others so he could keep his job," Chris replied.

"Don't worry about it. You might own the company and be their boss one day." Mr. Stewart paused. Just as Chris opened his mouth to respond to his confusing comment; Mr. Stewart spoke again. "I've got to get some rest," Mr. Stewart said. "I'm tired. Come to the house one day this week. I have some more important things to talk to you about."

"What can be more important than me getting my job back? Thank you very, very much Mr. Stewart. You're a good man."

Mr. Stewart began to cry as he drove away. Chris could hear him sobbing loudly through the open car window.

"It's OK to cry, Mr. Stewart," Chris said to himself as he watched Mr. Stewart drive away. "I know I want to. If I was rich or in a position to do good for people's families, I'd cry, too."

Later that night after everyone had left, Chris propped a couch pillow under his head and lay on his back on the floor close to Angel, who was sitting on the loveseat reading a book.

"I wonder why Bryan never showed up to pick up a plate for his wife," Chris said.

"Oh, yeah. You were going to tell me why they said they couldn't come," Angel reminded Chris.

"Oh, Bryan said that Cynthia had to work and he was meeting her for lunch. The other two both got into arguments with their other halves."

"You mean 'better halves,' smart dummy?" said Angel.

Knowing that Angel was only kidding, Chris continued. "Get this. Tony and Tina might be getting a divorce and you'll never guess why."

"Tony was unfaithful like most men are," said Angel, smirking. "Duh. That was easy."

"No, Tony has never been unfaithful. It's because he got laid off and Tina is fearful of spending money and starting up a new business that Tony wants to start. You ought a' be ashamed for stereotyping us men. Besides, a man can't be unfaithful by himself. It may be Adam's fault we all got in trouble, but Eve tempted him to do wrong with that skin suit she was wearing," said Chris.

"I am shame. Shame of a husband who stereotypes men as being victims of being stereotyped."

Out of nowhere, Jacob came running straight for Chris making a Tarzan yell mixed with an Indian whoop. Chris turned over on his stomach and braced for the impact as Jacob's little body came flying through the air and landing on Chris's back.

"Giddy-up, horsey! Yah! Yah!" he yelled. "Play with us Daddy, you said you were gonna play with us the other day and you didn't. Come on, horsey. We wanna play— we wanna play."

"Daddy's too full to play right now. Wait until I get done talking to Momma and resting a little bit more."

Jacob leaned over, put his nose to the back of Chris's neck, and then scooted down toward the middle of his back. Raising his head, he continued sniffing around with a look of confusion on his face.

"Daddy, why yo' neck and yo' back smell like that? It smells kinda weird." Without another word, Jacob put his right hand over his nose, slowly climbed off Chris's back, and walked back into the bedroom to play video games with Heath after figuring out that he had helped Chris relieve a little pressure off his full stomach.

Chris rolled back over onto his back and continued talking to Angel as if he had not been interrupted. "I've got my first preaching job coming up Sunday. Deacon Banks asked me to be their guest speaker."

"You're late. You know Idella Banks can't keep a secret. As soon as you all went outside she told me, "I bet you Eddie fixing to ask Chris about preaching Sunday,'" Angel replied.

"Did she tell you I'm probably getting my job back?"

"You're late again. She was standing at the window lip-reading when you were out there talking to Mr. Stewart."

"Unbelievable!" said Chris.

"I'm just joking. She was trying, though. If you hadn't had your back to her, blocking her view to Mr. Stewart's lips, I believe she would've decoded the message."

"I wouldn't be surprised if she placed bugs in the mailbox and all around the yard before she came in. She's probably at home now listening to everything she recorded."

"Are you serious about getting your job back?" Angel asked excitedly.

"Yes. Mr. Stewart's been in a hospital overseas getting treatment and trying new experimental drugs for about nine months and he just got back last week. He said he's got something more important than me getting my job back to tell me and to stop by his house one day this week."

"God is good. He's been good to us during these challenging times we've been in. It doesn't even seem like we're in a life storm because of the way we've been trusting in Him this time, does it?"

"They say storms are meant to get us closer to him. I'd say this one put us right in our His lap."

"I have a confession to make," said Angel.

"I'm listening," said Chris. Angel picked up the stereo remote on the end table next to the loveseat she was seating on and fumbled with it as she spoke. "I haven't been being honest with you and I hope you'll forgive me, but it was for a good reason. Saturday morning when I said I was going to the shoe store to get some shoes, I lied. I went to talk to a body shop that was in need of a donor car to work on to teach a class on doing bodywork. Before you ask, don't worry about how much it's going to cost or where the money's coming from to buy all the parts; I have that taken care of." Out of nervousness, Angel turned the stereo on to drown out all the objections she thought Chris was about to come up with.

In the background, the radio DJ was speaking live on the air to a young woman on the phone who had just won tickets to see a new movie release called *Chapters in Our Lives.*

"You mean to tell me that God is blessing me to get the dream car I've prayed for restored and I don't even have a job?" Chris asked.

"Yes," Angel said, surprised and relieved that he hadn't objected to her plan. "They said they could come pick it up this week if I talk you into it."

"They can come and get it tomorrow," Chris said excitedly. "I'll push it to the shop if I have to. How far is it, twenty, thirty miles? Hurry up and call them tomorrow and tell them come get it before they change their minds."

"You know, Angel," Chris said, getting up off the floor and sitting next to her, "at one point in my life, my troubles hurt me so bad that I couldn't cry. My pain was extreme. It was beyond crying. I even thought about suicide. Look at what I would've missed if I had committed suicide. I never would've got to experience what it's like to see God perform personal miracles for me in our lives. Nothing is worth ending life for. I wouldn't have met you or had the opportunity to be a father. For all that I've experienced and learned, I thank Him. I thank Him for the good and the bad times. I'm glad I waited until my life turned to the page called tomorrow. I used to wonder to myself when I looked at others who were doing well while I struggled, when am I going to get my happy ending? I know now that it's coming for all of us in the new life. If I don't get it down here, I still love Him. I just can't stop loving Him . . . and you, Angel."

"I love Him and you, too. I've seen how He can change a man."

"Forgetting somebody? One somebody? Hint, hint."

"And change a woman," Angel mumbled.

Chris tuned his ears in to the radio DJ in the background as she announced the next song she was about to play.

"Here again is 'I Belong to You' by Kathryn Scott," said the radio DJ.

"Come on, dance with me and God. I love this song," Chris said as he stood up and took Angel by the hand. "It comes from a verse that promises me that my dad is in heaven. Not one sin except for blasphemy against the Holy Spirit can separate us from God's love."

"Never in a million years did I think my husband would love God so much that he'd slow dance with me while listening to praise and worship music."

"What can I say? As Deacon Banks would say it, God's love has 'turched' me."

Each time the song reached its chorus, Chris and Angel gently sang the chorus to each other while dancing on what felt like clouds.

CHAPTER 21

Bryan's Sin

On his way to have a late lunch with his wife, Cynthia, that Monday evening around 5:45, Bryan had received a welcome call from her just as he had gotten within five minutes of the food manufacturing plant where she worked a twelve-hour shift.

"If I skip my lunch hour, I can get everything done and get off two hours early," said Cynthia. "I'd rather do that so I can gain two hours to spend with you."

"I'm not going anywhere, baby. I'm yours and yours only for life. You don't have to rush to come home. I'll be there. You get off at ten instead of twelve, so you should be home round 10:15 or so?"

"Yeah. And I can't wait, either, I'm tired. These twelve-hour-plus shifts are a killer."

"I'm a' just chill and read a little bit of the Bible tonight and wait patiently for you to come home. Having a preacher as a friend has gotten me kind of interested in the Bible," Bryan replied.

With a couple of quick flickers of his tongue, Bryan lied to his wife and prepared to take advantage of the opportunity to commit premeditated sin against himself, his wife, and God. Bryan didn't waste any time calling up his mistress and rushing to the hotel instead of staying home to read and study his Bible. He even sped up as he drove almost ten miles over the speed limit to gain more time for the premeditated sinful act he secretly and often committed while his wife Cynthia worked as a supervisor at night.

Standing at the front desk waiting for the clerk who was on the phone to assist him, Bryan thought back to Saturday morning when he had seen Angel sneaking around at the hotel and remembered overhearing a man's voice say that the rest of the crew were coming on the night of Memorial Day. He remembered that this unknown man had given Angel their departure time as a room number to meet him in instead of the correct room number, which was 310, and decided to try to rent a room on the third floor in hopes of running into the man he believed was Angel's pretend husband on the side.

Finally, the clerk got off the phone and assisted Bryan. "Do you have any rooms available on the third floor?" Bryan asked the new receptionist behind the counter. He gawked at her as she searched in the computer for available space. With her Hispanic accent, shiny jet-black hair, and multicolored eyes, she hypnotized Bryan, who processed her every word slowly. Her beauty slowed Bryan's perception of time so that it almost stood still.

"Room trey hundred five is available. Here is key. Enjoy you stay," she said.

"*Bonjour*," Bryan replied.

"*Gracias*," the clerk replied while laughing at Bryan's mix up of Spanish and French.

Before getting in the shower, Bryan called his mistress, Nicky to give her the room number and ask her to bring him a couple of beers and a bag of hot barbecued pork skins.

Nicky arrived a short time later wearing tight blue jeans with lightly faded sections on the front and back of her thighs and a black fitted T-shirt with rhinestone appliqué designs on the front that brought out the strawberry blonde hair she wore in braids. She charged in like a linebacker after a quarterback as soon as Bryan opened the door.

"I've got to use the bathroom!" she said as she set the six-pack of bottled beer on the table and made a mad dash toward the bathroom. She took her purse off her shoulder and threw it on the bed as she ran. Her unzipped purse bounced off the edge of the bed and fell on the floor. As Bryan kneeled down to pick up the purse and put it back on the bed, he noticed two bottles of prescription meds inside. Overcome by curiosity, he read and memorized the names of the medications and put the bottles back into her purse.

—

Around 9:30, Bryan returned home. He logged onto the Internet to Google the names of the prescription meds he had memorized.

"Atripla," Bryan said as he typed the first drug's name and clicked the Search button. As the search results appeared on the screen, Bryan flew backwards in his chair. His stiffened body shook violently as if he were dying in the electric chair. He took several deep breaths and began to moan and cry. It had been so easy to lie, cheat, and sin with all his wives and mistresses that he had gotten comfortable with his sinful lifestyle. Now, the consequences of his sins were written in capital letters on the subject line of the first web page the search engine had pulled up: "HIV."

He tried to stand, but he couldn't hold himself up and fell forward, catching himself with his forearms as he landed on the edge of the computer desk. Still very weak, he let his knees drop to the floor and he raised his head up to make sure that he was reading the consequences of his sin correctly. The words "HIV treatment pill" were still there; he had not read them wrong. He paced the floor in several rooms trying to convince himself that he might have escaped contracting the AIDS virus because he had used protection.

Suddenly, his expression changed from that of great fear and worry to an expression of positive hope. He wiped his tears with the back of his hand and went into the laundry room, coming out with a bath towel and one of two gallon-and-a-half bleach bottles, and went to the master bathroom. Bryan turned on the hot water and poured the entire bottle of bleach into the tub. While the water ran, he went into the kitchen to grab a bottle of hand sanitizer, stopping in the laundry room to pick up the second bottle of bleach. Reentering the bathroom, he poured it into the water as well, turning off the faucet because the tub was at his desired water level.

The bleach fumes were very strong. Bryan turned on the exhaust fans, then opened and closed the bathroom door several times to clear the air. It didn't help. After grabbing a hand towel and tying it around his nose and mouth, he took the top off the hand sanitizer bottle and dumped half of the contents onto a washcloth to use as soap before removing his clothing to purify himself of disease and reverse the consequences of the sins he had committed against God, himself, and his wife. Moments after getting in the hot water to scrub himself, his eyes began to burn and his vision blurred. Almost immediately, he began having double visions of the candles and bathing supplies Cynthia had stored on the ledge of the Jacuzzi bathtub.

When he woke up, Cynthia was by his side in the ambulance, crying.

CHAPTER 22

Angel's Servant

On Tuesday morning, Chris resumed his normal routine of cooking breakfast, packing lunches for Angel and the kids, and seeing Angel off to work and the kids off to the bus stop. After praying, and reading the Bible for over two hours nonstop, he decided to take a break and drive to Mr. Stewart's home to find out what information he had for him that was more important than getting his job back at Raven Jet.

At 9:30 A.M., Chris rang Mr. Stewart's doorbell but no one answered. He returned to his truck and headed back home. As he backed out of the driveway, he marveled the beauty of Mr. Stewart's twelve-thousand-square-foot home and wondered what could be inside the separate thirty-five-hundred-square-foot garage. The off-white stucco house with red Italian clay roof tiles was the biggest mansion in the neighborhood.

Just as he pulled into his driveway after the short drive home and pushed the button to enter the garage, Chris received a call from Tony.

"Bryan was rushed to the hospital last night. Cynthia found him passed out in the bathtub after putting too much bleach in his bathwater. He's back home now and he's going to be OK, but Cynthia needs our help."

"What does she need?" asked Chris.

"She didn't get any sleep because she was at the hospital all night with Bryan. Her boss won't let her off work to be with him, so she asked if we could bring him something to eat this evening and check on him for her. You know, change his diaper and stuff like that . . . the big baby. He goes to the doctor and gets a Band-Aid put on him then wimps out like he can't do nothing for himself. Ain't nothing wrong with him."

"That's ridiculous," said Chris. "These companies are taking advantage of this economy and treating their workers any kind of way they want. It's a shame."

"You think that's ridiculous. They're giving her four hours to get some sleep and ordered her to come in and work from 4:30 to 12 A.M. or lose her job. She said they even had the nerve to ask her if she could skip her lunch hour so she could give them a full eight hours."

"It wouldn't bother me one bit if Jesus came back tonight and made everything right," Chris said. "I don't even fear His return anymore. The Bible's not a lie, the Rapture is going to happen . . . and soon. Believing and knowing that the Rapture is coming is about the only thing that comforts and gives me hope now. I have dreams about it almost every night."

"Slow down, hot rod," responded Tony. "Let Jesus take His time and come when He wants to. I believe He's coming soon, too, but I still get nervous when I think about it. Shoot, I had me a drink last night; I'd be 'shamed if he came back tonight."

"Not me. I've given myself up both now in this life and forever in the next. Sounds like somebody might need to change *your* diaper, you big chicken. No need in being scared if you love Jesus; it's going to happen. If you read the Bible and get to know of God's loving nature, you wouldn't be scared." Chris paused and looked at his phone. "Anyway, Angel's hittin' me up on the other end, so I have to hang up. I'll be there around 4:30 and give him a couple of spoonfuls of applesauce, but I'm a' let you change his diaper." They both laughed as they disconnected. Chris parked in the garage, switched over to talk to Angel, and walked to the mailbox to get the newspaper.

"Shoemaker family servant speaking," said Chris. "How may your servant serve you today?"

"Ooh wee!" said Angel. "That's what I'm talking about. What a man, what a man! You make my heart beat out of place every time you say that. You can serve me by letting me take you to dinner this evening at the restaurant of your choice."

"Now look, woman. I'm the man . . . excuse me, I mean, I'm the servant. I can't be your servant or this family's servant if y'all serve me."

"Yes, sir. Humph, I'll be submissive forever if it means being treated like a queen. You can serve me anytime, my sweet servant husband."

"With pleasure," Chris replied.

"I'm motivated to quit my job right now and be totally submissive to you today."

"Ho-ho-ho-hold it. Wait a minute," Chris stuttered. "Now you know I'm in between jobs and God's moving me right now, so that wouldn't be a good idea."

Angel began to giggle, causing Chris to grin widely. "I'll pass on going out to eat tonight. I'll have something cooked for y'all when you get in from work. I had planned on visiting Bryan this evening. He was rushed to the hospital last night after he passed out from using too much bleach in his bathwater last night."

"Is he OK?" Angel asked.

"Yeah, he's fine. He had brain damage before he put that bleach in his water so I'm sure the bleach fumes didn't hurt him. We're just going over there and give him a hard time and make fun of him so he doesn't get the impression that we actually care about him," Chris responded.

"OK, well, what time are you going and when will you be back?" Angel asked.

"Around 4:15 and I'll be back around six or six thirty."

"OK. We'll just eat a little later than normal, which is fine by me. See you when you get in." As she ended the call, Angel smiled the same blushing smile that she'd worn when she met with her mystery friend at the hotel.

"Perfect!" she said out loud before making a phone call to the mystery guy who made her smile. "Hey, it's me, Angel. Be at my house at four thirty sharp. He'll be away for about an hour and a half. Is that enough time?"

"I can do it in twenty minutes or less," he said.

"Great! I am so, so excited! I'll see you at four thirty."

CHAPTER 23

Forgiveness

After the guys had talked for about forty-five minutes in Bryan's living room, Bryan requested them to move their male bonding meeting outside to the garage so he could breathe some fresh air. Chris, Harold, Tony, and Bryan all went out to the garage, pulled out Bryan's folding chairs from beside his toolbox, and continued with the two topics that they never got tired of discussing: sex and cars.

Tony and Tina had stopped having marital relations because Tina was planning on divorcing him. Tina didn't know how to handle or deal with the pressures of Tony being laid off and her weakness was tearing them apart. Frustrated and confused, Tony felt the need to vent with his friends about a few of his frustrations. "I stopped by the bank on my way over here to try and get some money from my unemployment debit card, man, and almost caught a public disturbance charge."

"What happened?" Harold asked.

"I went in, gave the teller my unemployment bank card that looks just like my regular debit card and told the teller I wanted some cash from the account the card was on, and he said out loud, 'This is a card for unemployment benefits. You're going to have to contact them to find out where you can get a cash advance.' Man, they made me so mad I almost came across the counter and separated them,"

"Separate them? Who was the other person?" Chris asked.

"Either a man was sharing a body with a woman or a woman was sharing a body with a man. I couldn't tell what he or she originally was, so I was gonna separate 'em and turn the volume down on the male side with his big mouth. It was embarrassing. On top of that, it was a nice future plus-size cutie in line behind me. And on top of that, Tina's been turning me off in all categories, worrying me about getting a job like I can make somebody hire me right now. I'd be committing suicide if I took just any old job. Nobody's paying anywhere near what I was making." A mask of contrition dried tight on Tony's face after he realized that he'd used the word *suicide* in Chris's presence. The word *suicide* had haunted Chris for years causing him to go into a deep state of depression.

"My bad, man," said Tony. He wiped his face a couple of times with both hands as he tried to remove his mask of sorrow.

"Ah, man, I'm good. The truth has set me free from the misery of thinking my dad automatically went to hell for committing suicide. No one can confuse me again by misinterpreting what Jesus died for anymore. As a pastor, I want to teach people things that will help them overcome their addictions and sinful ways and unconfused them. I'd like to lead as many as I can including confused Christians to Jesus so he can change the way they live like he's changed me," Chris explained.

"Even a cheater like me can make it to heaven?" Bryan asked. His friends didn't know why he had tried to take a bleach bath, but his frequent adultery was no secret.

"All the husbands, boyfriends, and families that you hurt may want you to go straight to hell, but God doesn't. There's no way they'd let you come and live with them forever in their home after you hurt them and destroyed their family. No one but God will invite a sinner who sinned against Him into his home to live with them forever. Nobody's love on earth is that deep," Chris explained.

"Speaking of sex, I'm so sexually frustrated right now it ain't funny," said Tony. "I think I'm developing genophobia," said Tony.

"Frustrated? Why? All you have to do is use your imagination and your fear of sex phobia is cured," said Bryan.

"It's hard to do that when you got Gospel music playing while you're trying to . . . trying to be mannish, know what I'm saying?"

"Shoot, man, ain't that much religion in the world to be listening to Gospel music when it's fixing to be some cussing going on, you heard me?" Harold said. "It's time to take a break from religion when you're in the bedroom. Huh. Know what I'm saying?" They all gave each other high fives except for Chris. "Know what I'm talking 'bout? Time and a place for everything. The bedroom ain't the place for getting that kinda Holy Ghost. Can I get a witness?" Everyone laughed except Chris.

"Aw, Chris don't think it's funny," said Tony.

"I don't know now. Sometimes you got to call God's name in the beginning, the middle, and the end of the . . . ." Bryan paused. "For Chris's sake, let's just continue calling it the cussing contest."

Tony chimed in and teased Chris out of brotherly love. He moved over closer to Chris and placed his hand on his shoulder as Chris sat on the mechanic's stool. "Yeah, I bet after about a month of preaching, Chris's gonna be reading his Bible and praying before he has sex."

All the guys laughed at Tony's joke. Even Chris snickered a little at Tony's idea of praying before sex.

"Y'all don't have to tone our guy talks down for me just because I'm a preacher now," Chris said. "The sex talks in the Bible are dirtier than any sex talks we've ever had. Just read Song of Solomon, the story of David and Bathsheba, and Abraham and Sarah just to name a few. With that said, I don't know if I can agree with you guys. Making love while Godly music is playing is the deepest level of sex I've ever experienced."

"What'd I tell you? He's already doing it," said Tony as they all laughed.

"Praise and worship music to be specific," continued Chris, "but I like to call them Jesus love songs. I'm not putting Gospel music down, but most of it makes me feel like I'm in church or on earth. Praise and worship music goes a little bit deeper. It makes me feel like I'm in the presence of God in heaven. Since He created sex for marriage; it makes it OK that He's watching. Maybe I'm comfortable because I truly love God and include Him in everything I do now. Or maybe it's—"

"OK, preacher," Bryan interrupted. "Now you're getting a little too much on the weird side."

"Seriously, man," Chris said, "we've had some gruesome sex discussions in the past as we tried to figure it all out, and figure women out, but I'm telling you. I stumbled on a sexual high like no other I've ever had in my life after reading the Bible one night before bed. I was studying to gain understanding of the Holy Trinity and I stumbled across several other verses that sparked a fire of appreciation for my wife that will never go out. When we got married, our wives became a part of us."

"Hold on. I didn't know you could get high off Viagra," Bryan jokingly said. The rest of the guys chuckled and snickered. "You smokin' it or shootin' up with it?" Bryan added as they all laughed again.

"You can't," Chris responded, laughing. "I'm talking about a sexual excitement you can't get from cheating, watching pornography, or lusting after women who are not your wife. But for me, there's nothing more exciting than making love God's way. When spouses cheat on each other, He's there. When you have lustful thoughts of other women besides your wife, He's there. He's right there in the room with us and He's not alone."

"Who, God? Are you serious?" Bryan asked with a stunned expression and his arms covering up his body as if he were standing there naked.

"Not just God, but all of heaven. Billions and billions of angels are watching us along with God. Not one of our thoughts is a secret. God knows everything from how many breaths we take in our lifetime to how many times everyone who's ever walked the face of the earth has blinked their eyes. Every detail and everything about us is very precious to Him. He loves us enough to care about even the smallest things. One of the biggest things he cares about is our thoughts. They reflect our hearts. And He listens to them daily."

"Oh, my God! Is that in the Bible?" asked Tony nervously. "The part about He knows all of our thoughts and secrets and the angels watching, and all that stuff?"

"Yes," answered Chris. "We've all put on quite a show for them when we thought no one was watching us. They're in the hotel rooms, the parks, and the strip clubs we sneak off to. God knows every so-called secret that we think we have. We're actors making a movie. Our words and actions are being recorded at all times. And *cut*"—Chris pretended to snap an invisible clapboard in his hands—"is not a word used in the heavenly video productions for unbelievers."

Bryan began to breathe very heavily.

Harold moved closer to Bryan and stood next to him.

"Recorded?" asked Bryan.

"You all right, man?" asked Harold. Bryan suddenly lost all control of his body and passed out, falling against the side of his '69 Boss Mustang and into Harold's arms. Harold caught Bryan and laid him gently on the floor. Seconds later, Bryan regained consciousness.

"Are you fifty percent sure or one hundred percent sure that's true?" Bryan asked Chris.

"I'm a trillion, trillion percent sure it's true."

Bryan started breathing heavily and was on the verge of passing out again. "I'm going straight to the bottom of hell y'all," Bryan said as he looked up at all their faces with watery eyes. Tears began to fall down his face. "I'm going to south hell. I wish I could never die. I don't want to ever die," he cried.

"That makes me uncomfortable knowing that God is watching me in my most private, intimate moments," said Tony. "That ain't fair for him to violate us anytime he wants to."

"He made our bodies. I'm pretty sure he's seen us naked, right Chris?" asked Harold.

"We are all one body. We totally belong to Him. The good thing about being a part of God's love is that Jesus edits the audition tapes we believers make to become characters in heaven before their shown to God the Father. He keeps God the Father from watching and remembering our sinful acts. Because of Jesus there is no evidence recorded of our sins. Jesus has written us into the next episode called forever in heaven. It doesn't mean we're free to sin because He promised us that we'll suffer consequences here on earth for our sins. His love is not of this world. Just like these old cars we love restoring; we gave up the title to our body and soul for Christ to restore when we said 'I do' to Christ and our wives. They're owner and co-owner of us men. Our bodies belong to our wives." He paused and looked at Tony. "Do you want Him to keep the title to your soul when you die?"

"Yeah, of course," Tony replied.

Chris smiled and gazed upward toward the ceiling like a little boy falling in love for the first time. "We've all called His name while being intimate in the wrong ways with no shame or remorse. When we were having sex before we were married and even while some of us were married . . . ." Everyone glanced over at Bryan, who shamely looked away. "We enjoyed it in a sinful way as if God and the angels weren't watching. We should have the love of God so deep in us that we feel comfortable doing something so sacred without embarrassment, knowing that were being recorded. When we lay with our wives the way He intended for us to, we're doing nothing wrong. He made sex for marriage. You can't make love without God because God *is* love."

"I love God," Tony said, "but you must *really, really* love God. You went from being a borderline atheist not wanting anything to do with God to doing nothing, and I do mean absolutely nothing, without Him after hearing that. How can we get to love God that deeply?"

"By reading the bible, the whole bible," Chris responded. There was silence for a brief moment.

"I wish I would've never divorced my first wife," said Bryan. "God's probably going to punch me for some of the stupid things I've done. I'm almost scared to go to heaven."

"Well, don't feel bad. None of us in this room has the right to look over at you like we did earlier as if we've done better than you because we're still with our wives. Any man who thinks about a woman lustfully has done the same thing you've done. Our souls can't blame everything on our bodies when we stand before God. We're not the bodies we live in. That's why our thoughts are also judged." Silence interrupted their conversations for a moment again.

"If our thoughts are judged then there's nothing we can do to please God. Everyone has evil thoughts," said Tony.

"We can please Him by believing he came as a man and died for our sins. He's never given any gift to anyone who has tried to please Him by giving Him something or doing something for him that's better than the life long gift of the Holy Spirit to everyone who believes. We can't do anything greater to please him than simply believing in Him. His Holy Spirit will do the rest at different time periods in our lives.

"What a super, merciful, God," said Harold.

"I agree," Bryan responded.

"Me too. Lord how Mercy," Tony added.

"Did you ever find out what happens after we die?" Harold asked Chris.

"I found what I believe is the answer while reading the Bible this morning. To be absent from our body is to be present with the Lord. I'd have to get my Bible out of the truck and explain how the verse applies to us, I'll be right back," Chris said as he stood up.

"You don't have to prove it to me. I believe you. I don't understand the Bible and it probably would've taken me ten years to find that answer. Keep doing what your doing man. So many of us are lost and need God to send us pastors like you to help us out. You're about to take the hardest job in the world. Let God use you and don't give up man. You know how church folks can be. They're the reason we all stopped going to church," respond Harold.

"What saddens my heart the most is that I know over half of the people God sends me to preach to aren't going to believe anything I tell them. Jesus already knows who listened and chose to accept Him. He teaches in Mathew 7:13-14 that their will be more people entering the gates of Hell than there will be entering the narrow gate to heaven. There are a lot of people who think their going to heaven who will not make it. Satin uses preachers and people who don't know their not really Christians to accomplish his goal of deceiving probably over half of God's greatest creation," Chris paused. "If it were possible for a spaceship to land and take us all to heaven right now would ya'll get on board?"

"Because of the sin's I've committed. I'd be very afraid and ashamed to get on board…but I'd get on board," said Bryan.

"I'd get on board. We got to leave here anyway, right," Harold replied.

"Count me in. I'll miss this place though. What about you Chris?" Tony asked.

"I'm already homesick."

CHAPTER 24

Teaching the Truth in Nineveh

The week leading up to Chris's first sermon went by quickly. That Saturday night after dinner, Chris sat down at his desk and studied all the important points he wanted to address in his sermon.

"What should I call my first sermon?" he asked himself. "'Blessings and tithing and laws, oh my?' Nah, that's too childish. 'Is the Bible talking to you?' Hmm, that fits! It's exactly what I'm covering in my sermon. That just might work."

—

On Sunday morning as Chris sat in the pastor's study wearing jeans and a black polo style knit shirt preparing for his first sermon, deacons Russ Justice and Phillip Walker approached him with an under-the-table proposition dealing with the money flow in the church. They were trying to find out if he was going to give them a percentage of the tithe offerings as Reverend Apostle Prophet Edgars had done as a bonus for the pressure they put on the members who were not quite giving 10 percent of their paychecks. They had convinced ninety percent of the congregation to submit copies of their W-2 quarterly statements throughout the year.

"I'm Deacon Justice and this is Deacon Walker," said Deacon Justice as they both shook Chris's hand. "I know you're trying to prepare the morning message you're going to bless us with, so we're going to get straight to the point. We're the workhorses behind the tithe offering staying out of the red, and staying in the black letters"

"Uh-huh. Economic increase," Deacon Walker added.

"Our last pastor gave us these positions that have no title for business purposes. You understand what I'm saying, huh?" said Deacon Justice with a smile.

"Yeah. We collect the W-2's from the members to make sure they don't miss out on their blessings. You don't happen to have a copy of yours with you do you?" asked Deacon Walker.

"He's the preacher you idiot. He doesn't have to tithe. God pays him for working for Him with the tithe money. Why don't you think sometimes? Excuse him pastor. Sometimes the liquor he dranks on Saturday nights affect his judgment on Sunday mornings," explained Deacon Justice.

"I understand. This morning's sermon is going to be very interesting," said Chris. "It's going to be on that very subject. Y'all are about to be blessed on another level that's far past tithing."

"Oh, so you with the program already on this, then! I told you, Walker. What preacher don't like money?" Deacon Justice said as they both smiled and gave each other a fist bump. "So you found some new promises in the Bible that's bigger than tithing, huh?"

"Um, it's not quite what you're thinking," said Chris. "I like money, but I like the truth even more, which is why I'm preaching on how it's impossible for Gentiles to tithe today and how Gentiles never were instructed by God to tithe a certain percentage of our income."

"Yeah, preach it to 'em," said Deacon Walker. "Sermons like that give 'em giving fever up in here. That'll make 'em so thankful God gave 'em the gift of tithing that they'll give even more. That's where we come in. We've been getting compensated with the overages for our names being on the mortgage, so if you can rally 'em up and motivate 'em to really give today, we might be able to give you a little extra on the side from our portion. Know what we mean?"

"Well, I hope not because that would mean that they've been clinging to the wrong promises. I'm hoping that after my message, they'll stop giving to get a blessing and realize they're Gentiles and not required to tithe ten percent, but to give from their hearts. Giving to give is better than giving to get."

Deacon Justice nodded. "Yeah, we definitely don't want that. Make sure you tell it right 'cause there's no need in lying in church about . . . ." He paused, scratching his head with a puzzled look on his face. "Run that by Deacon Walker again; he missed the part where you said something about him being a Gentile."

"You, us, me, we're Gentiles," said Chris.

"I don't know what Bible you're reading, but we're Blackile servants of the Lord," Deacon Justice explained, making up a word resembling *Gentiles* to make himself sound knowledgeable. "We ain't Gentiles or Jews."

"There you go; that's my whole point," answered Chris. "Let's say that that were true. Depending on what passage you're referring to, you might or might not be the group of servants God was talking to or about. If he was talking to the Blackiles, then he was talking to the Blackiles; if he made a promise or gave a command to the Jews, then that's who he made a promise and gave a command to. We can't apply God's covenant with another group of people to our lives by picking and choosing the part of their promise we like and putting ourselves under their covenant with God. When it comes to promises in the Bible, beware of how you pick it, choose it, and try to use it because God might not have promised it to you," said Chris.

For a moment, there was total silence in the office.

"I don't know why, but after years of hearing the different arguments between different churches on why we should tithe or shouldn't tithe, for some reason the way you put that just makes too much sense," said Deacon Justice.

"So what do we do to be blessed if we can't tithe? It's impossible to be blessed without giving God His portion back to him." asked Deacon Walker.

"The same thing you were doing while you were tithing to receive a blessing," Chris replied.

"Deacon Walker don't get it," said Deacon Justice.

"I'm pretty sure you said a prayer requesting what you wanted and expected God to give you behind every tithe offering y'all gave, didn't you?" asked Chris.

A light bulb came on inside Deacon Walker's head. "You mean we've been getting blessed with the things we requested simply because we've been praying for them and not because we gave ten percent?" he asked.

"That's right," said Chris. "We've got the best promise given to any group of people in the Bible, the promise of prayer. More powerful than the tithe promise or any other promise you can put on a balance scale and weigh against it."

"This all just makes too much sense," said Deacon Justice.

"Now, of course, the promise of everlasting life outweighs the promise of prayer because prayer isn't required in eternity. We'll talk to God face to face, and our talks won't be about our problems because we won't have any problems in heaven."

"Wow, we've been deceived all our lives," said Deacon Justice.

"Nothing God created is more intelligent than Satan. It's as easy as breathing for him to trick us. Which promise would you choose now that your eyes have been opened to Satan's deceptive schemes using God's words to make Him look like a liar, The promise of tithing or the promise of prayer?" asked Chris.

"The promise of prayer," they both said almost simultaneously.

"The gift of speaking in tongue and prophesying, or the gift of prayer that enables you to speak directly to God yourself without going through Reverend Apostle Prophet Edgars to hear and speak to God?" They both looked at each other and replied again simultaneously.

"The gift of prayer."

Chris looked at the clock on the wall and then at his watch to see if it was displaying the correct time. "It's almost time for me to give my first sermon. If y'all don't mind, I'd like to pray and read over my notes one more time before I set out on my new journey."

"Oh, of course. We apologize. We didn't mean to interrupt. Come on, Walker. Let's give him time to change his clothes and finish studying his lesson," said Deacon Justice who didn't know that Chris had planned on wearing the Jeans and polo shirt he had on.

On the way out the door, Deacon Walker turned around and told Chris, "This sermon is definitely about to change lives. Just that little bit of truth has already changed mine." He paused. "Other than praying, tell me one thing I can do for God and I'll try my best to do it?"

"Do the one thing Jesus asked us to do in the New Testament after He died on the cross for our sins. Love one another."

"Thank you, Jesus. Thank you, Pastor, for telling me the truth," Deacon Walker said before leaving Chris alone to meditate and pray.

After saying a quick prayer and looking over the notes he had written for his sermon one last time, Chris pulled out his IPod and meditated while listening to "Found" by Hillsong. What he liked to call the Jesus love songs always calmed his nerves and helped him focus on a purpose greater than his own life. "Found" reminded him of himself. It described what he had felt when he discovered that every word of the Bible was true and that God really did love him. He knew now that preaching and leading people to Jesus was the reason he was created. His father and his father's father and a long list of relatives had worked as earthly angels of God. Chris had run from the voice he heard that no one else could hear for years until he'd finally surrendered to it. It hadn't mattered to God that Chris claimed not to love him in the past. The moment Pastor Sanders had talked Chris into letting his guard down; God was able to enter his heart and show him the purpose in which he had for his life.

Chris was almost in tears listening to "Found" when Deacon Walker burst into the office to give him a five-minute warning. He turned off his IPod and went out to preach his first sermon expecting to change lives instantly the way he had done with Deacon Walker and Deacon Justice, but, instead, he got the shock of his life. He had five other deacons and the whole congregation to persuade that they had been bamboozled all of their life. Rather than jumping for joy and shouting Hallelujah!, Thank you, Jesus! At being set free from the Old Testament laws that they tried to follow, most of the congregation were staring at him angrily or talking among themselves, possibly quoting Bible passages that they thought contradicted what Chris was saying. Apparently, they didn't understand his message and refused to believe the truth. Many members walked out after he quoted Galatians 3:10 and 3:25.

Embarrassed by their hostile reaction but determined to continue, Chris summed up the message of Galatians 3:10-14. "So here in these verses we see the people God had told to tithe being reminded of what the old law required to be saved before the death of Christ Jesus. Then the good news was given to them in verse 25 that states that after his death, they no longer needed to tithe or count on the laws to enter the kingdom of heaven. Continuing to tithe meant that they didn't believe that Jesus died for their sins. If God promised us that we will suffer and be tempted and deceived by Satan, then his promise is true and doesn't contradict any other promise he gave. The Bible is not a lie. If everyone in this congregation who claimed to be a Christian looked past their pride and told the truth if they were asked if they had ever been deceived by what they thought was in the Bible, and what they thought was meant by a certain verse, one hundred percent of them would say yes, they had been deceived at some point in their lives. Be deceived no more. If you are led by the spirit . . . in other words, if you've accepted Jesus, then you are not—are *not*—under the law according to Galatians 5:18."

The volume of the congregation's voices grew louder. Some of them were on their feet, shouting "Antichrist!" and "Blasphemer!" and even "Call the police!" The uproar in the congregation drowned out Chris's voice and compressed it as if it were a grenade exploding at the bottom of the ocean. Almost in tears, Chris eased out of the sanctuary and ran to the pastor's study to gather his things to run out of the heart of what Chris now thought of as the city of Nineveh.

CHAPTER 25

The Deacons' Challenge

Reaching the pastor's study, he put his head down on the desk and took a loud, deep breath. All the embarrassing words and names some of the members called him during his sermon echoed in his mind, not just labels like "blasphemer" and "Antichrist" but accusations like "He's trying to steal our blessings from us!" He lifted his head, let it fall backwards as far as it could go without detaching itself from his neck, and cried out to God, "Why have you sent me to Nineveh?" He bowed his head, bracing his elbows on his desk, and let his forehead rest on his hands. "Lord Jesus, I have loved sin longer than I've loved you. I don't deserve nor am I worthy to preach your word. Send someone else to this church." While he was praying silently, several of the deacons burst into the office.

"That sermon stunk worst than uncleaned chitlins boiling in a' unvented outhouse!" said Deacon Dexter Ross. God a'mighty! You slapping the hand of God, who's trying to pour out blessing and prosperity on this church!"

"What-in-the-hell do you think you're doing?" asked Deacon Ron McKinney, the only Caucasian deacon on the deacon board. "How we goin' t' pay the bills for the church and keep it running with you preaching mess like that, huh?"

"First of all I'm teaching, not preaching," Chris responded. "And, second, you can try testing God the same way you tested Him when you were blackmailing Him for His grace and mercy with His sheep at this church that you've been using for a ransom. People have gone out and bought new houses and fancy cars and put themselves in bondage because of this false promise. Nothing in the Bible says that God won't forgive the heads of this church for misunderstanding His Word, but it does say that He'll judge leaders of the churches on a level higher than those He didn't choose to teach His Word. I bet you He'll make a way to pour out his grace and mercy on this church and others just the same if y'all stop blackmailing Him and admit that our enemy Satan fooled us with our Father's words just like he did Adam and Eve and almost half of the angels who were already in heaven."

"In case you didn't know, some of us deacons have our names on the mortgage and the church bus and are cosigners on Reverend Apostle Prophet Edgars's house, cars and a lot of other investments he promised us we'd make a lot o' money on," Deacon McKinney said as he started charging around the left corner of Chris's desk. "Our credit is on the line here and you want to make jokes! We can't afford for them to stop tithing right now! I done invested too much money in this church for you to come mess things up!"

Deacon Ross and Deacon Mookie Moore grabbed Deacon McKinney and held him back.

Furious, Chris stood up to accept Deacon McKinney's challenge which wasn't much of a challenge at all. He was sixty-two year old with a lot less muscle than Chris. "God's word is not a joke!" he yelled back. "You and the whole congregation are missing the point behind God's message. I'm not telling them not to give money! If I'm a' teach the word of God, I'm a' try my best to teach it right. I'm not going to sit here and play with God's Word and use it against Him! I'm not fixing to teach anyone how to blackmail God by twisting his words around just 'cause other churches do it! I ain't misquoting the Bible for nobody, and I didn't come here to be persecuted, ridiculed, and chastised against! I came here to teach the true word of God!" said Chris who now knew how Reverend Apostle Prophet Joe Edgars probably felt when he went into his office and unintentionally criticized his sermons and almost got into a physical discussion.

"Let's all sit down and discuss this like godly men," Deacon Moore suggested as he and Deacon Ross released Deacon McKinney who decided to give Deacon Moore's suggestion a chance. "If this is true about tithing, why in the world have we not ever heard about it? This is the twenty-first century. We've believed in tithing all our lives, and now you come here with this new Bible trickery stuff that goes against what we believe in and you expect us to believe you?"

"You've been bamboozled," Chris explained. "Confusion is the name of Satan's game. We've all been Bible-whipped with manmade Bible politics. The majority of churchgoers I know had me believing things the Bible didn't say for years. We've been misunderstanding the truth by trying to make the Bible say what we want it to say and we've got to do better than this. If we think like a child when we read the Bible, we'll understand it. God wrote it for his children to understand. Humble yourself and think like a child. If one part of the Bible is a lie, then the whole book is a lie. If the floodgates of heaven don't open up and pour out blessings on everyone who tithes, it's because God never promised us they would. He was talking to His people, the Jews. We Gentiles were still considered dogs and hell-bound sinners throughout the Old Testament until later on when a New and better covenant was made; A covenant that included us. By including us, he showed everyone that he's not a respecter of persons. He could have saved one group of us, but instead, he offered freedom to everyone, no matter what they've done. But he didn't offer us His salvation plan during Old Testament times, nor did He offer to open the floodgates of heaven for us if we tithed during that time or any other time throughout the Bible."

"Bamboozled or not, you should've ran this by us first and gotten our approval before you decided to go changing and adding to what the Bible say and jeopardizing our credit. I don't see what it would hurt to not tell the congregation they don't have to tithe. We could've made the decision to tell them after we got the church paid off. It's got nothing to do with their salvation so let them keep doing it," said Deacon McKinney.

"It may be a business deal to you, but eternity is too long for me as a pastor to jeopardize earning a crown along with others who may want to hear the truth and earn one too. If this church listens to what God has for me to say, then you'll see God's love a whole lot deeper than you did when you were in the dark about His true words written in this book." Chris held up his Bible and pointed to it.

Deacon Banks and Deacon Wright burst into the office and closed the door on several members of the church who had pursued and questioned them as they made their way to the pastor's study.

Deacon Banks looked at Chris with a look of total shock on his face. "It's total chaos out there," he said.

Deacon Wright cruised in behind Deacon Banks, trying to sound nonchalant. "When Eve made the biggest mistake that we all suffer for today—hear me now," Deacon Wright leaned forward as if he were getting ready to do the robot with his back slanted at a forty-five-degree angle and his hands in the ready-set-go position. "I mean the biggest mistake ever," he said before transforming back into human mode with his finger pointing at Chris. "God looked at Eve like I'm looking at you right now and asked her what I'm fixin' to ask you now . . . what is this you've done?"

"Eve explained that she was deceived by the serpent who twisted the words around to confuse her just like he's still twisting them around on us today," responded Chris. "We all have been deceived the same way as Eve. It's time for us men to take responsibility for our actions today. We've failed just like Adam with the women God gave us to take care of because we've been deceived. Blame it on Adam for making the big mistake we suffer for today. Not Eve. God wasn't talking to her; he never commanded her to eat or not to eat any fruit."

Deacon Banks looked at Chris with a frown on his face. "You playin' with the Striptures now! Its woman's fault and don't say nothing no differ'nt"—Deacon Banks lowered his voice and began to whisper—"out loud and let these women at this church hear you say that."

"You just plain crazy. In church on a Sunday, letting them lies stink up this office," Deacon Wright added. "Why you think God punished Eve if He didn't care if she ate the apple?"

"Because she disobeyed her husband that God put in charge of her. She disobeyed God when she disobeyed her husband." responded Chris.

"What! Say it louder so people listening in from outside can hear you, boy. Speak up," said Deacon Banks.

"You should've said something 'bout' that in the microphone this morning," said Deacon Wright. "The women might not have liked it, but that would've been something all the men would've wanted to hear; that's how you earn favor from your congregation. You cuttin' off your own paycheck with what you talkin' 'bout with yo' preaching," said Deacon Wright.

"Let's go back to this New Testimony talk," said Deacon Banks. "If I didn't know no better, I'd think you was tryin' to say the Old Testimony don't mean nothin' to us Christians. Now that's what we most strictly go by 'round here. And what kinda preacher come to church on Sunday morning disrespecting the house of God by not wearin' a suit or a robe?" said Deacon Banks.

"Wearing your Sunday best to church is a made-up myth just like tithing; it's not in the bible. We're free to wear what we want. I can wear a suit or a robe once a month or not at all if I want to, a lot of things that are believed to be in the bible aren't in the bible or misinterpreted," Chris responded.

"That's another thang," said Deacon Wright. "You done proved to us that if a preacher gotta go to school to learn how to preach, then it ain't no way a school-taught preacher could a' been called to preach. That school done confused you. If you don't want your reputation ruined, you better fix this sermon next Sunday and stop preachin' on what you were taught in school and listen to what God is puttin' in yo' heart to preach," said Deacon Wright.

"I'm not gonna blackmail God by holding his sheep ransom with a ten percent fee for their freedom," said Chris. "And I'm not going to give the members of this church false hope and hold ten percent of their income for ransom on a misunderstood promise of a law that Jesus died to condemn, which tithing was apart of."

"So you telling me that adultery and murder is OK?" asked Deacon Moore.

"Absolutely not," Chris said, looking directly at Deacon Banks, who he felt was betraying him by not backing him up and somehow forgetting their discussion on tithing at his Memorial Day dinner. "God commanded us to love one another, and we can't even follow that one command. Adultery and murder and other big sins like those are part of the moral laws that taught us how to love one another. We learned how to love from the Old Testament. If you love God you won't fight your battles using murder and revenge." He paused briefly. "I tell you what. I'm going to pray that God shows this church the power of prayer and that He'll allow this church to pay off its debts so that we can help those in need. Just because everyone can't afford to get an education and get a high paying job doesn't mean that they should be punished. Help pay for college for the members who've helped pay the bills at this church. Get them on their feet and empower them with true biblical teachings on money and how to spend it frugally so that they can live and enjoy life. That's how much I believe in the promise of prayer God gave us."

"I sho' want to see how much more powerful prayer is in this economy than the power of tithing," Deacon McKinney said, laughing.

"I don't know what poirn't you trying to make, but I think we should give him a few more chances to preach and try to make his point, said Deacon Banks. "Let's do this. If we can read our Bibles and prove him wrong, then we'll never invite him back to preach. Oh, excuse me, Pastor Shoemaker. I mean teach the word of God here at this church. If we can't prove him wrong, then we'll invite him back to preach—sorry, bad habit—*teach* at our annual revival coming up in a couple of weeks. That is, of course, if you accept the offer?" Deacon Banks looked at Chris and winked.

"I accept," said Chris. "And just to add to that and get you all to read your Bibles, I challenge you to find me one contradiction in the Bible anywhere. I'll condemn myself to hell by cursing God for lying if you find one lie."

All the deacons leaned back and mumbled to each other.

"Either I've gone mad and crazy or I truly believe that what God says is true. The Bible is not a lie is the song I sing. Prove me wrong."

The deacons mumbled louder, discussing how crazy and foolish Chris was for making what they thought was a risky challenge. All the deacons believed in God, but they also believed that the Bible had lots of contradictions and some of it wasn't true. Reverend Apostle Prophet Joe Edgars had never preached from the book of Revelations. He had taught them that God was a good God and that the white man added Revelation to the end of the Bible to try to scare, govern, and keep evil people in line. In their minds, Chris was a hell-bound soul for the challenge he had made.

"All in favor say aye," said Deacon Banks.

All the deacons said, "Aye."

"Looks like the ayes have it. We'll inform Deacon Justice and Deacon Walker of this later on. In the meanwhile, can you help us by writing down all the Bible verses that you think prove that we don't have to tithe or give us some literature defending your view on us Gentiles never being given a command to tithe?" Deacon Banks winked at Chris again and gave him a quick smile without anyone noticing.

Chris smiled back, knowing that Deacon Banks was still on his side. He pulled a copy of his father's essay on tithing, the same essay that he and Deacon Banks had discussed on Memorial Day, out of his briefcase and handed it to Deacon Banks, who gave Chris a nod of agreement.

"We'll see y'all direckly," said Deacon Banks. "We better get outta here before he change his mind."

"That was an easy way to run him off," responded Deacon Ross. "We've been tithing all our lives. He think we don't know what we doing or something. Humph. I guess we won't be seeing him anymore after we prove him wrong."

All the deacons began to leave the office. Deacon Banks was the last one to go. He turned around after letting the other deacons get a few steps ahead of him and went back in the office to talk to Chris.

"I love it when a plan comes together. Here's your copy back. I already have copies made to give 'em. This church needs a lot of teaching, doesn't it? The motivational preaching just hasn't been working."

"Not just this church but all churches," answered Chris. "The Bible is not a lie. Satan is the master of deception. He's been using churches throughout the world and God's Word right up under our noses as one of his better weapons for deceiving all mankind."

"I see that now thanks to you. God can easily answer your prayer for this church by placing you as pastor here and I pray that he does. If you'll take eighty-five thousand dollars a year until the church's debt is paid off and guide the church into spending the leftover from what we were paying Reverend Joe Edgars wisely, and for God's purpose, you and I both know He'll still provide you the desires of your heart. You might know how to handle understanding the Bible, but I got you when it comes to handling church folks. Let me handle these deacons for you. They'll eventually get it."

Chris walked out to his car thinking about Deacon Banks suggestion to consider becoming pastor of their church.

Angel and the kids were already loaded up in the car waiting for him.

Chris got in the car, took a deep breath, and exhaled hard enough to push their car backwards. "Well that didn't go anything like I thought it would. I don't understand why people don't want to hear the truth," he told Angel.

"I'm proud of you, Chris," Angel said as she reached her left hand around his neck to give him a hug. "You've come a long way as far as loving God. Seeing Him work in you has changed me and my love for Him. I know you want to cry because you feel like you let God down somehow by not convincing them of His truth. I'm a part of you . . . I feel it. I feel your disappointment, and I can't help but cry for you." Angel's eyes began to mist up. "I know it's very disappointing when you try to help people out of love and they do you like this. Correcting confused Christians is hard. I know we have the free will to choose to do many different things, but I understand that this is not your choice. God needs, and has chosen you. I know He's using your voice to spread the Word of his amazing love for us.

We didn't get it at first, either, remember? Give them time and pray about it. God's spirit will show them that you're telling the truth."

CHAPTER 26

Mr. Stewart's Surprise

The next morning; In search of good news to make him feel better after the chastising and persecution he'd suffered at True Saints church on Sunday, Chris pushed the button to open the door of the detached garage to get his bike. He fanned himself with his right hand and quickly changed his mind before the garage door finished opening.

"I think you'd better drive; it's too hot to ride in this heat," he said to himself. As he climbed into his Toyota Tundra, he was so preoccupied that he didn't even notice his '69 Camaro was not in the garage.

A few minutes later, Chris rang the doorbell to Mr. Stewart's house. A ten-inch monitor appeared inside the glass of the front door showing Mr. Stewart standing in his huge garage with dozens of antique cars and trucks gleaming under fluorescent lights behind him.

"I'm back here in my storage house," said Mr. Stewart. "Come through the gate I just turned the switch off, it's unlocked. I'll be standing outside the door." Slowly the monitor faded away, leaving no trace of existence inside the glass that concealed it. Chris put his face two inches from the glass, stepped back, and touched it with the tip of his finger. The new age technology was impressive, but Chris was more impressed with the vintage cars and trucks he had seen gleaming behind Mr. Stewart on the monitor. Chris quickly walked through the gate and to the back of Mr. Stewart's huge twelve thousand square foot home. He was overly excited to see all the antique cars and trucks in what Mr. Stewart called his storage house.

"I didn't know you liked old cars," said Chris. I've never seen you drive any of these beauties. About how many do you have here?"

"About thirty six I think. I can't even remember, I've been in and out of the hospital fighting this cancer since you moved into this neighborhood is why you hadn't seen me driving them. It looks like I'm not going to win," said Mr. Stewart.

Chris's excitement level plummeted to the ground and crawled under his feet as he tried to show compassion for Mr. Stewart's very serious situation. "I came by last week like you asked to get that good news you said you had for me that was better than me getting my job back," Chris said, "but you must not have been feeling to well,"

"Yeah. I wasn't feeling too good, so I went to the hospital and they kept me there a few days," said Mr. Stewart.

"Looks like we both have good news to share with one another. Since the news I have for you is more important, I'll go first." Chris looked toward heaven and breathed in deeply to clear away the lump that had risen in his throat at the thought of Mr. Stewart's situation. Gathering his composure he prepared to give Mr. Stewart, whose life story was near the end of its final chapter, some extremely good news. Chris was almost certain that Mr. Stewart wouldn't react like the True Saints Church Members, who had damned him to hell for sharing what he knew to be biblical truth.

"Have you ever heard the controversy on being absent from our body, present with the Lord?"

"No, I've never heard about that. I haven't waste a lot of time reading the Bible and going to church to be swindled out of my money."

Chris gave a confused shrug and kept talking. "OK . . . . Well, anyway, my dad had began studying and writing a sermon on what really happens after we leave this world. It was dated close to the time that he committed suicide and he never finished it." Chris paused and looked over at Mr. Stewart who's shoulders had began to shake rapidly. He then buried his face in his hands and covered it as he began to cry. "You're going to make me cry," Chris said as he quickly looked away from Mr. Stewart to stop himself from crying along with him. "But it's hard for me to cry tears of sadness now that I know the answer to the end of my dad's sermon he never got to preach. I found out the other morning while reading the Bible the truth behind this controversy. What made this so controversial is that nowhere in the Bible does it say that God promised us that when we are absent from our bodies, we're present with Him. Paul was expressing his desire to be absent from his body and present with the Lord. But the good news is, when Jesus died on the Cross—" Chris felt his heart pounding with excitement at the words. "When Jesus died on the cross, everything changed—every ceremonial practice, every law it took to obey to get into heaven, everything. He took control of death, Hades, the universe in which the fallen angels live. You name it; he took control of it. Old Testament believers who died before Jesus died on the Cross didn't die and go to heaven. Not one of them obeyed all the laws and commandments it took to get to heaven, but some of them believed that a savior was coming. It says in Luke 16:26 that their souls were being held in a pleasant, temporary heaven that was located in the center of the earth, separated by a 'Great Chasm' from the temporary holding place for those who didn't believe; Which is why for years it's been taught that hell is in the center of the earth. But the bible doesn't say were the permanent hell is…it may not be created yet or it could be on a burning star in outer space—but anyway. I found the answer in Ephesians 4. It fits what was said about how Jesus descended into the earth; then ascended into heaven. He took captive of the Old Testament souls who lived under the Old Testament laws and lead them in his train to heaven after He died. The believers' souls were held captive by death until Jesus died and took control over death. Do you know what that means?" Chris asked.

"What?" said Mr. Stewart as he wiped away his tears.

"Absent from the body, is to be present with the Lord," Chris said, smiling broadly and holding his hands out with his palms up in front of him. "All souls of believers in the Old and New Testament are instantly in the Lord God's possession when they die now. No more temporary heaven."

"I doubt that my soul is going to heaven," Mr. Stewart said. "I don't believe God's; going to let me in heaven to enjoy eternity with the people I sinned against."

"My dad's in heaven right now," Chris said, too excited by his message to take Mr. Stewart's remark seriously. "To know that he's with God Almighty and that you're going to be with God is the best news that can ever be reported to anyone here on earth."

Mr. Stewart began to get nervous and fidgety as Chris talked about his father and death, squeezing his eyes closed and hyperventilating.

"Mr. Stewart, you're going to heaven," Chris reassured him. "It doesn't matter what you did. You're forgiven simply because you believe. You do, believe don't you?"

Just as Mr. Stewart was about to speak, he quickly turned to his left side and began to vomit.

"Are you all right?"

"Can I get you something?" Chris asked, but Mr. Stewart was still trying to catch his breath and couldn't answer. Chris looked around the huge storage garage for a chair. Spotting a golf cart, he put Mr. Stewart's right arm around his shoulder and led him to the golf cart to sit and recuperate from his vomiting spell. Chris helped him onto the passenger side before climbing into the driver's seat next to him.

"Want me to drive you to the back door so you can go in and lay down for a minute?"

"Naw, I'm OK." There was a pause. "Drive down there and make a left by that black '57 Chevy. I want to show you something."

After rounding the corner, Chris drove the golf cart as fast as he could towards the end of the isle when he saw four of the most beautiful '69 Camaros he had ever seen parked side by side in front of him. He jumped off the cart before it came to a complete stop and stood with his mouth opened wide.

Mr. Stewart stayed seated on the golf cart with a sad look on his face. "I knew you'd like them. I passed your house one day and saw yours sitting in the garage."

"Sixty-nine Camaros are the baddest cars ever made," Chris replied. He turned around and looked at Mr. Stewart with an astonished expression. "This is the good news you had for me, isn't it? You're gonna let me pick one, aren't you?" The excitement Chris had buried under his feet earlier to be sympathetic to Mr. Stewart's situation had somehow escaped and displayed itself in his body language. An awkward feeling came over him. He felt that he was being rude for showing excitement over the possibly of getting the car of his dreams through Mr. Stewart's death, but he couldn't help the desire that came over him. For a short moment, his passion and love for old cars outweighed his compassion for Mr. Stewart, who was dying and preparing to leave everything he had on earth behind. A small voice inside his head spoke to him. "None of this stuff will ever be his again once he's gone. Shoot, I might as well take it and enjoy it while I'm here. Somebody's gonna get it; it might as well be me."

"Well, you're kind of right, but not quite. The news I have is better than getting all four of those Camaros. Let's go inside so I can give you the good news.

"Man, you need to stop playing. I know you're just messing with me now."

"I'm running out of time. Let's go inside. I'll tell you the secret to my success— and give it to you before I change my mind."

Mr. Stewart showed Chris around several rooms of his home before stopping to rest in the gun collection room. He sat down at a table he used to clean his guns and massaged the top of his shaved head. Then he began to tinker with a gun holder mounted toward the end of the three-by-five-foot table. There was a stack of papers, titles, and deeds on the center of the table with a pair of white gloves on top of them.

"Check out my gun collection. Here, put these on," said Mr. Stewart as he got up to give Chris the white gloves and to unlock several glass display cabinets that housed his guns. Chris put on the gloves and handled each gun Mr. Stewart handed to him very carefully. They looked at several shotguns, assault rifles, and handguns before Mr. Stewart handed him a particularly large revolver. "Now this one here is the 6.5-inch Smith and Wesson 500. The 357 model is a BB gun compared to this one."

"It's heavy," said Chris after grabbing it from Mr. Stewart.

"Tell me about it. I sat in here drunk many nights for hours holding that heavy thing pointed to my head. Evil as I am, I couldn't ever get the courage to do to myself what I done to someone else."

It took Chris about three seconds to process what Mr. Stewart had said. The colors on the wall and the lighting seemed to have darkened when Mr. Stewarts comment finally registered in his brain. Chris took four steps backwards and blurted out, "What!" Trying to think logically and rule out the possibility that Mr. Stewart was talking about murder, Chris released the tension in his muscles by moving his head from side to side and wiggling his left arm and tried to assure Mr. Stewart that whatever he had done could be forgiven by God. "You don't have to beat up on yourself. You're no more evil than anyone who claims to be holy. God doesn't punish soldiers who take a life in war."

"I've never been in the military, and I don't believe God's going to forgive me and put me in the same heaven as the man I murdered . . . and took away from his wife and kid," said Mr. Stewart.

Chris put his mind into overdrive as he tried to stay calm and think of an excuse to get him out of Mr. Stewart's house without running full speed through the first window he saw.

"If you knew what I did, you'd empty that clip out on me right now, which is what I hope you'll do before you leave here today," said Mr. Stewart. "I'm dying. I'm in more pain mentally than I am physically because of what I did. You're the only one I know, with the best reason in the world to help me die."

"I don't know why you're telling me your deathbed secrets, but you're really making me nervous. I'm going to walk out of here, OK? And I'm going to put this pistol in your mailbox 'cause I'm afraid that if I give it to you now, you might shoot me with it. There's nothing you can do or say to me that's worth me killing you for."

Chris began to walk away. Just as he walked through the doorway and made it a few feet down the hall, Mr. Stewart spoke loudly to get his attention. "It wasn't until I saw you being interviewed for that sales position that I started feeling remorseful. You and your mom were all your dad ever talked about."

Chris came back and stood in the doorway. All he'd had of his father most of his life were personal thoughts and memories. He couldn't resist the temptation to hear more about the father he'd never fully gotten to know. His desire to know his father even though he was gone was like the strong desire that true believers in God feel that causes them to seek after the love of their father whom they've never seen.

Mr. Stewart continued talking. "I've willed the company this house, my investments—everything—to you. It's yours. I know you'll do right by your mother if she regains her sanity and makes it out of that hospital. If you change your mind and decide to shoot me, I can show you how to make it look like I committed suicide so you don't go to jail."

"I don't understand. Why would you will all your possessions to me?" Chris asked.

"Because I made it look like a suicide."

"Made what look like a suicide?" Chris asked.

"Your father's death."

Startled, angry, and confused, Chris didn't know how to react to Mr. Stewart's confession. He flinched and dropped the pistol on the floor. He felt an instant pain in his stomach, legs, and chest. Even though his father had been dead for eighteen-years, the shocking news hit him as if it had just happened that moment. Chris dropped to his knees. With all his power, he reached over and struggled to pick up the gun. He held his stomach with his left forearm and struggled to lift up the huge revolver that seemed to weigh as much as he did to release his pain by firing several bullets into Mr. Stewart.

"You . . . ," he said, breathing heavily. "Did you kill my daddy, or are you pissing me off so I can help you die?" Chris asked.

"It wasn't a coincidence that I won Arkansas biggest lottery a few days after they said your dad committed suicide. While they were having choir practice that night, I went in the sanctuary to let Tom, the choir director, know that I had finished my janitorial work early and asked him if he could lock up for me. I left the back door unlocked and left through the front door. I walked around, came back in through the back door, and hid in a closet near the back door that had an offset hallway with no motion detector covering it with my ski mask on until they all left. The economy was bad like it is now. A lot of my clients were cutting back and I had lost several of my janitorial service contracts. Stealing had become my only option to survive.

"After Tom set the alarm, I deactivated it from the keypad at the back door. I went in your dad's office, started searching through his desk, and found a recently purchased lottery ticket. I'd heard on the news the day before that the winning ticket was purchased at a local gas station near his neighborhood. I turned on the computer to check the ticket, but before I could log on to the Internet, I heard your dad come into the church. I put the ticket in a drawer and ran across the hall to hide in the other the closet near his office. I realized I hadn't closed and locked the door and I hadn't put the ticket back in the right drawer, but it was too late. He noticed it, but I guess he thought nothing of it.

"While I waited in the closet for him to leave, I heard him yelling, saying he'd won the lottery. Something came over me and my plans to steal only a few things changed. At first, I planned on making a noise to get him out of the office, snatch the ticket out of his hand, or grab it off the desk and run, but I knew that wouldn't work. He would've known it was me when I cashed the ticket in and saw me on the news. So I knew what I had to do if I wanted that money.

"I snuck up behind him with a hammer from the closet and knocked him out. With a rag, I took his gun and made sure there were no signs that he'd been hit with a blunt object in the back of his head. I took his ticket and put mine in his pocket just in case he'd told someone he had gone to the church to get his lotto ticket. Before I knew it, that evil feeling that took over me was gone. I had done something that I thought I'd never do. It was all over. I'd staged everything perfectly to make it look like a suicide. It worked.

"After I got home, I realized I'd made two mistakes. After checking to make sure your dad hadn't signed the back of his ticket, I remembered that I'd signed the back of mine like I always did and thought I had messed up, but apparently, no one looked at it. I waited nervously for months for them to check with everyone who had keys and alarm pass codes to the church. I guess they figured your dad had taken the alarm off stay mode so someone could come in and find him. They never thought to question people who knew the alarm code. If they had, they would've probably caught me."

Still not certain whether Mr. Stewart's confession was true, Chris stood in the doorway tapping the barrel of the gun on the side of his right leg. He raised his left hand, opened his mouth, and tried to speak, but his words came out sounding as if he was choking or having convulsions. Suddenly, Chris closed his eyes, pointed the gun toward Mr. Stewart and fired two shots. He lowered the gun down by his waist and walked toward Mr. Stewart.

"Are you trying to tell me you killed my father?" Chris said with his teeth gritted together. He unloaded the rest of the bullets from the gun by firing them into the wall behind Mr. Stewart as he walked toward him. After hearing nothing but clicking sounds coming from the gun, Chris slammed the butt end of the pistol into the glass gun-display cabinet Mr. Stewart was standing beside, shattering it and cutting Chris's arm badly. Still in a rage, Chris grabbed Mr. Stewart by the throat with his left hand and pushed him up against the glass display cabinets. In a circular motion, Chris swung the butt end of the gun over his head and struck Mr. Stewart on the top of his bald head, jarring his teeth and his brain. He let go of the gun, sending it flying in back of him as he swung his fist into Mr. Stewart's mouth, knocking out three of his teeth and cracking the more durable tempered glass installed on the display cabinets mounted against the wall that Mr. Stewarts head was knocked into. Chris let go of Mr. Stewart's neck and stepped back to hit him again with his right hand but missed because Mr. Stewart had fallen to Chris's left. Chris stood over him and saw that he was unconscious.

"Wake up so I can see your eyes while you die!" Chris yelled in a strained voice as he began to choke Mr. Stewart with both hands. "You killed my father!"

Mr. Stewart woke up and grabbed Chris's arm's out of his natural self-protective instinct but stopped resisting seconds later when he realized that Chris was choking him to death, which was what he wanted.

"I suffered for years thinking that my father didn't love me because of you!"

Suddenly, Chris heard a voice reminding him that he was a child of God.

"You're a Christian—everlasting child of God." The voice said. Chris stopped choking Mr. Stewart, got up, and walked outside. Taking off his black T-shirt, he wrapped it around the cut on his arm and wiped the blood on his hands onto the white T-shirt he wore underneath the black one. With his fist clenched and his heart full of anger, he turned around and began walking back toward the house with the intent of honoring Mr. Stewart's wishes. On his seventh step, he heard the voice reminding him again of who he was. It was as if an invisible hand had reached out and stopped him in his tracks. He staggered forward, then took a few steps backwards and began to vomit.

CHAPTER 27

Ruining a Perfect Dream

Chris called the police as soon as he got home and told a detective about Mr. Stewart's confession. His cell phone rang while he was in the middle of reporting the incident and he let it switch over to voice mail. After being informed by the detective that the lottery ticket and all other evidence had not been kept or even looked at eighteen-years earlier because his father's death had been ruled a clear case of suicide, Chris slammed down the phone. Gripping it in his hands, he commenced to choke it before finally slamming it to the floor where it shattered into pieces. He sat down and tried to calm himself. Moments later, he checked his voice mail and listened to the message that Tony had left for him while he was on the phone with the police. "Chris! Bryan was telling the truth. I just passed Angel on the freeway driving some dude's '69 Camaro. I'm following them right now to find out where he lives. I'll call you when they get to his house.'

Mr. Stewart's confession and Tony's message sent Chris into a whirlwind of confusion. High at the top of his closet was a box of things he'd promised himself he was going to conquer and let go. Nervously shaking as he pulled the box down, he grabbed his father's obituary and a bottle of his favorite brand of whiskey that he'd sworn he'd never drink again and placed it on the countertop in his master bathroom where he and Angel had separate closets. He cleaned himself up, changed his clothes, and put a tourniquet on his wound before going to the great room and sitting on the couch.

With his father's obituary in one hand and the bottle of whiskey in the other, Chris had a private funeral for his father. The news that Mr. Stewart had promised to be good news really was good news because it meant that his father hadn't committed suicide and left his loved ones behind to suffer the way Chris had thought he had for eighteen-years. He began to miss him even more as he stared at his father's obituary picture. Finally, he no longer struggled with wondering if his father had lied to him when he said he loved him. With whiskey, he began to medicate one of several thorns in his side from his past that had finally been removed with Mr. Stewart's confession.

Feeling a slight buzz from the whiskey, Chris stretched out on the couch with his father's obituary on his chest and fell asleep. Fifteen minutes later, he felt someone shaking him and woke up to see Angel standing in front of him with a huge smile on her face.

"Come on. I have a big surprise for you outside," she said as she grabbed him by the hand and pulled him off the couch.

"Oops, I'm sorry," she said, laughing as she grabbed both his hands and helped him off the floor. Still smiling and very excited when Chris stood up, she hugged him tightly and gave him a kiss, but the smell of alcohol vanquished her excitement and her smile almost instantly.

"Of all the days you've been laid off, you choose to get drunk today. You've been doing so good. Why are you drinking, and what happened to your arm?"

"You didn't go to work today, that's why. Mm-hm. You thought you were hid, didn't ya? Don't worry 'bout my arm, acting like you care. I'm not your servant anymore," said a partially drunk Chris.

"How do you know I didn't go to work today?"

"Don't worry about how I know!"

"Calm down, Chris. It's been hard keeping this a secret, but today's the day I don't have to continue hiding anymore." Angel began to smile. "I think I know how you found out. Tony's outside talking to who you think is my mystery man right now." Angel began to laugh.

"Oh, you got the nerve to bring him home to meet me! After all that I've been through today! You and your little home wrecker picked the wrong day to come out the closet on me." Chris charged toward the garage door intending to fight the man he thought was Angel's new boyfriend, but Angel turned him around by grabbing his arm.

"No, of course not, I was test-driving your Camaro for you. Did he tell you a film crew was filming us while I was driving? Don't go out there and embarrass us."

"How did you test-drive my car when it's out in the garage with at least seven months of restoration work needing to be done to it?" Chris asked.

"That TV show you watch that restores old cars in a week chose my story I wrote on why my husband deserved free help with restoring his old car. This was all perfect; you didn't even know your car was missing for a week. Well, surprise. I hope you're happy."

"I can't be happy. I just found out that Willie Stewart killed my dad."

"What? Your dad's been dead for over seventeen years. I'm going to have to call this off. You've ruined it; you're drunk. How's it gonna look for a preacher to be on TV drunk?"

"I'm not drunk. He told me today; he killed my father for a winning lottery ticket. That was the good news he had to tell me that I was telling you about."

Angel hugged Chris and led him to the couch, signaling to him to sit down.

"I'm going to see if they can't film this another time or just cancel the filming part."

Before Angel could finish talking, Tony burst into their home excitedly. "Man, they hooked you up! You got a blinging pearl blue paint job with chromed twenties on the back and eighteens on the front. The engine compartment is cleaner than the outside with a picture of a big lion roaring on a custom made air filter cover and a 572 big block engine sittin' in it looking prettier than all the women in the world put together." Tony took a breath and glanced from Angel to Chris. "Except for your wife—oh! And my wife too. Ain't nothing prettier than our wives."

Tony turned his head to the side so Angel couldn't see his right eye and winked it a couple of times at Chris. After noticing that Chris wasn't smiling, Tony realized that something was wrong.

Angel explained to Tony how Chris had just found out how his father had really died. After Angel explained to the producers of the TV show that her husband had just received shocking news and was in no condition to appear on TV, they decided to skip the filming and parked Chris's car in the garage for him to drive another day.

CHAPTER 28

Confronting the Deacons

It was a very busy week for the deacons at True Saints Baptist Church. Revival week was right around the corner, and they were still without a head pastor. Instead of reading the Bible for themselves to find something untrue that would get Chris out of the head pastor pool and send him to hell, they all called around to different churches of other denominations who had different believes than that of their own in search of an untrue statement written in the Bible.

It was also a busy week for Chris. Early Tuesday morning, Mr. Stewart had turned himself in and confessed to murdering Chris's father eighteen years ago. He gave police specific details on how he had made the murder look like a suicide as evidence that he wasn't inventing his confession. Before he made his confession, Mr. Stewart had signed everything he owned over to Chris.

Now Chris was busy signing and accepting the titles for thirty-six antique cars and trucks and doing the paperwork to take possession of his new aircraft company, business investments, and twelve-thousand-square-foot home, but he couldn't bring himself to move his family into a house that had belonged to his father's murderer. He and Angel had decided to remain where they were. Mr. Stewart's confession to the police had put Chris in a fairly good mood. All the money he had received, along with ownership of the new house, company, and cars that Mr. Stewart had signed over to him contributed somewhat to his happiness, but finding that his father didn't committed suicide brought him the most joy. In a weird way, Chris was relieved that his father had been murdered rather than thinking he had committed suicide. Mr. Stewart's confession helped him to understand the confusing questions he asked himself for years of how someone as knowledgeable as his dad was of the Bible could commit suicide and purposely leave his family that he said he loved.

—

On Wednesday evening before Bible study began, all the deacons gathered together for a meeting to compare Scriptures they had found that they believed were untrue. After putting all of their findings together, they all agreed that Deacon Ross had found hardcore proof of a lie that Jesus Himself had spoken.

"If you will, call Pastor Shoemaker and see if he can meet us tomorrow before choir practice, Deacon Banks. And don't you dare tell him we found something untrue in the Bible. We want to see what a man's face look like right at the moment he discovers he's going to hell," said Deacon McKinney.

All the deacons snickered except Deacon Banks.

Deacon Ross, who sat next to Deacon Banks, elbowed him and told him, "We got that know-it-all now, don't we?" He snickered again.

"Sho' do, sho' do . . . and so does the devil," said Deacon McKinney. "It don't pay to be a know-it-all."

Deacon Banks contact Chris that Wednesday night and set up the meeting. Thursday evening before choir practice, all the deacons had gathered in the conference room and made jokes about Chris's salvation as they waited for him to arrive. They were confident, that they had found several things that were not true written in the bible.

"We oughta write up a fake contract and call it a soul contract for the devil and put it on the table," said Deacon Ross.

"Yeah, good idea. And put a knife on top of the contract so he can cut his finger and sign his name in blood. Here, I got one," Deacon McKinney added. He pulled out his pocketknife and slid it to Deacon Ross, who then wrote his fake contract idea on a piece of paper.

"Maybe we should let him sturdy what we come up with for a few days before we jump to conclusions, said Deacon Banks. I mean, he showed us some stuff we thought for twenty, thirty, and even fifty years was true that wasn't true." He pointed to several deacons as he spoke to emphasize the age difference between them. "We should at least consider that we might be misunderstanding the Bible. More importantly, if we have found something wrong, then not only is Pastor Shoemaker going to hell, but we all goin' t' be there with him if God told a lie. I'm starting to see the poirn't he's trying to make. What're we gonna do if y'all are right and God lied? Can we trust that He really forgave us for our sins?"

"Shut up! Just shut up!" said Deacon McKinney. "Don't start feeling sorry for Pastor Shoemaker. This is something he's doing to hisself. You can keep letting him play with your mind and confuse you if you want to, but we goin' t' stick to what the Bible say. I don't even know why we're wasting our time fooling around with him and his false teachings in the first place."

"Well, you know the old saying: If you can't beat 'em, join 'em," said Deacon Banks. "If we can't prove him wrong, then maybe we're the ones that are wrong and have been wrong along with past generations for over two thousand years on a lot of bible related believes."

"You're right," said Deacon Walker. "So much of what he's been saying just makes too much sense. For instance, I never paid any attention to the fact that I prayed about everything that I thought I got from tithing. How is God going to spend the trillions of dollars he gets from all the churches that tithe throughout the whole world? If God was getting all that money, it wouldn't be any hunger, homelessness or any of that."

"If you can't prove him wrong then join him, you say," said Deacon Ross. "Evidently, this theory has been proven wrong for thousands of years and that's why we've never heard of all this new stuff he's talking about. Majority rules, Brother Banks. I bet you there are more churches still practicing and believing in tithing today than there are churches that don't believe in its power. So how is it that our interpretation is wrong and his new interpretation is right?"

"All I know is that tithing contradicts a lot of—"

"Sh, sh. Let's stop talkin' 'bout how good heaven and a glass of cold water is, Chris is here; we don't want to drive him mad talking about things he's never going to get." said Deacon McKinney who restarted the salvation jokes.

Chris, who was standing in the doorway, laughed at Deacon McKinney's joke. "Thank God He's going to wipe certain parts of my memory away," he said. "If He didn't, then you're right. It would drive me mad to know y'all didn't make it to heaven after I told you over and over again how easy it was to get there. I wouldn't be able to enjoy one glass of water from the River of Life knowing you all would never be able to drink water again. If one doesn't believe that the bible is one hundred percent true with no contradictions, can he who claims to be a Christian—truly believe in God." He walked toward one of two empty chairs in the room. "I do apologize for being late. Truth is, I'm nervous and scared to death that one of you found something untrue that's going to prove once and for all that God is a liar." He paused as he sat down. "What's this?" he asked as he looked at the pocketknife and contract lying on the table in front of him.

"Let's just say before you read and sign that, be sure to get you one last ice cold glass of water and enjoy it for as long as you walk the face of this earth," said Deacon McKinney with a smug expression.

"Yeah. Drink up," Deacon Ross snickered.

"Oh, I get it," said Chris. "You must have found something that you think is a lie and contradicting in the Bible. Go ahead and condemn me. Let's hear it!"

"Did Jesus lie when he told the thief on the cross that he would see him in paradise?" Deacon McKinney asked.

"Absolutely not," Chris answered. "He can't lie. He's holy and true."

"Then save your soul and explain why he told the thief next to him that he'd see him in paradise on the day they both were crucified when he himself didn't go into paradise until over a month later?"

"Oh, my, my, my, Jesus! How could you not dot your I's and cross your T's?" Chris put his hands on top of his head and pretended to have agonizing thoughts of going to hell. "What's happening to me? It's so hot, it's so hot where I'm not going, I just don't know what I'm goin' t' do." Chris began to laugh. "I thought I'd mess with you since you're messin' with me. You are just kidding, right? That really wasn't what you came up with, is it?"

"Yeah, it is."

"Well, I'd better get serious and stop playing around and try to explain this, then." Chris cleared his throat and began to explain. "What we need to ask ourselves on a question like this that seems to be contradicting to earthly time and understanding is what God can do and where and when He lives. This is a good question for learning, Deacon McKinney; I'm glad you asked it. Now, when Jesus died, his soul entered into eternity, would you all concur?"

"Yeah, we agree with that," all the deacons said. There was a moment of silence as they all sat there staring at Chris.

"Well, finish explaining," ordered Deacon Ross.

"Y'all said you all agreed," said Chris. "I thought I was done."

"What kind of ridiculous answer is that?" Deacon McKinney responded.

"Eternity is outside of space and time. We live in space and time. The thief left this earth that same day with Jesus. The Bible says that one day with Jesus is like a thousand years. So it doesn't matter if Jesus hung around inside our space and time for forty days or one hundred days. Both his days and the thief's days never ended after they died on the cross. They were no longer human. The thief became what we'll become when we die. Everlasting, none sleeping, children of God who's day in his presents, will never end. There's no such thing as evening and night in eternity, is there?"

"Sho' ain't, according to the Word," Deacon Banks blurted out. "We'll never need to sleep."

"Time doesn't exist in eternity. One thousand years is a metaphor to show an example of how completely different time would be if it exist in eternity. When He told the thief he would be in paradise with him that day, He told the truth. The Bible is not a lie. Jesus has already seen and lived with us in our past, our present, and our future. Even after seeing every sin we committed, He sweat blood as he saw the sinful faces of everyone who has ever been created—He saw every sin we committed and still He died."

Silence burst into the room and interrupted their meeting again for a moment until Deacon Walker broke the silence and forced it out of the room. "Is it me, or is this stuff making sense for some reason?"

Deacon McKinney leaned inward toward the center of the conference table and looked over at Deacon Walker until he got his attention. Out of the corner of his eye, Deacon Walker could see Deacon McKinney tapping on his forehead signaling for him not to let Chris play with his mind.

"Not so fast. There's more than just this one contradiction in the Bible," said Deacon Ross. "To be fair, I think we should be allowed to run a couple more by you," said Deacon Ross.

"There are no contradictions in the Bible; contradictions are misunderstandings on our part, not God's," said Chris. "With that being said, run another misunderstanding by me and let's see if we can figure it out."

"You're right, you're right," admitted Deacon Ross. "Contradictions more than likely come from us misunderstanding what God said. For instance, you might not have read or maybe you misunderstood this passage here in Hebrews 7:10 that talks about the Levite priesthood being passed down to their descendants. This is how King Melchizedek became high priest forever. Abraham tithe to him before tithing began and this is why we are to still tithe today."

"What I don't know, I will study. I'm no smarter than any of you. This is elementary-level Bible learning. I believe God has sent me here to graduate this congregation from kindergarten to elementary school because you love Him dearly and you want to serve Him with all your heart. None of us will ever reach the college level of understanding God until heaven comes. He knows you've been taken advantage of for a large portion of your life just like I have. Not many who misinterpreted these contradictions to us did it on purpose. This is Satan's work, and now we know what it would be like if he was our god. What kind of god is a god that you can't trust? God wants to bring you out of darkness so you can see how awesome and amazing His love is. When it finally hits you as to what the Cross really means and what it changed, you'll never worry about getting a blessing here on earth again. All that God gives through Jesus is free of charge. It doesn't cost you anything to love Jesus, but it cost Him His life to love you forever. Everything is everything. All the ceremonial things you see churches doing today to get a blessing became unnecessary after He died. On top of that, we Gentiles were never commanded to do them, anyway."

Chris paused. "I'm sorry. When I think about His love for us, I tend to drift off in space. You asked me about Hebrews chapter seven, and I did a politician's moonwalk and made it look like I was going toward you, but Instead I slid by your question." Chris chuckled at his own joke.

Deacon McKinney didn't think it was funny and cut him off. "Well, moonwalk your way back to the question and try to stay on beat to Hebrews chapter seven. Have you read verses one through four to get the full understanding of the context?" said Deacon Ross with a snicker.

"Before I answer that, I'd like to take this opportunity to thank you all for allowing me the opportunity to become head pastor of this church. Today, I was blessed with millions of dollars, an aircraft company, a big, fine house, and enough cars to drive a different one every day of the month. I can retire and not have to worry with the headache of trying to help church folks learn the truth about how incredibly deep God's love is. This is a very stressful job, but you know what? No one will remember all that I have now forever. But if I teach you and those who are being deceived with the Word of God and become a nominee to earn a crown in heaven, that'll be remembered forever. I'd give all I have just to have God honor me. For God himself to place a crown on my head and for all the angels and the souls of everyone that makes it to heaven to see and remember that moment. . . ." Chris put his head down into the palms of his hands as he began to choke up. "I'd give up all I have and follow Him for that eternal opportunity. I know I'm not the only one who wants to earn a crown."

Deacon McKinney clapped his hands slowly. "Oh, that was touching. Could one of you deacons hand me a handkerchief or a Kleenex, please? My eyeballs are beginning to sweat." Deacon McKinney wiped his eyes as if he were crying while making sniffling sound with his nose. "It's so sad that not knowing the answer to the question is going to cause you to lose that opportunity. You said you'd give up heaven if we found one untrue statement in the Bible, remember? I pray that you can answer the question so you can still have a chance to see Jesus."

"The answer to your question is to keep reading. Don't jump into the middle of the passage. Read the whole book. What does Hebrews chapter eight say? What does chapter nine say? And more importantly, what does chapter seven, verses twenty-two, twenty-seven, and twenty-eight say? Jumping in the middle of anyone's conversation without getting the full story will always get you the wrong information. A large part of the answer is in verse five, the very next verse of the chapter in question . . . Abraham's descendants were the ones who lived under these laws. Gentiles never had the opportunity to live under these laws and earn their way into heaven because the way to enter heaven changed under the new covenant which included us. You can follow the old covenant road all the way to the gates of heaven, but you'll never get in. You can try to claim Abraham's blessings, but you won't get them all. Abraham's descendants are Jews. We got connected to the promise of salvation through Abraham's descendant, Jesus. Remember what God said in Galatians three, verses fourteen and sixteen? Why do you think God promised salvation to Abraham and his descendants?"

"Jesus didn't die and make everything official 'til way after Abraham and his descendants died," said Deacon Banks.

"Right. He knew before time began that He was going to save all who believed before and after He died on the Cross. We share the promise of salvation with the Jews and whoever else in this world that accepts God's gift. We'll never get every promise that God made to the Jews. Those old laws that no one completely obeyed were the only way they could get to heaven until Jesus came," Chris said with a smile. "Our promises began and some of theirs ended because Jesus offered us all a better promise—a promise that set us free if we just believe."

"Hebrews is in the New Testament," said Deacon Ross. "Some things changed, but not everything, evidently, so it must be possible that tithing didn't change."

"Hebrews is a New Testament book, but the passage is talking about an Old Testament event that Gentiles never took part in because we Gentiles couldn't do anything to earn our way into heaven until Jesus died. When you pay attention to the whole story of God's love, you'll see that He was showing us that He could've saved any group or race of people He wanted to save and been done with it. But our God is not a respecter of persons; He loves us all."

Chris opened his Bible to Hebrews chapter seven. "Verse eighteen says Jesus knew that the law didn't make anyone perfect. Verse twenty-two says that a better covenant was coming, one that included us. Verse twenty-seven says that no longer will we need any high priest to offer sacrifices for our sins, their sins, and the sins of the whole nation like the Jews did in the old days."

Chris looked up and glanced at the all deacons. "Ask yourselves why the priests and church leaders today who receive tithes and offerings are not offering blood sacrifices and the many other things that the tithe law required the Jews to do. In fact, chapter nine, verse twenty-two says that, according to the law, there is no forgiveness without the shedding of blood. We can jump right in the middle of any passage, but when we see what it says and not what we want it to say, we'll see that that Old Rugged Cross set us free from everything when the blood of Jesus was shed. We Gentiles were added into the new covenant at the crossroads of our eternal future where God allowed His love to hang as a symbol and a light to show us which way to go. The Book of Hebrews is not the whole story. But when you read the entire book of Hebrews, you'll see that in order for sins to be forgiven…they had to be cleansed with blood offered through a high priest. All the priest had to offer was the blood of animals to cleanse sins temporarily. No priest or any animal had perfect immortal blood to offer which is why King Melchizedek appeared this one time in the Bible. The reason King Melchizedek was able to become high priest forever is because he was Jesus, our Lord God in one of His many incarnated guest appearances. Jesus came as this high priest because the law according to Hebrew 9:22 required sins to be cleansed with blood in order for them to be forgiven for. And according to chapter eight— hold on, I have it highlighted in my Bible, let me find it," Chris said as he searched for the verse he was looking for. "Here it is. Verse three. All high priests had to have a gift, something to sacrifice or something to offer before the Alter. If Jesus hadn't came as King Melchizedek and appointed King Melchizedek as a high priest forever, then that small loop hole in the law would've caused Him to have to come back and die for our sins all over again. I'm pretty sure you all know about loop holes in the law—and Jesus does to which is why He did it right the first time. He came as a priest and offered perfect blood for the altar so that when His blood was shed years later, He had already fulfilled what the law required which was for a high priest to offer blood of an animal for everyone's sin. When His blood was shed on the cross, the temple was destroyed and the veil where His blood should've been placed behind as an offering was torn. It was a sign that God accepted the blood of His perfect Lamb...And after the cross."

Chris patted his hand on the table twice and paused. "No more ceremonial offerings of any kind. A new covenant isn't new if nothing has changed. New covenant, new promises, and a new way to get to heaven; everything changed. Hebrews chapter ten, verses eleven and twelve, seems to contradict what was said of how sins were forgiven through sacrificial offerings offered by priest."

Chris read the verses silently and then continued, "Says here that priests offer their daily religious sacrifices, which can never take sins away. But this priest, meaning Jesus, who offered one sacrifice for our sins, made other sacrifices unnecessary. The verses are true; sacrificial offerings for sins through earthly priest never took forgiveness of sins away completely. It was the blood offered by Jesus when He came as an everlasting high priest named King Melchizedek."

"Why does my Bible say when Jesus came as high priest here in Hebrews 9:11? I'm almost convinced that Jesus was King Melchizedek," said Deacon Walker who was reading the beginning of Hebrew chapter 9 to try and fully understand the context of verse 9:22 that Chris had mentioned.

"Sound better and make mo' sense than the contradictionary thangs we been learning," said Deacon Banks. "Look like to me what appeared to be a lie was just a misunderstanding. Welcome to True Saints Baptist Church is my ruling on that contrick."

"Conflict. It's conflict, not contrick," said Deacon Walker.

"That's what I said, contrick. Don't be tryin' ta correct me cause you finally learning how to read the Bible," Deacon Banks replied.

"I'm with Deacon Banks," said Deacon Wright. "I find no reason to continue to tithe and blackmail God, but give freely from our hearts. Reverend Shoemaker, welcome aboard."

"Thank you, Deacon, but call me 'Pastor,'" Chris responded. "We'll get into the controversy of calling me 'Reverend' a little further down the road. Get ready. We're fixing to learn some things about this God that we've given our lives to that's going to make your soul want to jump out of your body and not think twice about the things that have confused our understanding of His love for us all these years."

"So can we still tithe or not'"" asked Deacon Ross. "I guess I just don't get it. I mean, how are we supposed to pay the bills 'round here?"

"You might just not *want* to get it," said Deacon Wright. "You heard the man. Keep giving, but don't give to receive. We're going to continue to take care of the church by giving freely what we can even if it exceeds ten percent, because we love God. Since we all have been paying ten percent for years, there's no reason to stop now, but don't expect the floodgates of heaven to open because that promise wasn't promised to us. Right, Rev? I mean Pastor."

"You got it. Use the promise that was promised to you," Chris replied.

"Looks like we got ourselves a pastor," Deacon Banks said. "Now we can better prepare for revival next week. We need someone to head the refreshment committee and the advertisement committee and somebody to come up wit' a theme and Stripture to go long wit' it. Any voluntairs?" Deacon Banks pulled a pen from his white-red-and-black pinstriped button-up shirt pocket.

"How about this one that I was going to use for my next sermon: 'building up the Body of Christ by teaching others how to eat from the Tree of Life'?"

All the deacons sat quietly as they thought about the theme Chris had suggested.

"That's a good one," said Deacon Wright. "I get it. When we get to heaven, God will reverse the curse of learning the knowledge of good and evil that came from eating from the tree of the knowledge of good and evil. We'll all get to eat from the right tree and live forever like we were supposed to have done when Adam messed things up by listening to his naked wife."

"Right, I believe that's why we're here," Chris responded. God created us to worship Him forever when we get to heaven, but here on earth, we're just learning the knowledge of good and evil. Everything works for the glory of God. Heaven will be even sweeter because of our lives here on earth."

"I'll volunteer to head the advertisement committee," Deacon Moore offered. "I'm thinking we can put a fake tree in the sanctuary representing that we're learning the knowledge of good and evil through God's teaching in the bible. And we can have another tree in the banquet hall representing the Tree of Life while everyone enjoys refreshments," added Deacon Justice.

"Yeah! That's a great idea. We can have fruits in little baskets under the trees on all five days. Fake fruit under the Tree of Knowledge and real fruit under the Tree of Life," said Deacon Moore.

Deacon McKinney nodded to Deacon Ross, signaling him to step outside the conference room. Once they were outside, Deacon McKinney said, "Look at this mess. Somebody come along and make something sound good and these people believe it. If it wasn't for our secret operation, I'd resign as deacon right now and find another church that's Holy Ghost filled to join. This whole church is about to be cursed by God if they follow Pastor Shoemaker. Humph. You ain't thinking about following him and his fancy explanations to hell, are you?"

"They're some good ones, I ain't goin' t' lie to you. Part of me wants to take what we got and quit before we get caught. Another part wants to get just a little bit more to save for retirement, but I don't know. This whole incident is forcing me to read my Bible for myself, but I don't know if that'll do any good, because I just can't understand everything it say. I do have a heart and a conscience. Survival was the name of the game when we first started doing this, but something inside me keeps giving me this feeling that we're not gonna be able to prove him wrong," said Deacon Ross.

With the tip of his left index finger, Deacon McKinney touched the left side of his own temple as he placed his right index finger on Deacon Ross's left temple. "Let me transfer some positive brainwaves to your brain. Don't believe that stuff; we been doing fine without his kind for all these years. He ain't nothing, but a Bible politician. Stay focused; together we can overthrow him. What you wanna do? Let him come in and mess up what we been secretly doing for years or get him fired like we did Reverend Apostle Prophet Edgars? We'll find his weakness and get him outta here. Every man's got a weakness no matter how holy he claims to be. I can't prove him wrong with the Bible yet 'cause I haven't read it all. But it looks like it's time. He ain't right. I know we can get some of these preacher-loving women in here to distract him like we did Edgars and possibly run him outta here too. Either way, if we stick together and prove him to be a fraud with his fancy explanations, he'll be gone and we'll still be in business."

"Yeah, but if he's right, we'll be in the business of robbing God."

Without saying a word, Deacon McKinney placed the tip of his finger on Deacon Ross's temple again, but this time he tapped on it. "Ain't nothing true and believable in this world lessen you believe it to be true. I don't care what he says; I can speak anything into my life. I don't need God for every little old thing. Them flapjack Christians in there want his lies to be true 'cause they wanna keep their money in their pocket. When they stop tithing and get in need of a blessing, they goin' t' flip-flop back to tithing. You watch and see what I tell you. With the way this economy is, I don't expect this tithe problem to last long. Watch and see."

"I wonder why God done made him rich, though. If he was going around lying on God, it don't seem like he'd be getting blessed with the big blessings he just got."

"That money came from sinful gambling, and a sinful man who committed a sinful act to get that sinful money. The devil blessed him with that money. That man that gave it to him gave it away to get rid of the curse it put on his life. Trust me. You don't want that money made from sin. Don't covet that dirty money he got."

"Suppose he put some of it in church. How we goin' t' be able to tell the difference and separate it?" asked Deacon Ross.

"Once the money's placed in the basket, it's blessed. What we put in our pockets will be blessed. Just pray over it. It ain't like we're stealing it. It's being given to the church. This building ain't the church; we're the church."

—

Inside the conference room, Chris prepared to leave. "Wouldn't it be good to show Jesus that our Bible knowledge is past the pull-up stage?" he asked as he stood up. "Studying and trying to understand the Bible is not a waste of time. Do y'all know Jesus is going to give us crowns for our knowledge of the Bible?"

Deacon Moore rolled his eyes. "Everybody's gonna get a crown when we get to heaven," he said. He laughed and added, "I hope you got some other ways to motivate the members into staying members here."

"I'm afraid that's not true, Deacon. There's going to be a lot of disappointed believers standing before Jesus at the Bema judgment, forever regretting in heaven that they didn't do their best in this life to avoid sinning. There are plenty of things we can do to earn a crown, and I'm a' teach on that later. I'm afraid that giving to get some blessings by tithing is not one of them," said Chris.

"I didn't know that," Deacon Moore said. "Well, you need to preach on that soon, Pastor."

Chris looked at each of the deacons in turn. "I assume that I'm now the pastor of this church if you all agree that all Bible contradictions are human misunderstandings."

All the deacons expressed agreement, even Deacon McKinney and Deacon Walker who had just walked back into the conference room.

"Thank you for this opportunity," Chris said, standing up to leave. "This is going to be an awesome experience relearning the Bible! I can't wait to get started! We'll work backwards like God does. Yeah, that's what we'll do. We'll start with the New Testament and then go to the Old Testament. That way, we won't get confused and try to apply old covenant laws to our lives."

Chris shook everyone's hand and went home.

CHAPTER 29

The Rapture

"How did the meeting go?" Angel asked.

Chris smiled proudly. "God has given us a church. He's given me a job. I'm now officially an angel of the third kind."

"What?" asked Angel, looking puzzled.

"You know; a human angel. You know there are three kinds of angels: heavenly angels, fallen angels, and human angels who act as God's messengers on earth. So as the new pastor of True Saints, I'm an angel of the third kind."

"Oh! Congratulations!" Angel said, getting up from the couch to give him a hug.

"They don't know it yet, but I'm going to pay off the church's debt after we get the money that was rightfully my dad's. I know that's what he would've done."

Angel felt her jaw drop to the floor. She closed her mouth and frowned at what Chris had presented as wonderful news. "Uh, that church has got to cost and still owe over a million dollars," she said when she realized that he wasn't joking. "You need to pray about this. Some prayers take years to be answered. I feel it in my heart that this is one of them."

"This isn't our money, Angel. We're just stewards over it. God will take care of us; don't worry. I also want to give away the house or sell it cheap to someone. There's no way I can live in that house. I've always wanted to own my own business, but I consider preaching to be more important than being the owner of an aircraft company making millions of dollars.

204

So I'm going to sell it and just own part of it. I want to put all my time into teaching God's word."

After watching God transform her husband during what should've been his most difficult life storm, Angel had learned to trust in God.

"Well, you're the man, I see nothing wrong with any of that." she said, sitting down and picking up his father's notes to read. "I'm not going to come between my servant's decisions. I've learned to trust y'all," Angel said, referring to Chris and God.

"That's right. Why can't other women see the role y'all play in marriage that way? I'm proud of you, I'm a' mess around and polish your toenails tonight."

"Huh?" said Angel.

"Never mind, it's a guy joke. It's a figure of speech we say that means the wife is in control."

"I guess I missed the joke." Angel clapped her hands twice and stretched out on the couch. "Servant!" she said as she looked around the room. "Oh, there you are. Take off my socks and massage my bunions."

"I can fix your bunion problem permanently. I'll be right back with the hatchet."

"Mm-hmm, you done forgot your place already," Angel said as she sat back up and grabbed his father's papers again. "Speaking of being out of place, I've been reading your father's essays you left here on the table. This is some weird stuff." Angel began reading one of the essays. "'What if the whole entire Bible had already happened and the people and angels we read about in the Bible stories were us? Millions of theories could be developed to put the missing parts of the puzzle of life together. We could be the one third of the angels that God kicked out of heaven. That's almost half of the billions of heavenly angels that Satan fooled. There's evidence in the Bible that angels may have occupied this earth before us. Could this life be our second chance given by God to learn and choose our eternal fate because of His love for us? Nowhere in the Bible is there a salvation plan for angels. Is He giving us who were heavenly angels a second chance by teaching and exposing Satan's evil lies that got us kicked out of our Creator's presence? Could it be that we earn our rank as angels in heaven through our lives here on earth? Could the angels who come to take our souls to Jesus be our loved ones who died in the past? Will God give our memory of heaven back to us when we earn our way back to whence we came? Anything is possible with God.'" Angel shook her head in amazement at Chris's father's theories. "You oughta preach on this next week," she said.

Chris laughed. "That got me, too, when I first read it. But you just did what a lot of us do when we read everything in the Bible literally and don't read it in its entirety. Didn't you read the end of the essay where he explained that his made-up theory might sound good, but it isn't in the Bible? I believe he goes on to say that he was going to teach God's Word straight from the Bible instead of from conflicting opinions."

Angel ducked her head and tried to hide behind her right hand. "Oh." She took her hand down and added, "You didn't let me finish. I knew that."

"Have you ever read the entire Bible cover to cover?" Chris asked.

Angel ducked and hid behind her hand again.

"Never mind; I know what that means. Here I am trying to get other people to read the whole Bible and the preacher's wife hasn't read it. Shame on me . . . and shame, shame, shame on you, too," Chris teased. "You're going to have to do better."

"Will you read it to me tonight as a bedtime story?" Angel asked.

"I'd love to," Chris replied.

—

Later that night, Chris got into bed and began reading the Bible while Angel finished prepping for her beauty sleep. When she had finished and gotten into to bed, Chris told her a bedtime story based on the theories of humans being fallen angels in his father's essay that Angel had read earlier that day.

"Did you know that not even the angels in heaven have seen God the Father yet?"

"Now Chris, don't you start misinterpreting the bible. Did you forget about the story of Job and how Satan and all the angels presented themselves to God when he asked Satan, where he had been and gave Satan permission to test job?"

"No, I didn't forget. That was the Lord God Satan was talking to. Not God the Father."

"Oh…well continue," said Angel.

"The Lord God did everything and said everything in the Old and New Testament. What's most amazing to me is how Jesus is going to wash our sins away and present us as faultless before God the Father, the holiest part of God that I use to believe not even the angels have seen until I started studying to get an understanding of the trinity. There were a few verses I read that wow'd me. One of them was Mathew 18:10 where Jesus warned not to look down on little children and that their angels in heaven always see the face of His Father in heaven. I've been blown away by the amazing things that the Lord God has done throughout the Bible. The Lord God did everything and it just seemed strange to me that God the Father has done nothing and Jesus said they are one. There are so many contradicting verses about Jesus being God the Father that I just had to pray and search for my own understanding of the trinity."

"Yea, like the fact that you just said not even the angels have seen God the Father then showed proof that they have in Mathew 18:10."

"There is sort a' kind of no proof in the bible of the angels seeing and talking directly to God the Father other than what Jesus said in Mathew 18:10. But when I found out who God the Father was! Then it all began to make since. Since Jesus who is God never lies, a lot can be seen through His statement when you look at it with a magnifying glass."

"Don't tell me you can explain the trinity. I don't know anyone who can explain the trinity?" asked Angel.

Well I think I got it, but I'm not sure. Since I couldn't find many places where God the Father spoke much in the bible, I started thinking, maybe God the Father is not going to show up until we get to heaven or something. But I believe Jesus was referring to himself in Mathew 18:10. It seems to me that when Jesus refers to himself in heaven, He calls Himself the Lord God as He was called throughout the Old Testament. When He stepped into our time as Jesus, He was a real human living on earth; He referrers to the Lord God as being His Father just like we will when we get to heaven. When we see God the Father, we'll be seeing what Jesus looked like when He was the Lord God before time began. In Mathew 11: 25 which was apart of the verses that was in my dream. Jesus said 'I praise you Father, Lord of heaven and earth.'" Chris paused. "Now who did Jesus say was Lord of the heavens and the earth? Not God the Father, but the Lord God who we know is Jesus, and the Lord God is the one who sent Jesus to the earth to die for our sins. He sent Himself and made Himself a man. All throughout the Old Testament it was the Lord God who made all the promises and covenants remember."

"I'm with you," said Angel. Chris continued talking while he turned the pages of his bible in search of a verse. "Jesus said something about making a group of people a pillar in the temple of His God and writing the name and city of His God on them...here it is. Revelation 3:12. Jesus has to be saying that the Lord God is His Father because He says here that the name of His God's city is the New Jerusalem. Then Jesus said that He's going to write His new name on them that overcome. The temple is where Jesus will reign for a thousand years on this earth and the New Jerusalem is the city that the Lord God promised his people they would dwell with Him forever. Jesus just said right here that it's the Lord God that's his Father, you see that!" Chris said as he tapped and pointed on verse twelve. "God the Father is the same Lord God of the Old Testament who's changed name title is being mentioned to us in advance of what our Lord God will be called when we all get to heaven. Since the Lord God is God the Father of all mankind including Jesus, because He was a real man, this means that the angels have seen the future God the Father who is the same Lord God that they've been worshiping since they were created. But they haven't seen Him as God the Father with all of his children, because we are not all in heaven yet. I'm almost positive that this explains the Trinity, but I know for sure we all will understand it fully when heaven comes." Chris looked over at Angel who had fallen asleep with a smile on her face. He pulled the covers up to her shoulders, turned off the light with the remote and tried to fall asleep.

Angel dreamt sweet dreams of heaven all night long after Chris told her a bedtime story, but Chris was too excited by the idea of being in heaven with God to concentrate on sleeping. Tossing and turning at three A.M., Chris still struggled to fall asleep. The opportunity to be a multimillionaire was nice, but the excitement that kept him from getting a good night's sleep came more from his new job of teaching and saving souls. He was officially an angel of the third kind and indeed a candidate to earn the crown of glory promised to ministers who faithfully serve as shepherds of God's flock in 1 Peter 5:1–4. Becoming the pastor of True Saints Baptist Church had elevated his love for God beyond the normal limits of human love.

After several hours of tossing and turning, Chris finally fell asleep only to be awakened by a loud noise that sounded like fifty fighter jets passing over the roof of his home. Within five seconds, the air-tearing sound had faded to a faint echo as it passed and ascended through the darkness of space, leaving behind it a great sky quake that shook his home. Seconds before the sound ended, Chris somehow managed to hide under the bed, ready to jump out and surprise what he supposed must be alien invaders.

When the sound and rumbling of the sky quake faded away, Chris started to check on Angel although he knew he risked blowing his cover, but before he could crawl out from under the bed, the brightest white light he had ever seen poured through the windows, nearly blinding him. Chris put his hands over his eyes and closed them as tightly as he could, but the bright light penetrated through everything including his flesh and bones. His body slowly became transparent from the holiness of the light, and, for a moment, his body was covered with a new body that glowed as white as snow. As the light faded, Chris's new body faded as well. In a low voice, Chris spoke to the fading light. "Come back. Please, come back!"

When the light disappeared, Chris called from under the bed, "Angel? Are you OK?" When she didn't respond, he called again, "Angel? Angel!" and crawled from under the bed to find that Angel was gone.

Assuming that she had gone to check on the kids, Chris eased over to the kids' room only to find that they were nowhere to be found, either. Frantically, he began searching under the beds, in the closet, and in every room in the house. Not knowing what to expect, he snatched the door to the garage open quickly and readied his fists as if he expected someone to charge in to attack him. To his surprise, the cars were still in the garage with the doors down. There was no one keeping his family hostage in the garage like he had imagined. This could only mean one thing, he thought. The Rapture had come and gone. In the twinkling of an eye, his body had stayed the same while the bodies of his family had changed. His family must have been caught up in the rapture cloud and ridden it with Jesus to heaven.

Not wanting to believe that Jesus had broken His promise by not coming back for him, Chris decided to check the one other place he hadn't searched to find his family, the detached garage.

Chris hadn't cried since his father's death, but after entering the detached garage and finding no one there, years of tears began cracking the levies and floodgates of his eyes. A tear squeezed through the crack of his eyelid and streamed down his face as he stared at his reflection on his newly restored '69 Camaro. Heavy tears poured down his face as he pleaded with God, "Just like I restored old, broken down, good-for-nothing cars, I expected you to restore me the same way, Lord. Make my life brand-new. Restore me. Whenever it seemed like life wasn't going to get any better, my hope was in you." Chris scrunched up his face like a child mocking and teasing another kid on the playground. In a whiney voice, he made fun of himself as he repeated the phrase that had always given him comfort and helped him keep his faith. "The Bible is not a lie; the Bible is not a lie." He paused. "Humph. Well, if it's not a lie, why am I still here? I had no doubt that you loved me after I learned better, but it looks like you really don't love me. All I've done for many years of my life was suffer. Now you want me to suffer forever. Vengeance is yours for the sins I committed against you. Even though you've left me, I still love you."

Chris paused and began to think logically about his situation, which gave him hope. "Wait a minute. There's no way I can be on my way to hell if I love you. This is a big mistake. Wake me up from this dream." He began to smile. He stopped talking to himself and focused on a noise he heard coming from outside. Someone was coming.

"Angel, is that you?" Chris asked.

Suddenly, Angel walked like a ghost through the closed double garage door holding hands with Heath on her right side and Jacob on her left. "I loved the way you treated me when I was your wife," she said.

Jacob's and Heath's voices trailed behind Angel's. "When we were your sons, you treated us like Christ treated the church, with unconditional love and understanding of our weaknesses," they said together. "Thank you, brother for teaching us how to enter the new life we now live."

"I'm confused. We'll be brothers in heaven, but I'm not with you." Chris reached his hands out to touch Heath and Jacob but changed his mind and pulled back. "Did God say why I'm not with you now?" he asked in a very concerned tone.

A heavenly voice came from the four corners of the earth, speaking to Chris like a soft breeze. "I loved the thoughts you envisioned of me as your sister although we never met."

Chris did a three sixty to his left then to his right as he desperately tried to locate the heavenly voice of his little sister who had died when she was a seven-week-old embryo in their mother's womb.

Hearing what sounded like a crowd of people talking outside the garage, Chris walked over and pushed the button to raise the garage door. To his surprise, more people than he'd ever seen in his life were spread out for miles as far as his eyes could see.

His mother appeared on his left. "I love the way you treated me when I was your mother," she said.

Not too far off, he spotted his mother's father and his father's mother making their way through the crowd with as much energy as if they were in their twenties. All sickness and pain that slowed them down during their time on earth was gone. Grandma Mary and Grandpa Eddie had been dead for eleven years. In the same way that misunderstood Bible verses had disrupted Chris's life and his relationship with God, his grandparents' relationship with each other had been damaged and separated by color because of misinterpreted Bible verses that Satan used to deceive their generation as well.

Chris stumbled backwards into the shop and held himself up on the hood of his newly restored 1969 Camaro.

"I love the way you treated me when I was your grandmother."

"I love the way you treated me when I was your grandfather."

Grandma Mary, who was White, and Grandpa Eddie, who was Black, did something that Chris had never seen them do when they lived on earth. They hugged each other, a sign to Chris that all hatred and confusion had fled from their hearts. After seeing his grandparents, who had hated each other because of their different skin color, hugging each other, Chris desperately wanted his body to be changed so he could feel the everlasting happiness he knew they felt.

Slowly, he reached out his hand to touch Angel on her shoulder. Her holy body lit up into a soft, bright, snow-white glow. At the same time, the bodies of everyone Chris had ever seen in his life began to glow as they stood outside the garage behind her.

"We're all one body now," Angel said before leaning forward to kiss Chris on the lips. As soon as she pulled away, the ground slid from under his feet, causing him to fall to his knees. He quickly tried to stand back to his feet, but the ground snatched itself from under his knees and he found himself lying face down on the violently shaking ground that seemed about to swallow him. Unable to either walk or crawl, he could only writhe on the ground like a snake. At his first attempt to move forward, fifty feet by eighty feet of ground surrounding him collapsed. He closed his eyes tightly as he began to fall deep inside the earth. Through the loud, rumbling sound the earth made as it swallowed him, he heard Angel's voice calling out to Jacob and Heath, and he opened his eyes to find himself lying in bed with Angel beside him.

What a relief! He thought.

CHAPTER 30

Is This the End?

His relief didn't last long. His dream about the Rapture had been just a dream, but the earthquake was real. By the time Chris could make sense of what was happening, it was all over. The 2.8 earthquake had lasted only fifteen seconds, causing only minor damage to the drywall on the walls and ceilings. Chris and Angel hurried out of bed and rushed to Jacob and Heath's bedroom to check on them. To their surprise, they found them both asleep, cuddled up with their big Teddy bears.

The earthquakes, the bad economy, wars and rumors of wars, and other end-time Bible predictions were on everyone's minds after the New Madrid fault in the northeastern section of Arkansas produced a 4.6 quake that triggered the 2.8 quake that shook Little Rock and its surrounding areas. After watching the noon news to see if the earthquake had done any major damage in Little Rock, Chris grabbed his bible to see what the scriptures had to say about end-time signs that were happening all around the world. The index notes pointed him to several different passages, but the passages in Mark 13:5-14 were so interesting to Chris; he decided to make it the subject of his next sermon.

Chris had noticed that most of the sermons being preached on TV and around town gave false hope of a healthy, prosperous, miraculously happy lifestyle that promised earthly blessings and a problem-free life. Chris believed that God would give blessings along with suffering at their appropriate times in different chapters of everyone's life story. Because of his belief, he chose to preach sermons that dealt more with eternal life in heaven than with the temporary life on earth.

With a full week of teaching ahead of him at the revival, Chris asked Deacon Walker and Deacon Moore to find another pastor to preach that Sunday. On Monday evening, he arrived an hour before service began to meditate and focus on his sermon. It was six thirty-five when he decided to get a drink of water and walk around to stretch his legs after sitting for thirty-five minutes straight. Chris was on his way back to the pastor's study when he heard voices coming from the sanctuary. He walked over and stood along the side of double doors that lead into the sanctuary and listened in on three mothers of the church who were sitting with their backs turned toward him catching up on church gossip.

"That old sister really preached yesterday. We ain't had church like that in a long time," said Mother Bernice Honeywell.

"Sho' ain't, honey," said Mother Plumpy Magee. "It's been a long time since a pastor done brung the spirit in here wit' 'em. Cuttin' Doll say she ain't felt the spirit and shouted like she did yestiddy in a good long while. Humph. It's goin' t' be another long while now since we got Pastor Shoemaker here. All he do is talk. He don't get his soul in it like other pastors do."

"Yeah, I don't know why dem dumb deacons couldn't give the pastor that preached yesterday a chance," said Mother Honeywell. "She brought the Spirit with her. She cut loose and preached. You can tell the Word was in her. She was natu'al bow'n called to preach. All Pastor Shoemaker done brung with him is blasphemy and offensive ridicule of our knowledge of the Bible like we some fools or something. He gets on my nerves worst than my arthritis in my elbows. Don't do nothin' but criticize ever'thing we do. It wouldn't surprise me if next he claimed women ain't sa'spose to preach."

"What she preach 'bout yesterday?" asked Mother EssieMae Hebert.

"I don't know, but we had church 'cause a lot of people were shouting and crying and carrying on all over the church. You don't see none of that when Pastor Shoemaker preach," said Mother Honeywell.

"Rumor has it that Deacon Ross and Deacon McKinney goin' t' call him out and give him a taste of his own medicine," said Mother Magee. "He call hisself a pastor teacher when Matthew 23:10 strictly say not to call yourself a teacher. He think he know everything. Why don't he know that?"

With a confused look on his face, Chris answered Mother Magee secretively in a conversation with himself.

"It also says not to call yourself Rabbi or father. He was talking about the teachers of the law. Not teachers of the Bible. Seven times He strictly said woe to you teachers of the law and Pharisees. How did you miss that?" said Chris.

Hurt and embarrassed, Chris continued to stand quietly outside the doors eavesdropping on the mothers' conversation. As badly as he wanted to correct their numerous misunderstandings of the Bible, he decided to take the humble approach and back down. None of their misunderstandings condemned them to hell. They were just incorrect interpretations of what Chris called Bible politics. As he stood outside the doorway with his head drooping, he heard his dad's voice in his head speaking words from one of his essays. "There's never been a preacher in this world who hasn't been talked about by the people of the church that God gave him to lead. When I think about the humility that lies ahead on my name, because of the truth I teach, I think about who I'm suffering the embarrassment and shame for, and I still answer yes to His calling and purpose for my life. No one is greater than He is. His promise to give me a crown makes the road of humility ahead of me worth every embarrassing moment of my suffering for his name. I pray that I'm not alone when He steps down from his mighty throne to hand out crowns for our good works." Chris looked up toward heaven and whispered. "You won't be alone, Dad. I, too, have heard His call. I'd rather be talked about for His name's sake than for any other reason." With his eyes on the prize, he gathered up the strength to walk forward with God even though he wanted to quit because of his unpopularity in the church.

Inside the quiet four walls of what was now his pastor's study, Chris prepared to meditate and pray. Thinking of how far he used to be from God because of unintentional misunderstood teachings of God's truth, Chris prayed that his messages would break the cycle of misinterpreted Scriptures so that the people he taught the Word of God could understand God's love for them on a higher level.

He hooked up his IPod to the desktop computer and clicked Play. As "More Than Life" by Hillsong poured softly out of the speakers, Chris bowed his head and began to pray. "Help me, O Lord Jesus, as I teach your Word tonight. Help me convince my congregation that this life on earth is just a courtship for us to get to know the bridegroom we've agreed to marry and, more importantly, that you're coming to marry us soon. I pray that you'll come back today, but I know that if you did, many souls would be lost forever. May many souls be saved tonight, and may saved souls receive empowerment to go out and help both saved and non saved souls understand you better through your word. Amen."

Being a pastor was nowhere near as easy as Chris had expected it to be. Knowing that gossip and rumors about him were flying around the sanctuary like dust on a country road made it even harder for Chris to stand strong in the pulpit that night. Chris walked up to the pulpit as if he didn't know that many church members disliked his controversial sermons. Wearing blue jeans, dark brown loafers, and a blue-and-white horizontally striped knit pullover, Chris greeted the crowd and prepared to preach for the first time as the newly appointed head pastor of True Saints Baptist Church.

"Revival: Encarta dictionary defines it as a new presentation of something old or a renewal of interest in something that results in its becoming popular once more." Chris paused, stuck out his neck and lightly hammered his fist on the podium several times. "It is definitely time for a revival of Christianity and the teachings of God's word today." He paused again. "Welcome to revival week here at True Saints Baptist Church."

More than eleven hundred people including Bryan, Tony, Melvin, and their wives as well as Harold and his family had packed the sanctuary that night to hear Chris teach. Pastor Sanders's church, First Baptist, was one of two guest churches whose members had been invited to hear what many True Saints members thought for sure would be another controversial sermon. Many had showed up specifically for that reason. Deacon McKinney couldn't wait for Chris to embarrass the congregation in front of the guests so that many members would join him on his quest to have Chris removed. He looked all around the sanctuary with a smile on his face as Chris began to speak.

"Thursday morning's earthquake and all the earthquakes that have been shaking this old earth weekly and sometimes daily for the past eight months or more have definitely aroused some of us into blowing the dust off of our Bibles to see what God says about how much time we have left on this earth. Tonight, we'll find some of the answers in one of the most interesting and comforting books in the Bible, a book that many churches choose not to recognize because it seems to contradict the loving nature of our God. Turn, if you will, to the good Book of Revelation."

"Revelation is a prophecy about a time that is very near. All the wars, rumors of wars, and earthquakes that are happening today must be a sign that the world is about to end. The bad economy, the sinfulness of mankind, and all the other bad things that are happening are in line to send this world toward the Mark of the Beast, worldwide hunger and a one-world government. Lots of people believe that some things in Revelation have already happened, but Mark 13, along with Revelations, tells us differently. The wars and earthquakes that will be like that of a woman's birth pains that Jesus mentioned in Mark 13:5–8 are out of line with the time we're living in today. They are signs that the absolute end of time is near. We, the church of believers, will already be with God when the abomination of desolation occurs that our God mentions in verse fourteen. The Rapture is the end of living in this world without Jesus for believers. We're coming back with Jesus when He comes to end the tribulation period and bring one thousand years of peace as He rules this world. It should come as no surprise that the eschatology signs described in Mark 13 and the earthquakes like the one that shook us the other morning are coincidentally happening all over the world exactly as described in the Bible. We have plenty of evidence that Satan uses God's words to deceive and trick us. Satan has always tried to copy God to deceive us into believing he is God. He has his own evil trinity with the Antichrist being his only begotten son and the false Prophet who tries to attempt to copy the Holy Spirit. He has his own army of angels and humans that he deceived into following him. Satan also has the power to shake the earth in various places" Chris opened his eyes wide and looked around at each section of the congregation before continuing.

"All of the coincidental end of time signs that are going on around us today could very well be Satan copying the return of the real king with his many clever deceptions to fool many into believing that the Antichrist is Jesus. It's the perfect way to fool even the elect. Just like God, Satan will wrap himself up into a human body, perform miracles, and take control of the world. These signs we're seeing today are not coincidentally identical to how the bible says the world will end. If the signs we see today, are indeed the work of Satan, then what these signs mean is that this is the end of living in this world for all who believe in Jesus. The rapture of all believers is going to happen before the antichrist is revealed. According to these copy cat signs were seeing today, it looks as if the Antichrist is set up to appear at any day now. Jesus sent out these messages to warn us thousands of years ago.

"And now, it's time for them to come to pass. With Jesus, we'll come back to the this earth from heaven to reign with Him for a thousand years, singing songs of praise like the one that First Baptist is going to sing for us tonight. At the end of our Lord's thousand-year reign on earth, I believe that everyone who ever believed in God will get to see what Satan looked like at his defeat in the final war mentioned in Revelations 20:7-10. To see the face of the one who deceived us all our lives as he's cast into a fire so hot that it makes the heat from the sun feel like a cold winter day . . . priceless. Not only that—if he promised we'd be with Him forever after the rapture, then I believe it. There's no biblical evidence that says we'll be separated from God after the rapture. However, there is proof in 1Thessalonians 4:17 that we'll be with Him forever after we meet Him in the clouds. I believe that when He speaks…and creates a new heaven and earth; we'll be there watching and witness His awesome power just as the angels witnessed His power when He spoke our universe into existence at the beginning of time."

"Many were called, but zillions chose not to be chosen to see unimaginable events such as this. There are not enough people in this world believing in Jesus today . . . and we need to do something about it right now."

Chris held his Bible in the air and told the congregation, "In this Bible you'll find many things about our God. But you'll never, never *ever* find one contradiction or lie spoken by God. Look at how long it took for God to give what he knows is a fair punishment for Satan and his army. Now God has zillions times zillions of reasons to punish Satan after reviewing the evidence of who knows how many people God created multiplied by the zillions of sins that Satan caused us to commit during our entire existence. It's sad for me to have to say that some of our brothers, sisters, parents, and friends will be there in Satan's army that outnumbers all the sand grains of all the beaches on this earth as described in Revelations 20:8. I pray tonight that the Holy Spirit will take off the blinders Satan has put on the eyes of everyone who doesn't believe that everything in the Bible is true and allow them to see how good God is and how much He loves us. Believe tonight that the Bible is not a lie before you live out the last chapter of your life and your death make it a true story. Get to know Him and enjoy this life He's given you. Whosoever will, let him find a lie in God's Word. Whosoever can't find a lie, let him run to Jesus."

At the end of his sermon, Deacon Banks and Deacon Wright stood behind chairs they had placed in front of the stage and gave lost souls the opportunity to give their lives to Christ. Pastor Sanders's Praise and Worship Team began to sing "You Deserve" by Natalie Grant. Symbony led the song with her angelic voice as a culturally mixed choir of fifty voices backed her up. To Chris's disappointment, not one soul came up to be saved or to join True Saints Baptist Church that night.

—

On Tuesday night, Chris preached another sermon dealing with going to heaven. He preached as if the world were ending and he only had a few hours to help rescue as many souls as he could from eternal damnation. Chris felt strongly in his heart that the Rapture was very near and that teaching his congregation how to live on an earth that was near extinction was irrelevant.

On Wednesday night, Chris continued teaching on matters of the new life. After his sermon; Pastor Sanders's praise team, led by Symbony, began to sing "At the Cross" by Hillsong, Heath got up and began walking toward the chairs that the deacons had put out in front of the pulpit area. To Chris's surprise, seven-year-old Heath sat in one of the chairs and gave his life to Christ. For the first time in eighteen years, Chris had finally found something worth crying for, something worth living for, and something worth dying for—the everlasting freedom of the souls that he'd see and talk to again in heaven.

Chris cried through the entire song. His first-born son was the first soul that he had known of that he led to Christ to be saved. Chris never knew that he convinced DaFrenchy to give his live to Christ before he died in the aircraft accident. Fifteen people, including Heath, put their lives into the hands of Jesus Christ that night.

At the end of the song, Chris gathered his composure and gave the benediction. Still tearful, but able to speak, he said, "When Jesus died on the Cross, the very first thing he did was tear the veil that separated us from speaking to Him through High Priest. His death immediately enabled us to go directly to Him through prayer to ask forgiveness for our sins. He took control of the law, death, and the grave. He made the way easy. The price he had to pay for our sins was a load that no earthly man could carry. It was heavier than the weight of the universe. But when He saw a way to save all of us, the decision was easy. Jesus, the hero of heroes, is better than good. He is God, and God is love. Amen."

—

Revival week had ended. Despite a few rumors Chris heard about his preaching earlier that week from a few mothers on the mothers' board, Chris tried to convince himself that he had done a pretty good job for his first week as a pastor.

CHAPTER 31

Watching the Stars

The Shoemaker family arrived home from church around 9:30 Friday night. As they walked into the kitchen from the garage, Angel said to the boys, "Y'all get your nightclothes on and get in bed. I'll be there in a minute to kiss you night-night."

"Yes ma'am," both Heath and Jacob replied.

When they had disappeared to their rooms, Chris shared with Angel something that had been troubling him all week. "Why do people always get offended when you try to tell them the truth?" he asked, scratching his head in puzzlement.

"I don't know." Angel poured herself a glass of cranberry juice. "What makes you ask that?"

"Well, I overheard a few of the mothers talking about me and my controversial sermons earlier this week. Why don't they understand my sermons? I never said not to give any money to the church; I never even said not to give ten percent if they want to. All I'm trying to do is promote God's love, but to them, it seems as if everything I say is promoting sin."

"Have you thought of ways to soften your message a little bit? Think about the preachers who taught people that they had to tithe. We know most of them didn't mislead people on purpose. Satan knows the Bible better than the best pastor in the world, and he could probably fool you with it if he had a conversation with you. I've been learning a lot from you, but some of the things you talk about go over my head, Chris. I pretend to understand it sometimes, but I really don't."

A look of shock had frozen on Chris's face. "What's so hard to understand about all the contradictions and controversial issues in the Bible being centuries-old misunderstandings? Every word and sentence in the entire Bible is controversial when two or more people disagree on what God meant by what He said. God knows we'll never get everything in the Bible right. That's why He made the salvation plan so easy. It's probably too late to convince Christians today that separating into denominations centuries ago played a large part in keeping the confusion and misinterpretations of the Bible going still today. I doubt that we'll ever come together as one body in Christ like we're supposed to be, but it's worth a try."

"I guess all us Christians can do is pray that all the confusion doesn't lead anyone away from Jesus." Angel paused with a look of confusion. "Wait a minute? If all denominations and all religions came from disagreements over interpretations of the bible, then—why are we still Baptist?" she asked.

"The same reason why probably ninety percent of Christians are still separated into Catholic Christians, Pentecostal Christians, Episcopal Christians and the many other denominations that separate us Christians today—a master deceiver named satin has deceived us all. Chris replied. "Speaking of Satan, I'm always afraid that my sermons sound like they're promoting sin. Do they sound that way to you?"

"No. Not really. What I get out of your sermons is that we're all confused and messed-up people, Christians included. We all need Jesus to make us right. No matter how smart we think we are, we'll never fully understand the Bible because it's—it's so deep and beyond our world of understanding." Angel paused. "Another reason I think people are so confused is because they haven't completely read the Bible for themselves—me included. Everyone needs to read the entire Bible before choosing to say that they don't believe in God."

"You're exactly right. Not many Christians have made time to read the entire bible may be the answer to your question on denominations and religions. Baptist is the majority denomination here in Arkansas. I bet you if someone could convince the Baptist leaders to change over to non denominational Bible teaching churches; a major Christian revolution will get started and millions of people will start getting back into going to church. This is the information age. All the answers to every bible contradiction Satan used to separate us has been answered and were still separated. It makes no since to still agree to disagree." Chris replied.

"Why don't you go to the Baptist convention and talk to them about this?"

"Oh, no! God hadn't called me to do that and if He did I'm changing my number. It's hard enough being a pastor. I'm positive someone else will be called to do that."

"Since He put the thought of uniting churches as one body in Christ on your mind, He'll probably be calling you." Angel snickered. "I'm going to check on the kids. I'll be right back."

"I'll be on the back porch," said Chris.

As he had done almost every night since becoming an angel of the third kind, Chris went out on the back porch to gaze at the stars. The night sky fascinated him more than any work of creation except for woman, God's greatest and most beautiful creation in Chris's view. But unlike God, who loved man and woman equally, Chris loved his wife Angel more than he loved any other woman on the face of the earth, partly because God had asked him to and partly because he valued Angel as a gift from God along with the family that God had given him to serve.

Angel went out on the back porch after putting the kids to bed and hugged Chris from behind.

With tears in his eyes, he turned around and gave her a peck on the lips. Out of the blue, he said, "I love you more than the distance of all these stars you can see in this sky, even the ones too far in the past for you to see."

Angel looked up at the beautiful night sky with a lump in her throat. The night was so quiet and beautiful that they could almost hear God breathe. "Wow. You're going to make me cry," she said.

"It's what God said to all of us when he said he'd cast our sins farther than this sky that has no end," Chris wiped his face with his shirt. "I truly believe it now. That's why I'm crying."

Tears fell out of Angel's watery eyes. "I don't understand or know why you love me that much after how mean I use to be to you, but I love you, too," she said.

"Forgiveness and love. This sky says a lot about God's love. After all the sins we've committed and he saw us commit before He created the world, He still chose to die for us. I'll forever wonder what he saw in me that caused Him to trust me to teach His word. But at the same time, I know I'm not worthy enough to be a man of God. Not a preacher alive is worthy to do this job. But when I think about how I was deceived and how I almost rejected Jesus because of one small misunderstanding, one misinterpreted twist of His love—and when I understand how far in the past we look when we see these stars that are closer to us than our sins—I find strength that no one can take away. I want to do all I can to help those who are lost like I was because of what I'm sure is innocent misinterpretation of the truth." Chris wiped his tears away with the bottom of his shirt again.

"With all that said, I don't think I'll ever look at the sky the same way again," said Angel.

Chris stood behind Angel, put his arms around her, and looked back into the full moon that lit up the night sky. "How in the world can it take millions of years for the stars light to reach our eyes, and how could the tiny amount of light we see from them come from stars that could've disappeared millions of years ago?" He took a deep breath. "What a beautiful way to display how deep His love is."

Angel looked deeper into the beautiful night sky and shook her head. "Wait a minute. Are you saying those stars aren't really there?"

"Right. They're not there. I mean, they were there millions of years ago, but now they could very well be gone even though we still see their light. That twinkle we just saw right there—that happened millions of years ago before we were even born. The light from that twinkle is just now reaching earth for our eyes to see."

"Wow! God is amazing!"

"Yes, He is. One day, the light from His glory will light up this whole sky and defy the science of how light travels. The light of His glory is going to take out space and time like a nuclear bomb and bend around the entire earth, leaving not so much of as a shadow from our new bodies because of the bright light of His beautiful love. And we're going to live with Him forever."

"Amen," said Angel.

They walked over to the portable porch swing where they sat holding each other until 2:00 A.M., staring into the past where their sins and the sins of all Christians have already been cast away, never to be seen or heard of again."

Epilogue

As Chris and Angel stared into the heavens, Chris had no idea that I was smiling down at him, along with Jesus and the angels, as I finished viewing part of his life story. I'd been saddened to learn that Mr. Stewart, who I had helped by accepting a contract for him to provide janitorial services for my church, had taken my life just to steal my measly four-hundred-and-seventy-five-million-dollar lottery ticket. All the sadness I had ever felt in my life couldn't overcome my joy in knowing that my son, Chris, would stand in line to receive the crown of glory with me and others God trust to teach his word of truth.

All the struggles and disappointments that Chris and I had suffered, even the painful discovery of how my life on earth had ended, somehow made heaven much sweeter than it would've been if I had not experienced life on earth. Through zillions of galaxies, stars, black holes, and mysterious unknown wonders stretching zillions of light-years through space and time, I sat Indian style under what I assumed would be the Table that all the books of everyone's personal life story would be laid opened on when all humans stand before God to be judged. I turned to the next page of my son's life story that God had titled 'restoring dreams' and saw Chris and his family pulling out of their garage for their first ride in their 69 camaro. They were clapping their hands as they listened to Mighty to save by Hillsong while trying out the sound system. As I read more of his life story I learned that Mr. Stewart had died in jail two months later. Before he died, Chris had visited him in jail and told him that he had forgiven him. Despite the courage it took for Chris to attempt to lead him to Christ after learning that he murdered me; Mr. Stewart still refused to believe that Jesus was the hero of all heroes who died to save all sinners and refused to accept Him as his personal savior.

Eight months after Chris loaned Tony enough money to open his own auto customizing and restoration shop, he paid it all back in full. Tina never divorced Tony like she had threatened to after he lost his job. Just as she was about to give up, her prayer for her husband to somehow own his own business had gotten answered through Chris. Their shop quickly gained a reputation for being one of the best restoration shops in the state. Tina learned from Tony how to do upholstery work and decided to quit her job and help Tony with their business. Harold continued working as a mortician without the confusion of where the souls of the people went who no longer lived in the bodies he prepared for burial. Bryan attempted to have other affairs, but couldn't follow through with them because he knew that he was being watched. Bryan found it very difficult to sin comfortably after Chris informed him that everything everyone had done in secret had been recorded.

Eighty percent of True Saints church members had stopped believing in the power of tithing. They had been blessed to give ten percent of their income for years and chose to continue giving it when they could, but they never expected a blessing from tithing again. The other twenty percent who continued tithing didn't realize that by doing so, they were making a statement to God that they didn't believe in everything he died on the cross to fulfill.

I laid the book down and stood up to stretch when I noticed that the Book of Life was no longer lying closed on the table by itself. An angel of the Lord had slipped in and placed the Book of the Dead next to it while I was deep into my son's life story. It was much bigger than the book of life. The sight of it almost brought me to tears.

It appeared that all in heaven was preparing for the Judgment seat of Christ where the believers will stand to be judged for their good deeds and good works. Angels were busy working for Jesus preparing all the books of life that were to be opened on His judgment days when He will read over every detail of everyone's life. I sat back down on the floor, leaned my back against the leg of the Table and thought about how my life story had ended. What would've taken me eighteen years to watch on earth had taken me only a matter of seconds inside the Books of Life Library in heaven.

I started crying and I couldn't stop. Just as I was about to pick up where I left off viewing my son's life story; two angels of the lord appeared next to me wearing robes as white as snow. I looked up at the angel on my left and explained to him how I had died as if he didn't already know.

"I gave Willie Stewart a job and helped him when I couldn't help myself . . . and he murdered me. He killed me for a measly four-hundred-and-seventy-five-million dollars." I turned to the angel on my right and I said to him. "He took me away from my family."

In the blink of an eye, we left the Books of Life Library and appeared on the banks of the River of Life. Beside it, bigger than three genetically mutated Sequoia trees together, grew the Tree of Life. Its color was one that I've never seen. It was more beautiful than any color I had ever seen on earth. I could see its beautiful reflection cascading in the waters of the River of Life. One of the angels of the Lord dipped his right hand into the River of Life and poured water over my head.

"This is healing water," he said. "It will heal you of your earthly pains until you receive your glorified mind and body. Drink from the river and eat from the tree." I kneeled down and scooped up a drink of water with both of my hands. Painful anguish from my earthly thoughts quickly went away. One drink from the River of Life was better than all of the drinks I had ever had on earth. The fruits from the Tree of Life were so delicious and satisfying that I no longer felt any anger toward Willie Stewart. If he were to make it to heaven, I'd forgive him. Being in the presence of God makes death rewarding no matter what method it uses to cause us to die and appear in God's presence. It really doesn't matter how a believer dies. Whether death comes to a believer in a horrible car accident or through the method of murder like he came for me…death for a believer is the most beautiful, rewarding part of human life that one can ever experience. It's the day that will never end; and life with Jesus, the creator of all things… begins.